BARRON'S
BUSINESS
LIBRARY

Modern Cost Management & Analysis

Second Edition

Jae K. Shim, Ph.D.
Professor of Accounting and Finance
California State University, Long Beach

Joel G. Siegel, Ph.D., CPA
Professor of Accounting and Information Systems
Queens College of the City University of New York

BARRON'S

General editor for the first edition of *Modern Cost Management & Analysis* in *Barron's Business Library* Series is George T. Friedlob, professor in the School of Accountancy at Clemson University.

Copyright © 2000 by Barron's Educational Series, Inc.
Prior edition © Copyright 1992 by Barron's Educational Series, Inc.

All inquiries should be addressed to:
Barron's Educational Series, Inc.
250 Wireless Boulevard
Hauppauge, New York 11788
http://www.barronseduc.com

Library of Congress Catalog Card No. 99-86794

International Standard Book No. 0-7641-1397-6

Library of Congress Cataloging-in-Publication Data

Shim, Jae K.
  Modern cost management & analysis / Jae K. Shim, Joel G. Siegel.—2nd ed.
    p.   cm.—(Barron's business library)
  Includes index.
  ISBN 0-7641-1397-6
  1. Cost accounting.   2. Managerial accounting.   I. Title:
Modern cost management and analysis.   II. Siegel, Joel G.
III. Title.   IV. Series.
HF5686.C8S4774   2000
657'.42—dc21   99-86794
                                                           CIP

Preface

This book is a working guide to assist you in cost management, control, accumulation, and analysis.

A knowledge of your costs is needed to make intelligent managerial and financial decisions. Perhaps you are starting your own business, or have accepted or been promoted to a managerial position for which an understanding of cost information is crucial. Cost analysis helps to examine the effectiveness of cost incurrence, whether costs are excessive, how operations and activities are doing, how to formulate pricing, how to analyze cost data for short-term and long-term decisions, how to manage and control costs, how to set realistic profit goals, and how to develop a better mix of products and territories. Are cost-benefit relationships within reason? If not, what can be done about it and who is responsible? A comparison of actual costs to budgeted costs may be helpful in identifying problem areas. Effective cost control requires accurate information and continual monitoring.

Cost information is needed for planning, control, and decision making. Cost analysis looks at the different types of costs you are incurring and how they may be controlled. It examines what costs are associated with a particular decision and what may be done about those costs in the future. Cost behavior is also analyzed in this book: what effect does cost behavior have on total costs and costs per unit associated with a change in volume? Costs also need to be classified by type of expenditure or cost object.

Cost analysis is applied in appraising and evaluating costs associated with a decision or project. By knowing what the costs are and how they behave, you can take steps to improve efficiency and engage in cost-reduction programs. Cost analysis is needed for many reasons, including evaluating effects upon profitability, selection of the "right" orders, planning future directions, inventory valuation and pricing, cost allocation and minimization, determining break-even, what the financial effects might be from changing the selling price, budgeting, variance analysis, making nonroutine decisions such as make-or-buy and whether to sell a product at below the normal selling price, and transfer price determination.

Also covered in this book are important new developments in cost analysis and management, such as activity-based accounting (ABC) and the just-in-time (JIT) system. How they impact product costing accuracy and how they help managers control and manage their costs are explained and illustrated.

The purpose of the book is to provide a knowledge of cost management and analysis that can be applied in the "real world" regardless of firm size. The cost analysis and management techniques and approaches can be used by you irrespective of your primary duties.

The book will help to quickly identify and solve costing situations and problems. You will learn what you need to know, what to ask, what analytical tools are important, what to look for, what to watch out for, what to do with respect to accumulating and appraising costs, and when and how to do it. You will learn how to evaluate where your costs have been, where your costs are currently, and where your costs are headed.

This book contains measures, guidelines, procedures, techniques, and rules of thumb. It has many practical tips and applications. Those readers who do not have a background in algebra may skip Chapter 19; the material in that chapter is not crucial to development of cost-analysis expertise.

The book is organized with ease of use in mind. It is a valuable reference tool for your business library containing outlines, checklists, illustrations, step-by-step instructions, charts, sample documents, and other "how-to's." Throughout, you will find this book practical, up-to-date, comprehensive, and useful.

Keep this book handy in your library for easy reference on a daily basis throughout your professional business career. While the book does not contain "all you ever wanted to know about cost analysis," it is a foundation on which to build your knowledge of cost analysis and related managerial accounting topics.

We would like to thank our wives, Chung and Roberta, for their encouragement and patience during the writing of this book. We also thank Tom Friedlob of Clemson University, general editor of this series, for his outstanding input on technical and editorial matters. In addition, we greatly acknowledge the excellent editorial assistance of our editors at Barron's: Lynn Sackman and Grace Freedson.

Jae K. Shim, Ph.D.
Joel G. Siegel, Ph.D., CPA

Contents

1 Introduction / 1

2 Cost Concepts, Terms, and Terminology / 15

3 Job-Order Costing / 25

4 Process Costing / 39

5 Costing Joint Products and By-products / 51

6 Cost Allocation / 75

7 Activity-Based Costing and Activity-Based Management / 95

8 Just-In-Time Manufacturing and Cost Management / 117

9 Analysis of Cost Behavior and Cost Estimation I / 129

10 Analysis of Cost Behavior and Cost Estimation II / 137

11 Cost-Volume-Profit and Break-Even Analysis I / 153

12 Cost-Volume-Profit and Break-Even Analysis II / 167

13 Budgeting / 181

14 Cost-Center Control Through Standard Costs and Gross Profit Analysis / 205

15 Cost Analysis for Nonroutine Decisions / 239

16 How to Make Capital-Budgeting Decisions / 253

17 How Does Income Tax Affect Investment Decisions? / 263

18 Cost Analysis for Transfer Pricing / 275

19 Quantitative Applications for Cost Analysis / 283

20 Total Quality Management and Quality Costs / 309

Appendix / 323

Glossary / 335

Index / 343

Introduction

INTRODUCTION AND MAIN POINTS

How do American firms fare in the world market? Do they really measure the costs of products and services they offer *accurately?* Only recently has this question been seriously addressed. American managers are waking up to find themselves operating in a highly competitive global economy. Manufacturing and service industries are all seeing their profits squeezed by the pinch of foreign price and quality competition.

Even firms who do know how to accurately measure product costs will find the going tough, while firms who fail to recognize and solve cost-measurement problems and to analyze cost data are probably destined for extinction.

Today's cost analysts and cost managers have the tremendous responsibility for this task. They are the ones that ensure that the cost-accounting system produces accurate cost data for managerial uses, for performance measurement, and for strategic decisions on pricing, product mix, process technology, and product design. Cost analysts and cost managers are the ones that must know how to analyze cost information for operational planning and control and for making tactical decisions.

After studying the material in this chapter:

■ You will be able to understand what cost analysis is.

■ You will be able to distinguish between cost analysis and cost management and its related fields, such as cost accounting, managerial accounting, and financial accounting.

■ You will be able to describe the three broad purposes for which the manager needs cost information.

■ You will be able to identify the role of the controller.

■ You will be familiar with three certificates that recognize the expertise in the fields of cost analysis and managerial accounting—Certified Cost Estimator/Analyst (CCEA), Certified Management Accountant (CMA), and Certified Internal Auditor (CIA).

NATURE AND SCOPE OF COST ACCOUNTING

Cost accounting is the preparation of internal reports for use by management in planning, controlling, and decision making. A vital aspect in these internal reports is the management and analysis of costs. In that sense, cost accounting is a *combination* of managerial accounting and financial accounting, which will be discussed later.

Cost accounting consists of the following basic activities, whether it is for a manufacturing or service business or for a profit or nonprofit organization:

1. *Cost recording and reporting*, including classifying, summarizing, communicating, and interpreting cost data to interested parties, internal or external.
2. *Cost measurement or estimation* for specific products, services, or subunits of the organization.
3. *Cost management*, obtaining accurate product-costing data and managing it to assist managers in making critical decisions such as pricing, product mix, and process technology.
4. *Cost analysis*, analyzing cost data, translating them into the information useful for managerial planning and control, and for making short-term and long-term decisions.

More on Cost Management and Analysis

Cost management and analysis is a subset of cost accounting. It deals with cost data. Cost is the measurement of the sacrifice of economic resources that has already been made or is to be made in the future, in order to achieve a specific objective. Cost management and analysis deals with estimated future or planned costs as well as with past, historical costs. It involves the following basic phases:

1. *Cost planning*. Involves selecting the goals of the organization and its subunits, expressed as operating objectives, and then identifying the means of accomplishing them. Plans are summarized in budgets, which are expressed in terms of money and measurements. For example, a *cost budget* should be prepared so as to plan for expected expenditures. The *profit budget* outlines the planned revenues and expenses of the coming time period. The *production and cost of goods manufactured budget* shows planned inventory levels, units of product that the company plans to make, and the costs of the various types of inputs that will be needed in carrying out the production plans. A budget also achieves control through the comparison of actual and bud-

geted costs, providing variance determination and analysis.

2. *Cost control.* Sets predetermined standards (such as standard costs and budgets) by which performance can be measured. Cost control then reports differences between planned and actual performances to direct attention to what went wrong. Cost control aids in fixing responsibility for departures from a plan so that corrective actions can be taken. For example, a cost-accounting report to a production department manager may show that the cost of manufacturing one unit of output is significantly higher than the standard cost. Investigation may reveal that the higher cost is due to inefficient labor, excessive spoilage of materials, or use of faulty equipment and improper production methods.

3. *Cost management for decision making.* This phase involves the measurement of accurate and relevant cost data and analyzing such information for decision making. *Activity-based costing* (ABC) and *just-in-time* (JIT) costing are two new developments that enhance product-costing accuracy. Decision making, which can also be termed problem solving, is largely a matter of choosing between alternative courses of action. The questions that arise from time to time are many and varied. Should the new product be introduced? Should one of the products or services in a line be dropped? Should a special order be accepted at below the normal selling price? Should parts now being manufactured be purchased? Should the present equipment be replaced? Should equipment be purchased or leased? Should production capacity be expended? A cost-management system is used to support management's needs for better decisions about product design, pricing, marketing, and mix, and to encourage continual operating improvements.

Quantitative methods may be used in various phases of cost analysis to determine costs and their financial effects, correlations, and the financial feasibility of adopting alternatives. They include learning curves, linear programming, inventory planning techniques, and program evaluation and review technique (PERT).

Management Accounting and Cost Analysis

Management accounting as defined by the National Association of Accountants (NAA) is the process of identification, measurement, accumulation, analysis, preparation, interpretation, and communication of financial information, which is used by management to plan, evaluate, and control within an organization. It ensures the appropriate use of and accountability for an organization's resources.

Management accounting also relates to the preparation of financial reports for nonmanagement groups such as regulatory agencies and tax authorities. Simply stated, management accounting is the accounting method used for the planning, control, and decision-making activities of an organization. Unlike cost analysis, management accounting uses more of a variety of data, such as financial statements (including the statement of cash flows). It also uses qualitative (nonmonetary) data and financial data.

Financial Accounting vs. Cost Analysis

Financial accounting is mainly concerned with the historical aspects of external reporting—that is, providing financial information to outside parties such as investors, creditors, and governments. To protect those outside parties from being misled, financial accounting is governed by FASB (Financial Accounting Standards Boards) and what are called *generally accepted accounting principles* (GAAP).

Cost analysis, on the other hand, is concerned primarily with providing information to internal managers who are charged with planning and controlling the operations of the firm and making a variety of management decisions. Because it is used internally, cost analysis is not subject to GAAP. The differences between financial accounting and cost analysis can be summarized as follows:

Financial Accounting	Cost Analysis
1. Provides data for external users	1. Provides data for internal users
2. Is required by FASB requirements	2. Is not required by FASB requirements
3. Is subject to GAAP	3. Is not subject to GAAP
4. Must generate accurate and timely data	4. Emphasizes relevance and flexibility of data
5. Emphasizes the past	5. Has more emphasis on the future
6. Looks at the business as a whole	6. Focuses on parts as well as on the whole of a business
7. Primarily stands by itself	7. Draws heavily from other disciplines, such as finance, economics, and quantitative methods
8. Is an end in itself	8. Is a means to an end

The Work of Management and the Cost Analyst's Role

Cost information is vital for all phases of management. Cost analysis looks at the different types of costs a company or a segment within the company incurs and how they may be controlled. It examines what costs are associated with a particular decision or project and what may be done about those costs in the future.

Cost analysis enters into all phases of management. In general, the work that management performs can be classified as (a) planning, (b) coordination, (c) controlling, and (d) decision making.

Planning. The planning function of management involves the selection of long-range and short-term objectives and the drawing up of strategic plans to achieve those objectives.

Coordinating. In performing the coordination function, management must decide how best to put together the firm's resources in order to carry out established plans.

Controlling. Controlling entails the implementation of a decision method and the use of feedback so that the firm's goals and specific strategic plans are optimally obtained.

Decision making. Decision making is the selection of the best alternative choice to accomplish the company's goals. Although the cost analyst usually has no ready and easy answers, profitability will be a factor in each phase, and cost data, properly accumulated and applied, will play a large role in the ultimate answer.

The Organizational Aspect of the Management Function

There are two types of authority in the organizational structure: line and staff. *Line authority* is the authority to give orders to subordinates. Line managers are responsible for attaining the goals set by the organization as efficiently and profitably as possible. Production and sales managers typically possess line authority.

Staff authority is the authority to give advice, support, and service to the line departments. Staff managers do not command others. Examples of staff authority are found in personnel, purchasing, engineering, and finance. The management accounting function is usually a staff function with the responsibility for providing line managers and other staff people with a specialized service. The service includes (a) budgeting, (b) controlling, (c) pricing, and (d) special decisions.

Controllership

The chief management accountant or the chief accounting executive of an organization is called the *controller* (often called *comptroller,* especially in the government sector). The controller is in charge of the accounting department. The controller's authority is basically a staff function in that the controller's office gives advice and service to other departments. But at the same time, the controller has line authority over members of his or her department, such as internal auditors, bookkeepers, and budget analysts. (See Figure 1-1 for an organization chart of a controllership situation.)

The controller is basically concerned with *internal* matters—namely financial accounting, cost analysis, taxes, budgeting, and control functions. The Financial Executives Institute, an association of corporate controllers and treasurers, lists the controller's functions as follows:

> Planning for control
> Reporting and interpreting
> Evaluating and consulting
> Tax administration
> Government reporting
> Protection of assets
> Economic appraisal

COST ACCOUNTING STANDARDS BOARD

The Cost Accounting Standards Board (CASB), an agency of the U.S. Congress, was established in 1970 to promulgate cost accounting standards covering negotiated defense contracts in excess of $100,000. (Executive regulations have extended standards to cover nondefense procurements in excess of $100,000.) "Negotiated" means that the price is tied to costs rather than to competitive bidding.

The standards are mainly concerned with definitions, uniformity, and consistency in cost accounting practices. The standards begin with Number 400. Until the CASB's activities ceased in 1980, the Board had issued 19 standards. The Government Accounting Office (GAO) is now responsible for interpreting CASB standards. A list of CASB standards is presented below.

The standards are classified into the following three categories:
1. Standards addressing overall cost accounting matters
    400 definitions
    401 Cost accounting standard—consistency in estimating, accumulating, and reporting costs
    402 Cost accounting standard—consistency in allocating costs incurred for the same purpose

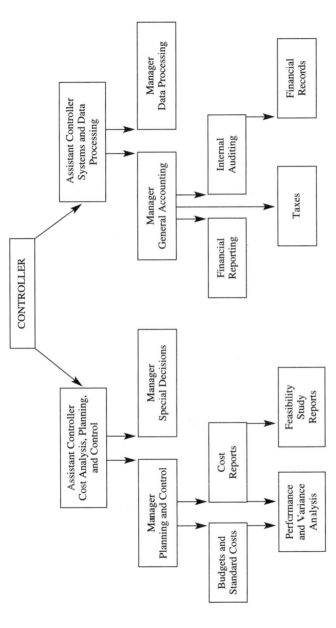

FIG. 1-1. *Organization chart for controllership functions.*

405 Accounting for unallowable costs

406 Cost accounting standard—cost accounting period

2. Standards addressing classes, categories, or elements of cost

404 Capitalization of tangible assets

407 Use of standard costs for direct material and direct labor

408 Accounting for costs of compensated personal absence

409 Depreciation of tangible capital assets

411 Accounting for acquisition costs of material

412 Composition and measurement of pension cost

413 Adjustment and allocation of pension cost

414 Cost of money as an element of the cost of facilities capital

415 Accounting for the cost of deferred compensation

416 Accounting for insurance costs

417 Cost of money as an element of the cost of capital assets under construction

3. Standards addressing allocation of costs

403 Allocation of home office expenses to segments

410 Allocation of business unit general and administrative expenses to final objectives

418 Allocation of direct and indirect costs (Proposed Standard 419 was combined with this standard)

420 Accounting for independent research and development and bid and proposal costs

Copies of CASB standards, rules, and regulations are available from the:

Superintendent of Documents,
U.S. Government Printing Office,
Washington, D.C. 20402.

COST/MANAGERIAL ACCOUNTING IN THE NEW PRODUCTION ENVIRONMENT

Over the past two decades, new technologies and management philosophies have changed the face of cost/managerial accounting. Following are the key developments that have reshaped the discipline. We will discuss these at length in future chapters. For example, where automation and computer-assisted manufacturing methods have replaced the workforce, labor costs have shrunk from between 30 and 50% of product and service costs to around 5%. Cost accounting in traditional settings required more work to keep track of labor costs than do present systems. On the other hand, in highly automated environments, cost accountants have had to become more sophisticated in finding causes of costs because labor no longer drives many cost transactions.

Total Quality Management and Quality Costs
In order to be globally competitive in today's world-class manufacturing environment, firms place an increased emphasis on quality and productivity. Total quality management (TQM) is an effort in this direction. Simply put, it is a system for creating competitive advantage by focusing the organization on what is important to the customer.

Total quality management can be broken down as follows:

Total. The whole organization is involved and understands that customer satisfaction is everyone's job.

Quality. The extent to which products and services satisfy the requirements of internal and external customers.

Management. The leadership, infrastructure, and resources that support employees as they meet the needs of those customers.

Market shares of many U.S. firms have eroded because foreign firms have been able to sell higher-quality products at lower prices. Under TQM, performance measures are likely to include product reliability and service delivery, as well as such traditional measures as profitability.

In order to be competitive, U.S. firms have placed an increased emphasis on quality and productivity in order to:
1. produce savings such as reducing rework costs, and
2. improve product quality.

Quality costs are classified into three broad categories: prevention, appraisal, and failure costs. Quality cost reports can be used to point out the strengths and weaknesses of a quality system. Improvement teams can use them to describe the monetary benefits and ramifications of proposed changes. Chapter 20 focuses on total quality management and quality costs.

Continuous Improvement (CI) and Benchmarking
Continuous improvement (CI), based on a Japanese concept called *Kaizen,* is a management philosophy that seeks endless pursuit of improvement of machinery, materials, labor utilization, and production methods through application of suggestions and ideas of team members. The CI utilizes many different approaches,

including: *statistical process control (SPC),* using traditional statistical control charts, and *benchmarking,* examining excellent performers outside the industry and seeing how you can use their best practices. Benchmarking typically involves the following steps:

1. Identify those practices needing improvement.
2. Identify a company that is the world leader in performing the process.
3. Interview the managers of the company and analyze data obtained.

Continuous improvement and benchmarking is often called "the race with no finish" because managers and employees are not satisfied with a particular performance level but seek ongoing improvement.

Business Process Reengineering (BPR)
TQM seeks evolutionary changes in the processes while the practice called *business process reengineering (BPR)* seeks to make revolutionary changes. BPR does this by taking a fresh look at what the firm is trying to do in all its processes, and then eliminating nonvalue-added steps and streamlining the remaining ones to achieve the desired outcome.

Just-In-Time and Lean Production
The inventory control problem occurs in almost every type of organization. It exists whenever products are held to meet some expected future demand. In most industries, cost of inventory represents the largest liquid asset under the control of management. Therefore, it is very important to develop a production and inventory planning system that will minimize both purchasing and carrying costs. Material cost, as a proportion of total product cost, has continued to rise significantly during the last few years and hence is a primary concern of top management.

Just-In-Time (JIT) is a demand-pull system. Demand for customer output, not plans for using input resources, triggers production. Production activities are "pulled," not "pushed," into action. JIT production, in its purest sense, is buying and producing in very small quantities just in time for use. JIT production is part of a "lean production" philosophy that has been credited for the success of many Japanese companies.

Lean production eliminates inventory between production departments, making the quality and efficiency or production the highest priority. Lean production requires the flexibility to change quickly from one product to another. It emphasizes employee training and participation in decision making.

The development of just-in-time production and purchasing methods also affects cost-accounting systems. Firms using just-in-time methods keep inventories to a minimum. If inventories are low, accountants can spend less time on inventory valuation for external reporting. Chapter 8 covers the JIT inventory system.

Theory of Constraints (TOC) and Bottlenecks Management

The theory of constraints (TOC) views a business as a linked sequence of processes that transforms inputs into salable outputs, like a chain. To improve the strength of the chain, a TOC company identifies the weakest link, which is the constraint. TOC exploits constraints so that throughput is maximized and inventories and operating costs are minimized. It then develops a specific approach to manage constraints to support the objective of *continuous improvement.*

Bottlenecks occur whenever demand (at least temporarily) exceeds capacity. For example, although a legal secretary has enough total time to do all her word processing, she may be given several jobs in quick succession, so that a queue (waiting line) builds up. This is a bottleneck, which delays the other activities waiting for the word processing to be finished. TOC seeks to maximize "throughput" by:

1. larger lot sizes at bottleneck work stations, to avoid time lost on changeovers,
2. small transfer batches—forwarding a small batch of work to the next workstation, so that the next operation can begin before the entire lot is finished at the preceding work station, and
3. rules for inserting buffer stock before or after certain bottlenecks.

THE CERTIFIED MANAGEMENT ACCOUNTANT (CMA)

Management accounting has expanded in scope to cover a wide variety of business disciplines such as finance, economics, organization behavior, and quantitative methods. In line with this development, the Institute of Management Accountants (IMA) created the Institute of Certified Management Accountants, which offers a program leading to the Certified Management Accountant (CMA) examination.

The objectives of the CMA program are fourfold:

1. To establish management accounting as a recognized profession by identifying the role of the management accoun-

tant and financial manager, the underlying body of knowledge, and a course of study by which such knowledge is acquired.

2. To encourage higher educational standards in the management accounting field.

3. To establish an objective measure of an individual's knowledge and competence in the field of management accounting.

4. To encourage continued professional development by management accountants.

The CMA program requires candidates to pass a series of uniform examinations covering a wide range of subjects. The examination consists of the following four parts:

1. Economics, Finance, and Management
2. Financial Accounting and Reporting
3. Management Reporting, Analysis, and Behavioral Issues
4. Decision Analysis and Information Systems

The exam is given twice yearly in June and December.

Note: For more information, call IMA at (800) 638-4427, ext. 141, or (201) 573-6300, or visit its web site: *http:// www.rutgers.edu/accounting/raw/ima/.*

The IMA has also created the new CFM (Certified in Financial Management) program to provide an objective measure of knowledge and competence in the field of *financial management,* only Part II (Financial Accounting and Reporting) is replaced with Corporate Financial Management. The CFM is approved by the prestigious Financial Management Association, whose web site is *http://www.fma.org.*

THE CERTIFIED INTERNAL AUDITOR (CIA)

This certification was created in 1974 by the Institute of Internal Auditors (IIA). The CIA exam is also broader than the CPA exam because it covers a broad range of areas, among them management, economics, finance, and quantitative methods. The CIA exam lasts 14 hours (four 3 1/2-hour parts) and covers the following areas:

1. Theory and Practice of Internal Auditing I
2. Theory and Practice of Internal Auditing II
3. Management, Quantitative Methods, and Information Systems
4. Accounting, Finance, and Economics.

Note: For more information, call IIA at (407) 830-7600 or visit its web site: *http://www.rutgers.edu/Accounting/raw/iia/.*

Society of Cost Estimating and Analysis (SCEA) Certification. The Society of Cost Estimating and Analysis administers a professional certification program to award the designation of *Certified Cost Estimator/Analyst (CCEA)* to qualified applicants. To be awarded the CCEA designation, an applicant must meet criteria of education and/or job experience in the area of cost analysis and pass a written examination conducted by the Society. The test is a four-hour, two-part examination intended to allow the candidates the opportunity to demonstrate their knowledge of both general theory and quantitative methods applicable to cost estimating or analysis. According to the SCEA, the body of knowledge of cost analysis includes:

1. Basic skills—background knowledge
2. Cost concepts
3. Cost theory
4. Data and measurement
5. Estimation and testing statistical theory
6. Analysis techniques

Note: For more information, call (703) 751-8069 or visit its web site: *http://www.erols.com/scea.*

CHAPTER PERSPECTIVE

This chapter outlines the "what and why" of cost management and analysis and the relationship between cost analysis and its closely related fields—cost accounting, managerial accounting, and financial accounting. Cost analysis applies to *appraising* and *evaluating* costs associated with a decision or project. By knowing what the costs are, how they behave, and how they effect profitability, you can take steps to improve efficiency and engage in cost-reduction programs.

Broadly speaking, cost analysis deals with budgeting, planning, control, coordinating, and decision making. The chapter also presents discussion of the roles of the cost analysts and the controller. Also covered is a brief outline of two certification programs that recognize expertise in the fields of cost analysis and management accounting.

Cost Concepts, Terms, and Terminology

INTRODUCTION AND MAIN POINTS

In financial accounting, the term *cost* is defined as a measurement, in monetary terms, of the amount of resources used for some purpose. In managerial accounting, the term *cost* is used in many different ways. That is, there are different types of costs used for different purposes. Some costs are useful and required for inventory valuation and income determination. Some costs are useful for planning, budgeting, and cost control. Still others are useful for making short-term and long-term decisions.

After studying the material in this chapter:

■ You will be able to identify and give examples of each of the basic cost elements involved in the manufacture of a product.

■ You will be familiar with various cost concepts and be able to define them.

■ You will be able to distinguish between variable costs and fixed costs and explain the difference in their behavior.

■ You will be able to explain the difference between the financial statements of a manufacturer and those of a merchandising firm.

COST CLASSIFICATIONS

Costs can be classified into various categories, according to:

1. Their management function
   a. Manufacturing costs
   b. Nonmanufacturing (operating) costs
2. Their ease of traceability
   a. Direct costs
   b. Indirect costs
3. Their timing of charges against sales revenue
   a. Product costs
   b. Period costs

4. Their behavior in accordance with changes in activity
   a. Variable costs
   b. Fixed costs
   c. Mixed (semivariable) costs
5. Their degree of averaging
   a. Total costs
   b. Unit (average) costs
6. Their relevance to planning, control, and decision making
   a. Controllable and noncontrollable costs
   b. Standard costs
   c. Incremental costs
   d. Sunk costs
   e. Out-of-pocket costs
   f. Relevant costs
   g. Opportunity costs

We will discuss each of the cost categories in the remainder of this chapter.

COSTS BY MANAGEMENT FUNCTION

In a manufacturing firm, costs are divided into two major categories according to the functional activities they are associated with: (1) manufacturing costs and (2) nonmanufacturing costs, also called operating expenses.

Manufacturing Costs

Manufacturing costs are those costs associated with the manufacturing activities of the company. Manufacturing costs are subdivided into three categories: direct materials, direct labor, and factory overhead. Direct materials are all materials that become an integral part of the finished product. Examples are the steel used to make an automobile and the wood to make furniture. Glues, nails, and other minor items are called indirect materials (or supplies) and are classified as part of factory overhead, which is explained below.

Direct labor is the labor directly involved in making the product. Examples of direct-labor costs are the wages of assembly workers on an assembly line and the wages of machine tool operators in a machine shop. Indirect labor, such as wages of supervisory personnel and janitors, is classified as part of factory overhead. Factory overhead can be defined as all costs of manufacturing except direct materials and direct labor. Some of the many examples include depreciation, rent, taxes, insurance, fringe benefits, payroll taxes, and cost of idle time. Factory overhead is also called manufacturing overhead, indirect manufacturing expenses, and factory burden. Many costs overlap within their categories.

One important category of factory overhead is that of *quality costs*. Quality costs are costs that occur because poor quality may exist or actually does exist. These costs are significant in amount, often totaling 20 to 25% of sales. The subcategories of quality costs are prevention, appraisal, and failure costs.

Prevention costs. These are costs incurred to prevent defects. Amounts spent on quality training programs, researching customer needs, quality circles, and improved production equipment are considered in prevention costs. Expenditures made for prevention will minimize the costs that will be incurred for appraisal and failure.

Appraisal costs. These are costs incurred for monitoring or inspection; these costs compensate for mistakes not eliminated through prevention.

Failure costs. These may be internal, such as scrap and rework costs and reinspection, or external, such as product returns or recalls due to quality problems, warranty costs, and lost sales due to poor product performance.

Direct materials and direct labor combined are called *prime costs*. Direct labor and factory overhead combined are termed *conversion costs* (or processing costs). This term reflects the fact that these costs are incurred to convert raw materials into finished goods.

Nonmanufacturing Costs

Nonmanufacturing costs (or operating expenses) are subdivided into selling, general, and administrative expenses. Selling expenses are those associated with obtaining sales and the delivery of the product. Examples are advertising and sales commissions. General and administrative expenses (G & A) include those incurred to perform general and administrative activities. Examples are executives' salaries and legal expenses. Other examples of costs by management function and their relationships are found in Figure 2-1.

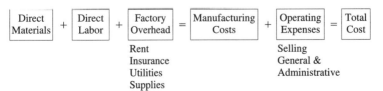

FIG. 2-1. *Costs by management function.*

DIRECT COSTS AND INDIRECT COSTS

Costs may be viewed as either direct or indirect, based on the extent they are traceable to a particular object of costing, such as products, jobs, departments, and sales territories. Direct costs can be directly traceable to the costing object. For example, if the object of costing under consideration is a product line, the materials and labor involved in the manufacture of the line would both be direct costs. Factory overhead items are all indirect costs, since they are not directly identifiable to any particular product line. Costs shared by different departments, products, or jobs—called *common costs* or *joint costs*—are also indirect costs. National advertising that benefits more than one product and sales territory is an example of an indirect cost.

PRODUCT COSTS AND PERIOD COSTS

By whether they relate to the manufacture of a product, costs are classified into: (a) product costs and (b) period costs.

Product costs are inventoriable costs, identified as part of inventory on hand. They are treated as an asset until the goods they are assigned to are sold. At that time they become the expense, or cost of goods sold. All manufacturing costs are product costs.

Product costs   ⟶   Asset (inventory)   ⟶   Expense (cost of goods sold)

Period costs are all expired costs that are not necessary for production and hence are charged against sales revenues in the period in which the revenue is earned. Selling, and general and administrative expenses are period costs.

Period costs   ⟶   Expense

Figure 2-2 shows the relationship of product and period costs and other cost classifications presented thus far.

From a planning and control standpoint, perhaps the most important way to classify costs is by how they behave in accordance with changes in volume or some measure of activity. By *behavior,* costs can be classified into the following three basic categories:

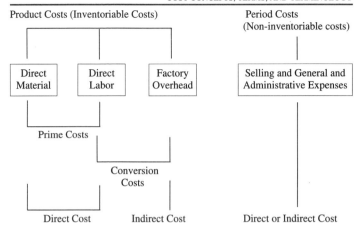

FIG. 2-2. *Various classifications of costs.*

Variable Costs
Costs that vary in total in direct proportion to changes in activity. Examples are direct materials and gasoline expense based on miles driven.

Fixed Costs
Costs that remain constant in total regardless of changes in activity. Examples are rent, insurance, and taxes.

Mixed (or Semivariable) Costs
Costs that vary with changes in volume but, unlike variable costs, do not vary in direct proportion. In other words, these costs contain both a variable component and a fixed component. Examples are the rental of a delivery truck, where a fixed rental fee plus a variable charge based on mileage is made, and a telephone bill having a fixed monthly charge plus a charge based on the number of calls.

UNIT COSTS AND TOTAL COSTS
For internal reporting and pricing purposes, we are interested in determining the unit (average) cost per unit of product or service. The unit cost is simply the average cost, which is the total costs divided by the total volume in units. Alternatively, the unit cost is the sum of (a) the variable cost per unit, and (b) the fixed cost per unit. It is important to realize that the unit cost declines as volume increases, since the total fixed costs that are constant over a range of activity are being spread over a larger number of units.

EXAMPLE 1

Fixed costs are $1,000 per period and variable costs are $.10 per unit. The total and unit (average) costs at various production levels are as follows:

Volume in units	Total fixed costs	Total variable costs	Total costs	Variable cost per unit	Fixed cost per unit	Unit (average) cost
			(b)+(c) = (d)	(c)/(a) = (e)	(b)/(a) = (f)	(d)/(a) or (e)+(f)
(a)	(b)	(c)				
1,000	$1,000	$100	$1,100	$.10	$1.00	$1.10
5,000	1,000	500	1,500	.10	.20	.30
10,000	1,000	1000	2,000	.10	.10	.20

The increase in total costs and the decline in unit costs are illustrated in Figure 2-3. Also note the relationships for variable and fixed costs per unit:

Behavior as Volume Changes from 5,000 to 10,000

	Total Cost	Unit Cost
Variable cost	Change ($500 to $1,000)	No change ($.10)
Fixed cost	No change ($1,000)	Change ($.20 to $.10)

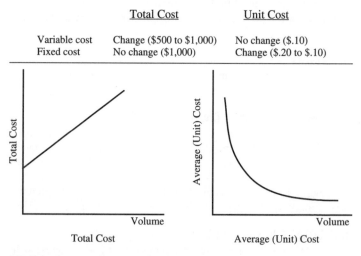

FIG. 2-3. *Total and unit (average) costs.*

COSTS FOR PLANNING, CONTROL, AND DECISION MAKING
Controllable and Noncontrollable Costs

A cost is said to be controllable when the amount of the cost is assigned to the head of a department and the level of the cost is significantly under the manager's influence. Noncontrollable costs are those costs not subject to influence at a given level of managerial supervision.

All variable costs, such as direct materials, direct labor, and variable overhead, are usually considered controllable by the department head. On the other hand, fixed costs, such as depreciation of factory equipment, would not be controllable by the department head, since he/she would not have power to purchase equipment.

Standard Costs

Standard costs are predetermined costs that serve as goals to be achieved. They are based on the quantities of manufacturing inputs needed to produce output efficiently.

EXAMPLE 2

The standard cost of materials per pound is obtained by multiplying standard price per pound by standard quantity per unit of output in pounds. For example, the standard price and quantity of material might be determined as follows:

Purchase price	$3.00
Freight	0.12
Receiving and handling	0.02
Less: Purchase discounts	(0.04)
Standard price per pound	$3.10
Per bill of materials in pounds	1.2
Allowance for waste and spoilage in lbs.	0.1
Allowance for rejects in lbs.	0.1
Standard quantity per unit of output	1.4 lbs.

Once the price and quantity standards have been set, the standard cost of material per unit of finished goods can be computed, as follows:

$$1.4 \text{ pounds} \times \$3.10 = \$4.34 \text{ per unit}$$

Incremental (or Differential) Costs

The incremental cost is the difference in costs between two or more alternatives.

EXAMPLE 3

Consider the two alternatives, A and B, whose costs are as follows:

	A	B	Difference (B – A)
Direct materials	$10,000	$10,000	$ 0
Direct labor	10,000	15,000	5,000

The incremental costs are simply B – A (or A – B), as shown in the last column. The incremental costs are relevant to future decisions, which will be discussed in detail in Chapter 15.

Sunk Costs

Sunk costs are the costs of resources that have already been incurred whose total will not be affected by any decision made now or in the future. Sunk costs are considered irrelevant to future decisions since they are past or historical costs.

EXAMPLE 4

Suppose you acquired an asset for $50,000 three years ago which is now listed at a book value of $20,000. The $20,000 book value is a sunk cost which does not affect a future decision.

Out-of-Pocket Costs

Out-of-pocket costs, also known as outlay costs, are costs that require future expenditures of cash or other resources. Noncash charges such as depreciation and amortization are not out-of-pocket costs. Out-of-pocket costs are usually relevant to a particular decision.

EXAMPLE 5

A capital investment project requires $120,000 in cash outlays. $120,000 is an out-of-pocket cost.

Relevant Costs

Relevant costs are expected future costs that will differ between alternatives. This concept is key to short- and long-term decisions and is discussed later (Chapter 15).

EXAMPLE 6

In a decision on whether to replace an existing business with a new one, the cost to be paid for the new business is relevant. However, the initial cost for the old business is not relevant.

Opportunity Costs

An opportunity cost is the net benefit foregone by rejecting an alternative. There is always an opportunity cost involved in making a decision. It is a cost incurred relative to the alternative given up.

EXAMPLE 7

Suppose a company has a choice of using its capacity to produce an extra 10,000 units or renting it out for $20,000. The opportunity cost of using the capacity is $20,000.

INCOME STATEMENTS AND BALANCE SHEETS— MANUFACTURER

Figure 2-4 illustrates the income statement of a manufacturer. An important characteristic of the income statement is that it is supported by a schedule of cost of goods manufactured (see Figure 2-5). This schedule shows the specific costs (i.e., direct materials, direct labor, and factory overhead) that have gone into the goods completed during the period. Since the manufacturer carries three types of inventory (raw materials, work-in-process, and finished goods), all three items must be incorporated into the computation of the cost of goods sold. These inventory accounts also appear on the balance sheet for a manufacturer, as shown in Figure 2-6.

For the Year Ended December 31, 20X1

Sales		$320,000
Less: Cost of goods sold		
Finished goods, Dec. 31, 20X1	$ 18,000	
Cost of goods manufactured		
(see schedule, Fig. 2-5)	121,000	
Cost of goods available for sale	$139,000	
Finished goods, Dec. 31, 20X1	21,000	
Cost of goods sold		$118,000
Gross margin		$202,000
Less: Selling and administrative		
expenses		60,000
Net income		$142,000

FIG. 2-4. *Manufacturer's income statement.*

Direct materials		
Inventory, Dec. 31, 20X1	$23,000	
Purchases	64,000	
Cost of direct materials		
available for use	$87,000	
Inventory, Dec. 31, 20X1	7,800	
Direct materials used		$79,200
Direct labor		25,000

Factory overhead		
Indirect labor	$3,000	
Indirect material	2,000	
Factory utilities	500	
Factory depreciation	800	
Factory rent	2,000	
Miscellaneous	1,500	9,800
Total manufacturing costs incurred during 20X1		$114,000
Add: Work-in-process inventory, Dec. 31, 20X0		9,000
Manufacturing costs to account for		$123,000
Less: Work-in-process inventory, Dec. 31, 20X1		2,000
Cost of goods manufactured (to income statement, Fig. 2-4)		$121,000

FIG. 2-5. *Manufacturer's schedule of cost of goods manufactured.*

	December 31, 20X1	
Current assets		
Cash		$25,000
Accounts receivable		78,000
Inventories:		
Raw materials	$7,800	
Work-in-process	2,000	
Finished goods	21,000	30,800
Total		$133,800

FIG. 2-6. *Manufacturer's current asset section of balance sheet.*

CHAPTER PERSPECTIVE

Cost analysis is the accumulation and analysis of cost data to provide information for internal planning and control of an organization's operations, and for short-term and long-term decisions. It is important to realize that there are different costs used for different purposes. The management/cost accountant must determine the use to be made of cost data in order to supply the most appropriate cost information.

Job-Order Costing

INTRODUCTION AND MAIN POINTS

Job-order cost accounting accumulates costs by specific jobs, contracts, or orders. This costing method is appropriate when the products are manufactured in identifiable lots or batches, or when the products are manufactured to customer specifications. Job-order costing is widely used by custom manufacturers such as printing, aircraft, construction, auto repair, and professional services.

In this chapter, you will learn:
- When a job-order cost system would be appropriate.
- What a job cost sheet looks like.
- The preparation of journal entries for a job-order system.
- The determination of applied overhead.
- How to determine unit cost.
- The computation of the total cost of a job.
- How to dispose of overapplied or underapplied overhead.
- The different concepts of capacity.
- The integration of job order costing and standard costing.

JOB COST SHEET

A *job cost sheet* is used to record various production costs for work-in-process inventory. A separate cost sheet is kept for each identifiable job, accumulating the direct materials, direct labor, and factory overhead assigned to that job as it moves through production. The form varies according to the needs of the company. A sample job cost sheet is presented in Figure 3-1.

PRODUCT_____

DATE STARTED_____

DATE COMPLETED_____   JOB NO. _____

	Direct Material				Direct Labor				Overhead	
Date	Reference (Material Requisition No.)	Amount		Date	Reference (Employee Work Ticket No.)	Amount		Date	Amount (Based on predetermined overhead rate)

FIG. 3-1. *Job cost sheet.*

COST ACCUMULATION

Job-order costing keeps track of costs as follows: direct material and direct labor are traced to a particular job. Costs not directly traceable—such as factory overhead—are applied to individual jobs using a predetermined overhead (application) rate. The overhead rate is determined at the beginning of the year as follows:

$$\text{Overhead rate} = \frac{\text{Budgeted annual overhead}}{\substack{\text{Budgeted annual activity units (direct-}\\ \text{labor hours, direct-labor cost, machine-}\\ \text{hours, etc.)}}}$$

For example, the budgeted overhead for a department for the upcoming year is $1,000,000 and the expected direct-labor cost for the year is $2,000,000. Assuming the applied overhead rate is based on direct-labor cost, the applied overhead rate equals:

$$\frac{\text{Budgeted annual overhead}}{\text{Budgeted direct-labor cost}} = \frac{\$1,000,000}{\$2,000,000} = 50\%$$

An applied overhead rate is needed for a *seasonal* business so as to derive more uniform monthly unit-cost figures. If actual overhead was used rather than applied overhead, a seasonal business may have distorted monthly unit cost figures. This is illustrated below.

The following information applies to a seasonal business:

	Actual factory overhead			Actual machine-hours	Applied overhead rate per machine-hour
	Variable	Fixed	Total		
High-volume month	$20,000	$30,000	$50,000	5,000	$10
Low-volume month	$5,000	$30,000	$35,000	1,250	$28

The presence of fixed overhead results in overhead costs vacillating from $10 to $28 per machine-hour. The variable element is $4 per machine-hour in each month ($20,000/5,000 and $5,000/1,250). However, the fixed element is $6 per machine-hour in the high-volume month ($30,000/5,000) and $24 per machine-hour in the low-volume month ($30,000/1,250).

It is not logical that an identical product should be charged with a $10 overhead rate during one month and a $28 overhead rate during another. These different overhead rates are not reflective of typical, normal production conditions. An average to total annual volume is more representative of typical relationships between total overhead costs and volume than is an actual monthly rate.

FACTORY OVERHEAD APPLICATION

The production surrogate used to determine the applied overhead rate may vary between departments, depending upon what is most realistic for that department and the cost/benefit associated with it. In one department direct-labor hours might be the best indicator of utilization, while in another department machine-hours might make more sense because it is most reflective of production activity.

A comparison of applied overhead and actual overhead will reveal whether too little (underapplied) or too much (overapplied) was charged as inventoriable costs during the year.

Underapplied overhead and overapplied overhead results as follows:

Underapplied overhead = Applied overhead < Actual overhead
Overapplied overhead   = Applied overhead > Actual overhead

Assume that two departments have prepared the following budgeted data for the year 20X1:

	Dept. X	Dept. Y
Predetermined rate based on	Machine-hours	Direct-labor cost
Budgeted overhead	$200,000 (a)	$240,000 (a)
Budgeted machine-hours	100,000 (b)	
Budgeted direct-labor cost		$160,000 (b)
Predetermined overhead		150% of
rate (a/b)	$2 per machine	direct-labor cost

Now assume that actual overhead costs and the actual level of activity for 20X1 for each department are as follows:

	Dept. X	Dept. Y
Actual overhead costs	$198,000	$256,000
Actual machine-hours	96,000	
Actual direct-labor cost		$176,000

Note that for each department the actual cost and activity data differ from the budgeted figures used in calculating the predetermined overhead rate. The computation of the resulting under- and overapplied overhead for each department is:

	Dept. X	Dept. Y
Actual overhead costs	$198,000	$256,000
Factory overhead applied to work-in-process during 20X1:		
96,000 machine-hours × $2	192,000	
$176,000 direct-labor cost × 150%		264,000
Underapplied (overapplied) overhead	$6,000	$(8,000)

Harris Company uses a budgeted overhead rate in applying overhead to production orders on a *labor-cost* basis for the Assembling Department (Dept. A) and on a *machine-hour* basis for the Finishing Department (Dept. F). At the beginning of the year, the company made the following predictions:

	Assembling Dept.	Finishing Dept.
Factory overhead	$72,000	$75,000
Direct-labor cost	$64,000	$17,500
Machine-hours	500	10,000

The budgeted overhead rates for each department are:

Dept. A: $72,000/$64,000 = 1.125 times direct-labor cost
Dept. F: $75,000/$10,000 = $7.50 per machine-hour

During the month of January, the cost record for a job order, i.e., number 105, that was processed through both departments shows the following:

	Assembling Dept.	Finishing Dept.
Materials issued	$30	$45
Direct-labor cost	$36	$25
Machine-hours	6	15

The total applied overhead for job order no. 105 follows:

Dept. A: $36 × 1.125	$40.50
Dept. F: 15 × $7.50	112.50
Total	$153.00

Assuming job order no. 105 consisted of 30 units of product, what is the unit cost of the job?

	Assembling Dept.	Finishing Dept.
Direct material	$30	$45
Direct labor	36	25
Applied overhead	40.50	112.50
Total	$106.50	$182.50

Total cost: $106.50 + 182.50 = $289

Unit cost: $289/30 = $9.63

Assume that at the end of the year it was found that *actual* factory overhead amounted to $80,000 in the Assembling Department and $69,000 in the Finishing Department. Assume that the actual direct-labor cost was $74,000 in the Assembling Department and the actual machine-hours were 9,000 in the Finishing Department. The overapplied or underapplied overhead for each department would be:

Dept. A:	Applied overhead (1.125 × $74,000)	$83,250
	Actual overhead	80,000
	Overapplied overhead	$3,250
Dept. F:	Applied overhead ($7.50 × 9,000)	$67,500
	Actual overhead	69,000
	Underapplied overhead	$1,500

At the end of the year, the difference between actual overhead and applied overhead is closed out to cost of goods sold, if an immaterial difference. If a material difference exists, work-in-process, finished goods, and cost of goods sold are adjusted on a proportionate basis based on units or dollars at year end for the deviation between actual and applied overhead.

PLANTWIDE VERSUS DEPARTMENTAL OVERHEAD RATES

As the degree of aggregation increases from simply combining related cost pools to combining all factory overhead, information may become more distorted. The following information is used to provide a simple example of the differing results obtained between using a departmental and plantwide overhead rate.

EXAMPLE 1

Allison Company has two departments: Assembly and Finishing. Assembly work is performed by robots, and a large portion of this department's overhead cost consists of depreciation and electricity charges. Finishing work is performed manually by skilled laborers, and most charges in this department are for labor, fringe benefits, indirect materials, and supplies.

The company makes two products: A and B. Product A requires five machine-hours in Assembly and one direct-labor hour in Finishing; Product B requires two machine-hours in Assembly and three direct-labor hours in Finishing.

Figure 3-2 provides information about estimated overhead costs and activity measures, and shows the computations of departmental and plantwide overhead rates. Product overhead application amounts for A and B are also given.

Note the significant difference in the overhead applied to each product using departmental versus plantwide rates. If departmental rates are used, product cost more clearly reflects the different amounts and types of machine/labor work performed on the two products. If a plantwide rate is used, essentially each product only absorbs overhead from a single department—from Assembly if machine-hours are used and from Finishing if direct-labor hours are used. Use of either plantwide rate ignores the dissimilarity of work performed in the departments.

	Assembly	Finishing	Total
Estimated annual overhead	$300,200	$99,800	$400,000
Estimated annual direct-labor hours (DLH)	5,000	20,000	25,000
Estimated annual machine-hours (MH)	38,000	2,000	40,000

(1) Total plantwide overhead = $300,200 + $99,800 = $400,000
Plantwide overhead rate
using DLH ($400,000/25,000 = $16.00)

(2) Departmental overhead rates:
Assembly (automated) $300,200/38,000 = $7.90 per MH
Finishing (manual) $99,800/20,000 = $4.99 per DLH

	To Product A	To Product B
(1) Overhead assigned using plantwide rate: based on DLH	1($16.00) = $16.00	3($16.00) = $48.00

(2) Overhead assigned
using departmental rates:

Assembly	5($7.90) = $39.50	2($7.90) = $15.80
Finishing	1($4.99) = 4.90	3($4.99) = 14.97
Total	$44.99	$30.77

FIG. 3-2. *Plantwide versus departmental overhead rates.*

Use of plantwide overhead rates rather than departmental rates may also contribute to problems in product pricing. While selling prices must be reflective of market conditions, management typically uses cost as a starting point for setting prices. If plantwide rates distort the true cost of a product, selling prices might be set too low or too high, causing management to make incorrect decisions.

EXAMPLE 2
Assume in the case of Allison Company that direct materials and direct labor costs for product A are $5 and $35, respectively. Adding the various overhead amounts to these prime costs gives the total product cost under each method. Figure 3-3 shows these product costs and the profits or loss that would be indicated if Product A has a normal market selling price of $105.

	Departmental rates	Plantwide rate (DLH)
Direct materials	$ 5.00	$ 5.00
Direct labor	35.00	35.00
Overhead	44.49	16.00
Total cost	$84.49	$56.00
Selling price	$105.00	$105.00
Gross profit (margin)	$20.51	$49.00
Profit margin	19.5%	46.7%

FIG. 3-3. *Total product costs and profits.*

Use of the product costs developed from plantwide rates could cause Allison management to make erroneous decisions about Product A. If the cost figure developed from a plantwide direct labor-hour basis is used, management may think that Product A is significantly more successful than it actually is. Such a decision could cause resources to be diverted from other products. If the cost-containing overhead based on the plantwide machine-hour allocation is used, management may believe that

Product A should not be produced, since it appears not to be generating a very substantial gross profit.

In either instance, assuming that machine-hours and direct-labor hours are the best possible allocation bases for Assembly and Finishing, respectively, the only cost that gives management the necessary information upon which to make resource allocation and product development/elimination decisions is the one produced by using the departmental overhead rates.

JOURNAL ENTRIES IN A JOB-ORDER COST SYSTEM

Typical journal entries required to account for job-order costing transactions are as follows:

1. To apply direct material and direct labor to Job X.

Work-in-process (WIP)—Job X	xx	
Stores control (materials and supplies)		xx
Accrued payroll		xx

2. To apply overhead to the job in process.

WIP—Job X	xx	
Overhead applied		xx

3. To record actual overhead.

Overhead control	xx	
Stores control, accrued payroll, other liabilities		xx

4. To transfer completed goods.

Finished goods—Job X	xx	
WIP—Job X		xx

5. To record sale of finished goods.

Cost of goods sold	xx	
Finished goods		xx
Accounts receivable	xx	
Sales		xx

Figure 3-4 depicts a system flow chart for job-order costing.

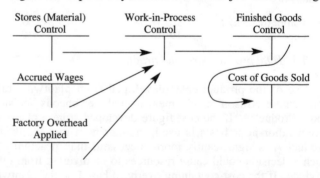

FIG. 3-4. *Job cost system—flow of ledger account relationships.*

The following transactions took place:

1. Materials and supplies bought on credit were $15,000.
2. Materials were issued to production consisting of direct materials of $6,000 (job 1 $3,000, job 2 $3,000) and indirect materials of $2,000.
3. Direct labor paid was $7,000 (job 1 $4,000, job 2 $3,000) and indirect labor was $3,000.
4. Miscellaneous factory overhead was $500 paid in cash.
5. Overhead is applied at 50% of direct-labor cost.
6. Job 1 consisting of 1,000 units were completed.
7. 300 units were sold. The selling price was $15 per unit and sales were on credit.
8. The difference between actual overhead and applied overhead is deemed immaterial.

The journal entries to record the above transactions in a job-order cost system follow:

Transaction Number	Account	Debit	Credit
(1)	Materials and supplies	$15,000	
	Accounts payable		$15,000
(2)	Work-in-process	6,000	
	Factory overhead	2,000	
	Materials and supplies		8,000
(3)	Work-in-process	7,000	
	Factory overhead	3,000	
	Cash		10,000
(4)	Factory overhead	500	
	Cash		500
(5)	Work-in-process	3,500	
	Factory overhead		3,500

Computation:

Direct-labor cost	$7,000
Applied rate	× 50%
Applied overhead	$3,500

Transaction Number	Account	Debit	Credit
(6)	Finished goods	9,000	
	Work-in-process		9,000

Computation:

$$\text{Unit cost} = \frac{\text{Total cost of job 1}}{\text{Total units of job 1 completed}} \quad \frac{\$9,000}{1,000} = \$9 \text{ per unit}$$

Cost of job 1 completed = 1,000 units × $9 = $9,000
(see ledger account for job 1)

(7)	Cost of goods sold	2,700	
	Finished goods		2,700
	300 units × $9 = $2,700		
	Accounts receivable	4,500	
	Sales		
	300 units × $15 = $4,500		4,500
(8)	Cost of goods sold	2,000	
	Factory overhead		2,000

These transactions would be posted to the following selected ledger accounts as follows:

LEDGER PAGE

Work-in-Process

(2) Direct material	6,000	(6)	9,000
(3) Direct labor	7,000		
(5) Applied overhead	3,500		
	16,500		

Job 1

(2) Direct material	3,000	(6)	9,000
(3) Direct labor	4,000		
(5) Applied overhead	2,000		
	9,000		

Job 2

(2) Direct material	3,000		
--------------------	-----		
(3) Direct labor	3,000		
(5) Applied overhead	1,500		
	7,500		

Factory Overhead

Actual Overhead		Applied Overhead	
(2) Indirect material	2,000	(5)	3,500
(3) Indirect labor	3,000	(8) To close	2,000
(4) Miscellaneous	500		5,500
	5,500		

Finished Goods

(6) 1,000 9	9,000	(7) 300 9	2,700

Cost of Goods Sold

300 9	2,700
To close	2,000

Assume instead that transaction 8 stated that the difference between actual overhead and applied overhead is deemed material. In that case, the underapplied overhead would be adjusted to work-in-process, finished goods, and cost of goods sold based on either the units or dollars associated with those accounts at the end of the year.

If units are used to allocate the difference, the following adjusting entry would be made (assume the ending work-in-process has 600 units):

Finished goods	$875	
Work-in-process	750	
Cost of goods sold	375	
Factory overhead		2,000

Computation:

	Units	Allocation of Underapplied Overhead
Finished goods	700	$875
Work-in-process	600	750
Cost of goods sold	300	375
	1,600	$2,000

CAPACITY MEASURES

The term *capacity* means "constraint," "an upper limit." A shortage of machine time, materials, etc., may be critical in limiting production and sales. Management specifies the upper limit of capacity for current planning and control purposes after taking into account engineering and economic factors. Management, not external forces, typically imposes the upper limit for capacity. In determining capacity size, management considers its decisions regarding the purchase of capital facilities. In turn, managers reach decisions in plant and equipment after studying the expected effect of these capital outlays on operations over a number of years.

It is important to define different capacity (denominator) measures, since they affect planning and performance evaluation. It also impacts under- and overapplied factory overhead.

Capacity is the ability to produce during a given time period. An upper limit is imposed by the availability of space, machinery, labor, materials, or capital. Capacity may be expressed in units, weights, size, dollars, worker-hours, labor cost, etc. There are typically four capacity levels:

Theoretical Capacity. The theoretical capacity is the volume of activity that could be attained under ideal operating conditions, with minimum allowance for inefficiency. It is the largest volume of output possible and may be called *ideal capacity, engineered capacity,* or *maximum capacity.*

Practical Capacity. The highest activity level at which the factory can operate with an acceptable degree of efficiency, taking into consideration unavoidable losses of productive time (i.e., vacations, holidays, repairs to equipment). Also called *maximum practical capacity.*

Two variations of the practical capacity concept are widely used as the denominator volume. They are *normal capacity* and *expected annual activity.*

Normal Capacity. The normal capacity is the average level of operating activity that is sufficient to fill the demand for the company's products or services for a span of several years, taking into consideration seasonal and cyclical demands and increasing or decreasing trends in demand.

Expected Annual Activity. Similar to normal capacity, except that it is projected for a particular year, this measure is also called *planned capacity.*

The choice of activity level used in determining the overhead application rate potentially will have a large effect on over- or underapplied overhead.

Standard Costing Integrated with Job-Order Costing

Standard costing is an "accessory" that may be added to job-order costing. With job-order costing, individual jobs consist of a single complex unit or a small batch of complete units. The units are customized to meet particular specifications. Standard setting may be used in formulating "custom-made" direct material, direct labor, and factory overhead standards prior to starting each job.

CHAPTER PERSPECTIVE

A job-order cost system is used when heterogeneous products are involved. In this case, the unit cost for each job differs. Job cost sheets should be prepared. The production costs charged to the job are direct material, direct labor, and applied overhead. The applied overhead rate should be the one most realistic for a particular department. Some surrogates of production include direct-labor hours and machine-hours. A capacity measure should be chosen that best suits the company's planning and performance evaluation objectives. For example, if management wants to establish a more rigid production goal to increase productivity, it would use practical capacity rather than normal capacity.

In a service industry, a surrogate measure for output must be determined. For example, job-order costs that may be used by health-care institutions might be cost per patient day, cost per diagnostic related group, or cost per patient care unit of time.

Process Costing

INTRODUCTION AND MAIN POINTS

In Chapter 3, we learned about the job-order cost system, in which costs for dissimilar products are accumulated by job. In this chapter, we look at another cost system, one in which manufacturing costs are accumulated for similar products. A company can use *process costing* for some products and job-order costing for others. For example, Honeywell, Inc., a high-technology company, uses process costing for most of their furnace thermostats and job costing for their specialized defense and space contracting work.

Process costing aggregates manufacturing costs by departments or by production processes. Total manufacturing costs are accumulated under two major categories—direct materials and conversion costs (the sum of direct labor and factory overhead applied). Unit cost is determined by dividing the total costs charged to a cost center by the output of that cost center. In that sense, the unit costs are averages. Process costing is appropriate for companies that produce a continuous mass of like units through a series of operations or processes. Process costing is generally used in such industries as petroleum, coal mining, chemicals, textiles, paper, plastics, glass, and food processing.

In this chapter, you will learn:
- What process costing is.
- How to estimate the degree of completion.
- How to determine equivalent production.
- How to calculate unit cost.
- How cost of goods manufactured is determined.
- How to value ending work-in-process.
- The types of product flow.
- The difference between the first-in, first-out and weighted-average process costing methods.

IDENTIFICATION OF SYSTEM PROBLEMS AND CHOICE OF A SYSTEM

Since the unit costs under process costing are more like averages, the process-costing system requires less bookkeeping than does a job-order costing system. A lot of companies prefer to use a process-costing system for this reason. However, before any particular system is chosen, the principal system problem(s) must be identified in a broader perspective. Typically, which method of costing to use depends more upon the characteristics of the production process and the types of products manufactured. If the products are alike and move from one processing department to another in a continuous chain, a process-costing method is desirable. If, however, there are significant differences among the costs of the various products, a process-costing system would not provide adequate product-cost information and a job-order costing method is more appropriate. For example, a job-order costing system would invariably be used if the customer paid for the specific item, production order, or service on the basis of its cost, which is often the case in repair shops and custom work.

Some companies might find it necessary to use a hybrid of these two systems, depending on how a product flows through the factory. For example, in a parallel processing situation, which is discussed later, some form of hybrid of the two systems has proved to be the optimal system.

Those industries that are most suitable for process costing have the following characteristics:
- Production quantity is uniform.
- One order does not affect the production process.
- Customer orders are filled from the manufacturer's stock.
- Continuous mass production through an assembly line approach.
- A standardization of the process and product exists.
- Cost control on a departmental basis rather than on a customer or product basis is desired.
- Continuity of demand for the output.
- Quality standards can be implemented on a departmental basis—for example, on-line inspection as processing proceeds.

PRODUCT FLOW

There are three different types of product flow involved in process costing, as shown in Figure 4-1:
- Sequential
- Parallel
- Selective

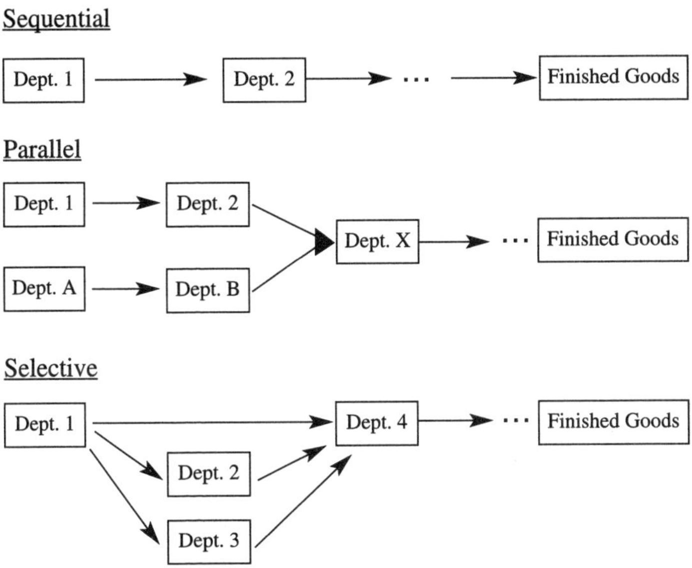

Sequential

Parallel

Selective

FIG. 4-1. *Types of processing flow.*

In *sequential flow,* each product goes through the same set of operations. In a textile industry, for example, a typical plant operates a dyeing department and a spinning department. The dyeing department receives yarn from the spinning department and then transfers it to finished goods. The product flow is sequential.

In *parallel flow,* certain portions of work are done simultaneously and then brought together in a particular process in chain form. The portions of work done simultaneously may require a job-order type of costing to keep track of the differences in costs between the portions of work done simultaneously. Canned-food processing industries employ this type of system. In manufacturing fruit cocktail products, different kinds of fruits are peeled and processed simultaneously in different locations in a factory. They are then brought together in a final process or processes for canning and transferred to finished goods inventory.

In *selective flow,* the product goes through a selected set of processing departments within a factory, depending on the desired final product. Meat processing and petroleum refining fall into this category. In meat processing, for example, after initial butchering, some of the meat product goes to grinding, then to packing, and on to finished goods. At the same time, some goes to smoking, then packaging, and on to finished goods. Selected flows may take a wide variety of forms.

PROCESS-COSTING CALCULATIONS

There are four basic steps in accounting for process costs:

1. Summarize the flow of physical units.

   The first step will encompass a summary of all units on which some work was done in the department during the period. Input must equal output. This step helps detect "lost units" during the process. The relationship may be expressed in the following equation:

   > Beginning inventory + units started for the period =
   > Units completed and transferred out + ending inventory

2. Compute output in terms of equivalent units.

   In order to determine the unit costs of a product in a processing environment, it is important to measure the "total amount of work" done during an accounting period. A special problem arises in processing industries in connection with how to deal with work still in process—that is, work partially completed at the end of a period. Partially completed units are measured on an "equivalent whole unit basis" for process-costing purposes.
   Equivalent units are a measure of how many whole units of production are represented by the units completed plus partially completed units. For example, 100 units that are 60% completed are the equivalent of 60 completed units in terms of processing costs.

3. Summarize the total costs to be accounted for and compute the unit costs per equivalent unit.

   This step summarizes the total costs assigned to the department during the period. The unit costs per equivalent is computed as follows:

   $$\text{Unit cost} = \frac{\text{Total costs incurred during the period}}{\text{Equivalent units of production during the period}}$$

4. Account for units completed and transferred out, and units in ending work-in-process.

   The process-costing method uses what is called the "cost of production report." It summarizes both *total costs* and *unit costs* charged to a department and indicates the allocation of total costs between work-in-process inventory and the units completed and transferred out to the next department (or the finished-goods inventory).

The "cost of production report" covers all four steps and is the source for monthly journal entries. It is a convenient compilation from which cost data may be presented to management.

WEIGHTED-AVERAGE VERSUS FIRST-IN, FIRST-OUT (FIFO)

When there is a beginning inventory or work-in-process, the production completed during the period comes from different batches, some from work partially completed in a prior period and some from new units started in the current period. Since costs tend to vary from period to period, each batch may carry different unit costs. There are two ways to treat the costs of the beginning inventory: the weighted-average (WA) costing method and the first-in, first-out (FIFO) method.

Weighted-Average Method

Under the *weighted-average* method of costing, costs of work-in-process at the beginning of the period are combined with costs of production units started in the current period. An average cost is computed. In determining equivalent production units, no distinction is made between work partially completed in the prior period and the units started and completed in the current period. There is only one average cost for goods completed.

Equivalent units under weighted-average costing may be computed as follows:

Units completed + [ending work-in-process × degree of completion (%)].

First-in, First-out Method

Under FIFO, beginning work-in-process inventory costs are separated from added costs applied in the current period. There are two unit costs for the period: (1) beginning work-in-process units completed, and (2) units started and completed in the same period. Under FIFO, the beginning work-in-process is assumed to be completed and transferred first. Equivalent units under FIFO costing may be computed as follows:

Units completed + [Ending work-in-process × degree of completion (%)]
– [Beginning work-in-process × degree of completion (%)]

The following data relate to the activities of the Assembling Department during the month of January:

	Units
Beginning work-in-process (100% complete as to materials; 2/3 complete as to conversion)	1,500
Started this period	5,000
Units to account for	6,500
Completed and transferred	5,500
Ending work-in-process (100% complete as to materials; 60% complete as to conversion)	1,000
Units accounted for	6,500

Equivalent production in the Assembling Department for the month is computed, using *weighted-average costing,* as follows:

	Materials	Conversion costs
Units completed and transferred	5,500	5,500
Ending work-in-process		
Material costs 1,000 × 100%	1,000	
Conversion costs 1,000 × 60%		600
Equivalent production	6,500	6,100

Equivalent production in the Assembling Department for the month is computed, using FIFO costing, as follows:

	Materials	Conversion costs
Units completed and transferred	5,500	5,500
Ending work-in-process		
Material costs 1,000 × 100%	1,000	
Conversion costs 1,000 × 60%		600
Equivalent production used for WA	6,500	6,100
Minus: Beginning work-in-process		
Material costs 1,500 × 100%	1,500	
Conversion costs 1,500 × 2/3		1,000
Equivalent production for FIFO	5,000	5,100

The following example illustrates process-costing calculations:

Processing operations at the Portland Cement Manufacturing Company involve quarrying, grinding, blending, packing, and sacking. For cost accounting and control purposes, there are four processing centers: Raw Material No. 1, Raw Material No. 2, Clinker, and Cement. Separate cost of production reports are prepared in detail with respect to the foregoing cost centers. The following information pertains to the operation of Raw Material No. 2 Department for July 20X1:

	Materials	Conversion
Units in process July 1		
800 bags	Complete	60% complete
Costs	$12,000	$56,000
Units transferred out		
40,000 bags		
Current costs	$41,500	$521,500
Units in process July 31		
5,000 bags	Complete	30% complete

Using weighted-average costing and FIFO costing, we can compute the following:

(a) Equivalent production units and unit costs by elements.
(b) Cost of work-in-process for July.
(c) Cost of units completed and transferred.

Computation of Output in Equivalent Units

	Physical flow	Materials	Conversion
WIP, beginning	800(60%)		
Units transferred in	44,200		
Units to account for	45,000		
Units completed and transferred out	40,000	40,000	40,000
WIP, end	5,000(30%)	5,000 × 100% = 5,000	5,000 × 30% = 1,500
Units accounted for	45,000		
Equivalent units used for weighted average		45,000	41,500
Less: Old equivalent units for work done on beginning inventory in prior period		800 × 100% = 800	800 × 60% = 480
Equivalent units used for FIFO		44,200	41,020

Cost of Production Report, Weighted-Average
Raw Material No. 2 Department for the Month Ended July 31, 20X1

	WIP beginning	Current costs	Total costs	Equivalent units	Average unit cost
Materials	$12,000	$41,500	$53,500	45,000	$1.1889
Conversion costs	56,000	521,500	577,500	41,500	13.9156
	$68,000	$563,000	$631,000		$15.1045

Cost of goods completed
(40,000 × $15.1045) $604,180

WIP, end:
  Materials
  5,000 × $1.1889 $5,944.50
  Conversion
  1,500 × 13.9156   20,873.40 $26,817.90
Total costs
  accounted for $631,000 (rounded)

Cost of Production Report, FIFO
Raw Material No. 2 Department for the Month Ended July 31, 20X1

	Total costs	Equivalent units	Unit costs
WIP, beginning	$68,000		
Current costs:			
Materials	41,500	44,200	$.9389
Conversion costs	521,500	41,020	12.7133
Total costs to account for	$631,000		$13.6522

WIP, end:
  Materials
  5,000 × $.9389 $4,694.50
  Conversion
  1,500 × $12.7133   19,069.95   23,764.45

Cost of goods
completed, 40,000 units:
  WIP, beginning to be
  transferred out first   68,000
  Additional costs to
  complete conversion

$800 \times (1 - .6) \times \$12.7133$

4,068.26

Cost of goods started
and completed
this month
$39,200 \times \$13.6522$

535,166.24 $607,234.50

Total costs accounted for   (rounded) $631,000

Answers are summarized as follows:

		Weighted Average		FIFO	
		Materials	Conversion	Materials	Conversion
(a)	Equivalent units	$45,000	41,500	44,200	41,020
	Unit costs	$1.1889	$13.9156	$.9389	$12.7133
(b)	Cost of WIP	$26,817.90		$23,764.45	
(c)	Cost of units completed and transferred	$604,180		$607,234.50	

ESTIMATING DEGREE OF COMPLETION

Estimating the degree of completion for work-in-process is critical. Inaccurate estimates will lead to inaccurate computation of unit costs, especially for conversion. Estimating the degree of completion is easier for materials than for processing or conversion costs. The degree of completion for materials is usually 100% unless the material is added during or at the end of a process. The stage of completion for conversion costs requires specific knowledge about the conversion sequence. The sequence consists of a standard number of processing operations or a standard number of days, weeks, or months for mixing, refining, aging, and finishing, etc.

To estimate the degree of completion for conversion, determine what proportions of the total effort (in terms of direct labor and overhead) are needed to complete one unit or one batch of production. Industrial engineers should be able to measure the proportion of conversion needed with reasonable accuracy.

Instead of putting effort into estimating the actual stage of completion, the assumption is often made that work still "in process" at the end of the accounting period is 50% complete. Some companies ignore the work-in-process completely and show no work-in-process inventory account. However, this approach is acceptable only if the work-in-process inventory is insignificant in amount or if it remains relatively constant in size.

USING PROCESS-COST DATA

A process-costing system, like a job-order costing system, is a cost-accumulation system that produces *the unit manufacturing cost* for a given process. Per-unit manufacturing costs are used primarily for product costing, inventory valuation, and income determination. Per-unit cost data are vital for pricing purposes. They are used not only for pricing finished products but also for selecting the "right" product mix in order to maximize profits and for determining ways to maximize production. Perhaps the most effective way to utilize process-cost data is to integrate the output into the standard costing system of the firm. Combined with standard costing, the process-cost data provides the basis for management to judge the *cost performance* of a processing department as a cost center in all categories, such as direct material, direct labor, and overhead. An increase in any one of these cost components is a "red light" to management, indicating inefficient operation in a department.

Process-cost data also aids management in processing decisions. In a multiproduct and joint-product situation, management is often faced with the decision about selling the product at the "split-off point" (juncture of production where joint products become individually identifiable) or processing it further. For external reporting purposes, process-cost data, whether in total or in units, help management allocate joint manufacturing costs to different joint products so that they can produce income statements by product.

In designing the system to meet the needs of both product costing and cost control, management should identify *cost centers*. Cost centers may be assigned to each division, department, or section. The number of processing departments designated as cost centers will depend on the detail desired by management. Cost centers should be set up along organizational lines for control purposes. Management weighs the cost-benefit relationship in deciding on the number of cost centers desired.

PROCESS COSTING AND DECISION MAKING

Process costing has many advantages for management decision making, including:

■ Monitoring production of component parts and subassemblies.

■ Providing good inventory management by retaining accurate records of the amount of materials, labor, and overhead on an equivalent unit basis.

■ Assisting management in the evaluation of the performance of processing departments and product managers.

■ Helping to determine the most efficient or least costly alternative production methods or processes. The information may assist management in deciding to invest in a new plant, new machinery, or repair existing machinery.

■ Revealing to management the number of unfinished "period-end units" so management can anticipate how quickly those units will be completed in the next period.

While process costing requires less paperwork and detail than job-order costing, it also has drawbacks. Under a process-costing system, management is unable to identify actual costs explicitly with individual items. If a particular product incurs any unusual costs, such as excessive spoilage or rework, its costs would be averaged in with other products' costs. Averaging simplifies but also makes process costing less specific and less informative.

CHAPTER PERSPECTIVE

Process costing is a primary approach to assigning manufacturing costs to units produced. It is used by manufacturers whose products are produced on a continuous basis, with units receiving equal attention in each processing center. The four steps in process costing are the computation of equivalent units, calculation of the unit cost, figuring the cost of completed production, and the valuation of the ending work-in-process. If units are spoiled or defective, the per-unit cost of good units will increase.

Costing Joint Products and By-products

CHAPTER

5

INTRODUCTION AND MAIN POINTS

Joint products are two or more products produced simultaneously by a common manufacturing process. The common manufacturing costs, called *joint costs,* have to be allocated on some basis to these products. Each joint product is *significant* to total revenue. By-products are two or more products produced from a common source that are *not significant* to the makeup of total revenue. By-products have a relatively low sales value in relation to the firm's other products.

In this chapter, you will learn:
- What joint products and by-products are.
- The methods that may be used to allocate costs to joint products, and how these methods work.
- How to determine a joint product's unit cost.
- What happens when multiple split-off points exist.
- Whether a joint product should be processed further or sold at a split-off point.
- How to assign costs to by-products.
- How to account for the value of by-products.

ALLOCATION OF COSTS TO JOINT PRODUCTS

A joint product, unlike a by-product, has a high sales value and is marketable. For example, gasoline, heating oil, and kerosene are joint products in oil refining. An item can go from a by-product classification to a joint product as technology and market conditions change. For example, sawdust and wood chips are examples of by-products that become joint products.

Joint-cost allocations may be necessary for inventory valuation, determination of cost of goods sold, deriving selling prices, meeting regulatory agency requirements, and taxation. Joint cost information assists you in looking at the effect of altering the output mix on costs and profitability, establishing a selling price for the product, determining the relative profitability between products, and controlling and evaluating the production and distribution processes. *Processing efficiency* may be appraised by determining the physical yield for each product. An index of production (i.e., weighted-average index) may be computed to evaluate output efficiency.

Some ways to allocate costs among joint products are:
- Market value at the split-off point
- Net realizable value (final sales price less separable costs)
- Final sales price
- Physical measure (e.g., units, feet, pounds)
- Unit cost
- Gross margin
- Chemical property
- Energy potential
- Opportunity cost
- Arbitrary mathematical techniques
- Judgmental allocation

Commonly used allocation methods are based on sales value, market value, and physical measure.

Allocation Based on Sales Value

A popular method of joint-cost allocation is based on *net realizable value*. The net realizable value at the split-off point is determined by subtracting the separable costs from the sales value. This method is widely used because of the desire to value inventory based on the relative income-generating ability of the inventory items.

The method of allocation of joint costs according to the ability of each product to absorb these costs will result in the same gross profit margin for each product when there are no separable costs. This is generally called the *relative sales value method*.

The use of *final selling price* as a basis for joint-cost allocation is feasible when a close relationship exists between cost and selling price. It may be advisable when the company must justify its selling prices, based on price-cost relationships, to governmental agencies. It may also be used when there is a rapid inventory turnover or a low normal profit percentage. When there is a wide vacillation in selling price, *average anticipated prices* for the period may be used.

Allocation Based on Market Value

The market value at split-off point method is recommended when market values are available for raw materials at the separation point. The market-value allocation ratio equals:

Market value of each item × Joint cost = Market value of all items

Allocation Based on Physical Measure

Joint-cost allocation using a *physical measure* is feasible when there is homogeneity of units in physical terms, the market potential of the products is similar, new products are involved (since a current selling price does not exist), and when net realizable values of the products are approximately the same. A major limitation of the physical-measure method is that it bears no relationship to the revenue-producing ability of the products. There is also a distortion in the gross profit computation any time the sales price per unit of quantity is not the same for the joint products.

COMPARING THE METHODS OF JOINT-COST ALLOCATION

The allocation of joint costs by physical units results in an equal cost per unit for each product.

EXAMPLE 1

Assume a refining process produces two products—gas and oil—in quantities of 2,000 gallons of gas and 4,000 gallons of oil. Since gas represents 2,000 gallons out of the total 6,000 gallons, gas would be assigned one-third of the joint costs of the process of refining. Oil would be assigned the other two-thirds. If the process costs $36,000, gas would be charged one-third of these costs—or $12,000. Oil would be assigned the remaining $24,000—or two-thirds of the joint costs. Since 2,000 gallons of gas was produced for $12,000, the unit cost is $6 per gallon. The 4,000 gallons of oil was produced at $24,000, resulting in the same unit cost of $6 per gallon.

After joint-cost allocation, one product could show a profit while another one could show a loss. This is illustrated in the next example.

EXAMPLE 2

Assume that gas could be sold at $14 per gallon, while oil could be sold at $5 per gallon at the split-off point. Since the costs of producing gas and oil are $6 per gallon each, gas shows a profit of $8 per gallon while oil shows a loss of $1 per gallon. It seems less than desirable to consistently sell a product for less than its cost.

In many cases in which the net realizable values of the product are not close, one could use the method of allocating joint costs according to the ability of a product to absorb these joint costs.

EXAMPLE 3

Let's assume that gas could be sold for $14 per gallon and oil for $5 per gallon after the joint refining process. Therefore, the 2,000 gallons of gas could be sold for $28,000 while the 4,000 gallons of oil could be sold for $20,000. Gas would absorb $28,000 divided by the $48,000 total sales value, or seven-twelfths, of the joint costs. Oil would absorb $20,000 divided by the $48,000 total sales value, or five-twelfths, of the joint costs. The total joint cost was $36,000. Gas would absorb seven-twelfths of $36,000, or $21,000. Oil would absorb five-twelfths of $36,000, or $15,000. This results in gas selling for $28,000 and costing $21,000, for a profit of $7,000. This is 25% of the sales price. Oil sells for $20,000 and costs $15,000, for a profit of $5,000. This is also 25% of its sales price.

The computation of net realizable value and the gross profit margin is as follows:

EXAMPLE 4

Assume that 2,000 gallons of gas could be sold for $14 per gallon and 4,000 gallons of oil could be sold for $5 per gallon. After the split-off point, gas undergoes further processing and incurs $4 per gallon of separable costs. Oil undergoes no further processing and incurs no separable costs. To determine the net realizable value of gas at the split-off point, the $4 per gallon separable cost is subtracted from the $14-per-gallon sale price. The net realizable value of gas at the split-off point is $10 per gallon for the 2,000 gallons. Gas has a *total net realizable value* of $20,000 (2,000 × $10) at the split-off point. The 4,000 gallons of oil sells for $5 per gallon at the split-off point and also has a total net realizable value of $20,000 (4,000 × $5). Since gas and oil have the same net realizable value at the split-off point, they share equally in the $36,000 of joint costs and are each allocated $18,000 of the joint costs.

The *profit margin* no longer would be the same for the two products. Gas has separable costs of $4 per gallon (or $8,000), and joint costs of $18,000. The total cost is $26,000 with a sales value of $28,000, giving a profit of $2,000. This is a 7% gross profit margin. Oil has joint costs of $18,000 and sells for $20,000. The profit of the same $2,000 is just a coincidence. The gross profit margin of oil is 10% larger than the 7% gross profit margin of gas. The reason the profit margin of oil is less than it was in the previous example is that oil absorbs a larger share of the joint costs than before.

ILLUSTRATION OF UNIT COST AND WEIGHTED-AVERAGE UNIT COST METHODS

The unit cost of a joint product has to be determined based upon a simple unit cost or weighted-average unit cost. The joint cost of manufacturing products alpha, beta, and gamma is $150,000. The units produced are (1) alpha, 20,000; (2) beta, 25,000; and (3) gamma, $30,000.

The cost per unit is

$$\frac{\$150,000}{75,000} = \$2$$

Using the unit-cost method, the joint cost is allocated in the following manner:

Product alpha	=	$2 × 20,000	=	$40,000
Product beta	=	$2 × 25,000	=	50,000
Product gamma	=	$2 × 30,000	=	60,000
Total				$150,000

The weighted-average unit cost method should be used when complexities exist regarding the joint products. Examples of such complexities are production problems, time required to produce, and the quality of materials or labor. Taking these complexities into account requires weighing the factors in order to arrive at a reasonable allocation basis. The weights may be based upon (1) the importance of the products, (2) time required to produce, or (3) expected value.

Using the weighted-average method, the allocation of the joint cost is as follows:

Product	Units	Weight	WAC*	AR+	Total joint cost	Assigned cost
Alpha	20,000 ×	2.8	= $56,000	$\frac{\$56,000}{218,500}$ ×	$150,000 =	$38,444
Beta	25,000 ×	2.3	= 57,500	$\frac{\$57,500}{218,500}$ ×	150,000 =	39,474
Gamma	30,000 ×	3.5	= 105,000	$\frac{\$105,000}{218,500}$ ×	150,000 =	72,082
Total			$218,500			$150,000

*Weighted average cost
+Allocation ratio

ILLUSTRATION OF JOINT-COST ALLOCATION BASED ON BOTH PHYSICAL AND NET REALIZABLE VALUE

The allocation of joint costs using both physical measure and net realizable value can be shown in the following example.

The Audio Processing Company refines two products, gas and oil, by a joint process in quantities of 2,000 gallons and 4,000 gallons, respectively. Joint costs are $36,000.

1. Use the allocation by physical units to determine the portion each product will absorb.

	Number of units	Fractional part of total units	Joint costs to be allocated	Allocated joint costs
Gas	2,000 gal	1/3	$36,000	$12,000
Oil	4,000 gal	2/3	36,000	24,000
Total	6,000 gal			36,000

The allocated joint costs for gas and oil are $6 per gallon.

2. Assume that gas sells for $14 per gallon and oil for $5 per gallon at the split-off point. Find the gross profit for each product based on the physical allocation of joint costs.

	Number of units	Sale price per gallon	Total sale price	Allocated joint costs	Gross margin
Gas	2,000 gal	$14	$28,000	$12,000	$16,000
Oil	4,000 gal	5	20,000	24,000	(4,000)

The gross margin of gas is $8 per gallon.
The gross margin of oil is a loss of $1 per gallon.

3. Assuming the same information in 2, use the net realizable value at split-off method to determine the allocated costs and gross profit for each product.

	Net realizable value	Fractional part of total net realizable value		Joint costs to be allocated		Allocated joint costs
Gas	$28,000	7/12	×	$36,000	=	$21,000
Oil	20,000	5/12	×	36,000	=	15,000
	$48,000					$36,000

	Sales price	Allocated joint costs		Gross margin		Gross margin percentage
Gas	$28,000 −	$21,000	=	$7,000	$\dfrac{\$7,000}{\$28,000}$ =	25%
Oil	20,000 −	15,000	=	5,000	$\dfrac{\$5,000}{\$20,000}$ =	25%

4. Assume the same information as in 2 except that gas must undergo $4 per gallon in separable costs before it can be sold for $14 per gallon. Use the net realizable value at the split-off point method to allocate the joint costs and find the gross profit. (See Figure 5-1.)

The gross margin of gas is $1 per gallon ($2,000 gross margin/2,000 units).
The gross margin of oil is $.50 per gallon ($2,000 gross margin/4,000 units).

A machine of the Berry Machine Shop cuts nails of two different sizes, small and large, and then packages them. A box of large nails sells for $1.75 and a box of small nails sells for $1.30. During the month of June, the machine cut and boxed 10,000 boxes of small nails and 8,000 boxes of large nails. The cost of running the machine for the month was $9,000.
We find the allocated joint costs to each type of box of nails using:
1. The number of units.

Berry Machine Shop Allocation
of Joint Costs Physical Units Method
for the Month of June

Type	Units	Fractional part of joint cost			Total joint cost		Allocated joint cost
Small nails	10,000	$\dfrac{10,000}{18,000}$	= 5/9	×	$9,000	=	$5,000
Large nails	8,000	$\dfrac{8,000}{18,000}$	= 4/9	×	9,000	=	4,000
Total	18,000						$9,000

Divide the number of units of each type by the total number of units. Multiply the fractional part of joint costs times the total joint cost to be allocated.

	Sales price		Separable costs		Net realizable value	Fractional part of total net realizable value			Joint costs to be allocated		Allocated joint costs
Gas	$28,000	−	$8,000	=	$20,000	$\frac{\$20,000}{\$40,000}$	=	1/2	$36,000 × 1/2	=	$18,000
Oil	20,000	−	-0-	=	20,000	$\frac{\$20,000}{\$40,000}$	=	1/2	36,000 × 1/2	=	18,000
					$40,000						$36,000

	Sales price		Separable costs		Allocated joint costs		Total costs			Gross margin
Gas	$28,000	−	($8,000	+	$18,000)	=	$26,000			$2,000
Oil	20,000	−	(-0-	+	18,000)	=	18,000			2,000

FIG. 5-1. *Net realizable value at split-off point.*

Type	Sales value or net realizable value				Fractional part of joint costs		Total joint costs		Allocated joint costs
Small nails $1.30 × 10,000	=	$13,000	$\frac{\$13,000}{\$27,000}$	=	13/27	×	$9,000	=	$4,333
Large nails $1.75 × 8,000	=	$14,000	$\frac{\$14,000}{\$27,000}$	=	14/27	×	9,000	=	4,667
		$27,000							$9,000

FIG. 5-2. *Berry Machine Shop allocation of joint costs net realizable value method.*

Answer: $5,000 allocated to the boxes of small nails or $.50 per box ($5,000/10,000), and $4,000 allocated to the boxes of large nails, or $.50 per box ($4,000/8,000).

2. The net realizable value method of costing for joint products. (See Figure 5-2.)

Divide the net realizable value of each product by the total net realizable value. Multiply the fractional part of joint costs times the total joint costs.

Answer: $4,333 for the boxes of small nails, or $.43 per box ($4,333/10,000), and $4,667 for the boxes of large nails, or $.58 each box ($4,667/8,000).

The DuPont Chemical Company manufactures three products—caustic soda, chlorine, and chloride—using the same machinery. Chlorine is sold at the split-off point while soda and chloride are processed further. For the month of November, the joint costs for the three products are $48,000, and the costs after the split-off for soda are $6,000 and for chloride are $10,000. Soda sells for $36,000, chlorine sells for $20,000, and chloride for $20,000.

1. Use the net realizable value at split-off to allocate the joint costs.

DuPont Chemical
Allocation of Joint Costs
Net Realizable Value Method
for the Month of November

Product	Sales value	Separable costs	NRV*	Fractional part of joint cost		Total joint cost		AJC
Caustic soda	$36,000	$6,000	$30,000	$\frac{\$30,000}{\$60,000}$ =	1/2 ×	$48,000	=	24,000
Chlorine	20,000	—	20,000	$\frac{\$20,000}{\$60,000}$ =	1/3 ×	48,000	=	16,000
Chloride	20,000	10,000	10,000	$\frac{\$10,000}{\$60,000}$ =	1/6 ×	48,000	=	8,000
Total			$60,000					$48,000

*Net realizable value

FIG. 5-3. *Net realizable value at split-off.*

2. Find the gross margin for each product.

	Caustic soda		Chlorine		Chloride	
Sales Value		$36,000		$20,000		$20,000
Costs:						
Joint	$24,000		$16,000		$8,000	
Separable	6,000	30,000	—	16,000	10,000	18,000
Gross margin		$6,000		$4,000		$2,000

Illustration of Multiple Split-Off Points

When more than one split-off point exists, management should:

1. Diagram the physical flow and cost incurrence of products.
2. Determine the net realizable values at each split-off point.
3. Allocate joint costs based on relative net realizable value.

The following data are given for Westinghouse Manufacturing for the month of December:

In Department 1, 5,000 feet of A are converted into 4,000 feet of B and 1,000 feet of C. In Department 2, 3,000 feet of X were added to the 1,000 feet of C to manufacture 1,000 feet of D, 2,000 feet of E, and 1,000 feet of waste. Before sale, D had to be further processed in Department 3.

Production costs are as follows:

	Department		
	1	2	3
Material	$50,000	$10,000	—
Labor	20,000	8,000	$5,000
Overhead	20,000	3,000	6,000
	$90,000	$21,000	$11,000

Unit selling prices per foot are:

B	$20
D	45
E	15

The diagramming of the process follows:

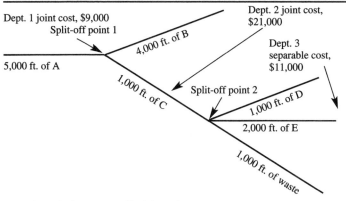

The relative net realizable values are:

	Sales value		Separable cost	=	NRV*			Relative NRV*
Split-off point 2								
D	$(1,000 \times \$45)$	–	$11,000	=	$34,000	$\dfrac{\$34,000}{\$64,000}$	=	53.1%
E	$(2,000 \times \$15)$	–	0		30,000	$\dfrac{\$30,000}{\$64,000}$	=	46.9%
					$64,000			100.0%
Split-off point 1								
B	$(4,000 \times \$20)$	–	0	=	$80,000	$\dfrac{\$80,000}{\$123,000}$	=	65.0%
C	64,000	–	$21,000		43,000	$\dfrac{\$43,000}{\$123,000}$	=	35.0%
					$123,000			100.0%

*Net realizable value

The allocation of joint costs is as follows:

Allocated joint cost	+	Additional joint cost	=	Total	Relative NRV*	Allocation of joint cost
Split-off point 1:						
B }	0	+	$90,000	= $90,000	X 65.0%	$58,500
C					X 35.0%	31,500
						$90,000

61

Split-off point 2:

$$
\left.\begin{array}{c} D \\[2mm] E \end{array}\right\} \quad \$31{,}500 + \$21{,}000 \;=\; \$52{,}500
$$

$\overset{X}{}$ 53.1%		$27,878
$\overset{\overline{X}}{}$ 46.9%		24,622
		$52,500

The final total and per-foot product costs are:

		Total cost		Feet		Cost per foot
B		$58,500	÷	4,000	=	$14.63
D	27,878 + $11,000	38,878	÷	1,000	=	38.88
E		24,622	÷	2,000	=	12.31
		$122,000				

*Net realizable value

Deciding Whether a Joint Product Should Be Processed Further or Sold at Split-Off Point

A joint product should be processed further when the incremental revenue exceeds the incremental costs. Some considerations regarding the decision to sell or process further are the impact on profitability, the market for the intermediate product versus the final product, sales volume, the advertising effort needed, time required and risk involved of additional processing, and the ability to obtain materials or labor for further processing.

Production of joint product Alco is 200 units having a selling price of $.90 per unit. Alco may be further processed into 200 units of Devo having a selling price of $1.05. The additional processing cost is $35.00. Should Alco be sold at the split-off point or processed further?

Computation:

Additional revenue 200 × $.15	$30
Additional cost	35
Loss	$5

Answer: Alco should be sold at the split-off point.

The next example illustrates that the simplistic use of cost-accounting allocations may result in incorrect management decisions. The purpose of the example is to show that management's cost allocation may not generate useful information. It is an illustration of what not to do and why not to do it.

Harvester Company has five products produced from a joint process. The joint cost is allocated based on the sales value of each product at the split-off point. Waste arises from the joint process, which is discarded. However, the company's research division has now found that the waste could be salable as fertilizer with additional processing at a cost of $200,000. The sales value of fertilizer is $280,000. Management has decided to allocate the joint cost based on relative sales value at split-off of the five products and the waste. As a result of this allocation, the waste product was assigned a joint cost of $110,000. The fertilizer thus showed a net loss of:

Sales value	$280,000
Assignable	310,000
Loss	$30,000

Because of this loss, management decided not to process the waste further.

Management has made the wrong decision. The joint cost is the same whether or not the waste product is further processed. In other words, the joint process involves the same total cost for the five products. It is, in fact, financially advantageous to process the waste further as fertilizer since there exists an incremental profit of $80,000 ($280,000 – $200,000).

Management must recognize that joint product costs incurred up to the point of split-off are *sunk costs* (costs incurred in the past whose total will not be affected by any decision made now or in the future) and are irrelevant in decisions regarding what should be done subsequent to the split-off point.

Dow Chemical produces three products from a process involving a vat and a furnace. A diagram of the flow process follows:

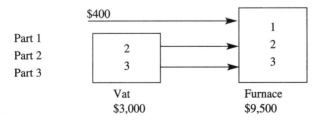

Before going into the furnace, part 1 has a separable cost of $400. Parts 2 and 3 go through a vat prior to being put in the furnace. In addition to the $3,000 vat costs of processing, parts

2 and 3 each require "dipping" at $.30 per cubic foot. The volume of cubic feet per unit of parts 2 and 3 are .6 and .8, respectively. Information regarding selling price per unit and production follows:

Part	Selling price	Production
1	$4	800
2	5	1,000
3	7	1,200

Management decides to allocate the vat cost based on cubic feet and the furnace cost based on the relative sales value before the parts are placed in the furnace.

1. Determine the profitability of parts 1, 2, and 3. (See Figure 5-4.)
2. Management has an opportunity to sell part 2 undipped at $4.60. Should management sell part 2 undipped or fully processed?

Reduction in selling price if part 2 is sold undipped:

		Per Unit
Selling price for part 2 fully processed	$5.00	
Selling price for part 2 undipped	4.60	$.40

Savings in dip costs if part 2 is sold undipped:

Total dip cost for part 2	$180	.18
Total units for part 2	1,000	
Decline in profitability		$.22

Part 2 should be processed further, since profitability per unit will decline by $.22 if it is sold undipped. Note that the vat and furnace costs are still the same even if part 2 is sold undipped.

Costs Assigned to By-products

Generally speaking, if a product's value is too small to affect the decision to produce, it is a by-product. By-products are produced in limited quantity, and result from the manufacture of main products. Examples of by-products are sawdust in lumber mills and bone in meat-packing plants.

The method used for by-product valuation depends on whether:
■ The by-product's value is uncertain when produced.
■ There is an established market for the by-product. Market sta-

Part		Sales value	−	Separable costs and allocated vat costs	=	Sales value before furnace	Allocation percent based on sales value	Allocated furnace cost	=	Profit
1	($4 × 800) =	$3,200	−	$400	=	$2,800	—	$2,090[a]	=	$710
2	($5 × 1,000) =	5,000	−	(*Dip + **Vat) ($180 + $1,154)	=	3,666	—	2,735[b]	=	931
3	($7 × 1,200) =	8,400	−	(288 + 1,846/2) $3,868	=	6,266	—	4,675[c]	=	1,591
		$16,600				$12,732		$9,500		$3,232

Dip and Vat Costs

Part	Cubic volume		Dip cost at $.30		Allocation of vat cost based on cubic feet	×		Allocated vat cost
2	1,000 × .6 =	600	× $.30	$180	600/1,560	×	$3,000	$1,154
3	1,200 × .8 =	960	× $.30	288	960/1,560	×	$3,000	1,846
		1,560		$468				$3,000

[a] $\dfrac{\$2,800}{\$12,732} \times \$9,500 = \$2,090$

[b] $\dfrac{\$3,666}{\$12,732} \times \$9,500 = \$2,735$

[c] $\dfrac{\$6,266}{\$12,732} \times \$9,500 = \$4,675$

FIG. 5-4. *Profitability calculations.*

bility and the reliability of market values determine whether a value should be placed on the by-product before sale. If there is a very unstable market, the sale of the by-product should be reflected in income with no value assigned to the by-product inventory.

▬ The by-product can be used as a substitute for other raw materials.

▬ The by-product is a possible alternative to the main product.

▬ The by-product can be used as an energy source for the firm.

▬ The external outlet for by-products cannot be used internally.

▬ The market is characterized as a long-term rather than a temporary short-term situation.

Note: If there is an abnormal increase in by-products, one may infer that production inefficiencies exist.

When there is an internal transfer of a by-product, the transfer price should preferably be its market value at the separation point.

By-products may be accounted for by the following methods:

1. Income from by-products may be reported as "other income."

2. Income from by-products may reduce cost of sales or the manufacturing cost of the main product.

3. Income from by-products is reflected in the foregoing methods except that the by-product income is reduced by appropriate expenses, such as marketing and administrative costs.

When a by-product is used internally (e.g., for fuel or as a new raw material for the main product), it may be valued at net realizable value or replacement cost. Under the latter method, the production cost of the principal product is reduced by the replacement cost of the by-product materials.

Illustration of the Accounting for By-products

Since by-products are incidental to the manufacturing process, they usually do not share in the joint costs. The net realizable value of a by-product is the sales value, less any separable or disposal costs. This value is either accounted for as "other income" on the income statement, or subtracted from the joint costs of the production process before these joint costs are allocated among the joint products. If one is to recognize a profit on by-product sales, the net realizable value could be reduced by an allowance for the profit. The result would be subtracted from the joint costs.

Assume that 6,500 gallons of a product is refined to produce 2,000 gallons of Alco, 4,000 gallons of Devo, and 500 gallons of Halo. Also assume that the revenue produced by Halo is insignificant relative to the revenue produced by Alco and Devo, and therefore Halo is a by-product. Halo could be sold for $1.50 per gallon at the split-off point. The net realizable value of the 500 gallons of Halo at $1.50 per gallon is $750. The refining process costs $36,000.

Under the first method, the entire $36,000 joint costs would be allocated between Alco and Devo. The $750 would be recorded as "other income" on the income statement.

Under the second method, the $750 would be subtracted from the $36,000 joint costs, and the remaining $35,250 would be allocated between Alco and Devo. The method used to allocate the joint costs between Alco and Devo does not affect, and is not affected by, the method chosen to account for by-product revenue.

Under the third method, assume a normal profit margin of 30% in sales. Thirty percent of the sales value of $750 is $225. The $225 would be recognized as profit from the sales of the by-product. The remaining $525 would be deducted from the $36,000 joint costs. The difference of $35,475 would be allocated between Alco and Devo. This assumes no identifiable separable costs for the by-products.

If a by-product has separable or disposal costs, these are subtracted from the sales revenue to reach the net realizable value. Assume the 500 gallons of Halo could be sold for $4 per gallon after separable costs of $1 are incurred. The net realizable value would be $3 per gallon, giving a total net revenue of the by-product as $1,500. This $1,500 net revenue could be shown as other income or subtracted from the $36,000 joint costs. If subtracted, the sum of $36,000 less the $1,500 revenue from the by-product gives $34,500 to be allocated between the joint products. The net realizable value of $1,500 could be further reduced by a profit margin. Taking the same 30% of the sales price as before, the profit margin is $600, 30% of $2,000. The separable costs were $500. The sum of the two, $1,100, would be subtracted from the sales value of $2,000 to get a remainder of $900. This $900 would be subtracted from the joint costs. The $36,000 minus $900, or $35,100 would be allocated between the joint products Alco and Devo.

Recognition of Net Revenue. The net revenue of the by-product could be recognized when produced or when sold. If the net revenue is recognized when the by-product is produced, an estimated sales value is used as the sales price. If the actual price is different, an account called gain or loss of sales of by-product could be used to record the difference. If the net revenue is recognized as sold, the actual sales price would be used. When the salability of the by-product is uncertain, or price is unstable, it would be better to defer revenue recognition until sold.

The value of the inventory of the by-product could be found by calculating the cost per unit, using any of the foregoing methods, and assigning this amount times the number of units in inventory to get the inventory value. Also, if the value of the inventory is so small as to be immaterial, it could be simply ignored.

Valuation of By-products. Certain by-products are not sold, but are used in the manufacturing process within the plant. In these cases, the value assigned to the by-product would be its replacement value. This value would be equal to the price the company would have to pay to purchase the by-product in the open market.

Scrap material is actually a by-product that is disposed of at the split-off point. It usually has a very minor sales value and would follow one of the previous accounting methods described for the by-product.

Recommendation: Choose the method that is most feasible and logical, but that would also enhance the profits of the company. Since in most cases by-products are relatively insignificant, the most convenient method may be used. If the values associated with the by-product are significant, it is possible that the by-product has moved into a position where it should be considered a joint product.

In the next example we present the allocation of joint costs under varying methods.

Dart Refinery produces 2,000 gallons of lube, 4,000 gallons of maxi, and 500 gallons of mini. The revenue produced by mini is insignificant relative to the revenue produced by lube and maxi. Therefore, mini is a by-product. Mini sells for $1.50 per gallon at the split-off point, while lube and maxi sell for $14 per gallon and $5 per gallon, respectively. The refining process costs $36,000.

1. Allocate the joint costs if the revenue from mini is listed in "other income." The net realizable value of the split-off point method is used to allocate joint costs.

Joint products	# of gallons	Price per gallon	NRV*	Fractional part of total NRV*	Joint costs to be allocated	Allocated joint costs
Lube	2,000	× $14 =	$28,000	$\frac{\$28,000}{\$48,000}$ =	7/12 × $36,000 =	$21,000
Maxi	4,000	× $5 =	$\frac{20,000}{\$48,000}$	$\frac{\$20,000}{\$48,000}$ =	5/12 × 36,000 =	$\frac{15,000}{\$36,000}$
Mini	500		$750			

$750 listed as "other income."

*Net realizable value

2. Allocate the joint costs if the revenue from mini is used to reduce the costs of the joint process. The net realizable value at the split-off point method is used to allocate the joint costs.

   Mini: 500 gallons at $1.50 per gallon, total revenue $750. Subtract $750 from the joint costs of $36,000, leaving $35,250 to be allocated.

Joint products	Net realizable value	Fractional part of total net realizable value	Joint costs to be allocated	Allocated joint costs
Lube	$28,000	7/12	$35,250	$20,562.50
Maxi	20,000	5/12	35,250	14,687.50
	$48,000			$35,250.00

3. Assume a 30% profit on the sale of by-products. Allocate the joint costs using the net realizable value at the split-off point method. The remainder of the sales price of the by-product is subtracted from the joint costs.

$750	Sales price for the by-product
× 30%	Profit on by-product
$225	Profit recognized as "other income" on sale of by-products
$750 – $225 = $525	is subtracted from $36,000 joint costs.
$35,475	Joint costs must be allocated between Lube and Maxi.

Product	Net realizable value	Fractional part of total net realizable value	Joint costs to be allocated	Allocated joint costs
Lube	$28,000	7/12	$35,475	$20,693.75
Maxi	20,000	5/12	35,475	14,781.25
	$48,000			$35,475.00

4. Assume mini undergoes $1 per gallon of separable costs and can then be sold for $4 per gallon. Also, lube undergoes $4 per gallon of separable costs before it can be sold for $14 per gallon. Allocate the joint costs and find the gross profit when the joint costs are allocated using the net realizable value at the split-off point, and the revenue from the by-product is:

  a. Subtracted from the joint costs
  b. Considered as "other income"
  c. Subtracted from the joint costs after a 30% profit is recognized for the by-product.

The total sales price for mini is $4 per gallon times 500 gallons, or $2,000. The only costs to consider are the separable costs of $1 per gallon, or $500. The net realizable value of the by-product is $1,500.

  a. The $1,500 would be subtracted from the $36,000 joint costs, leaving $34,500 to be allocated as in Figure 5-5.
  b. The $1,500 is recognized as "other income."
  c. $1,500 net realizable value for the by-product

30% profit on by-product

$450 Profit recognized as "other income"

($1,500 – $450) = $1,050 is subtracted from the $36,000 joint costs

($36,000 – $1,050) = $34,950 Joint costs must be allocated between lube and maxi, yielding a gross profit of $10,525, ($28,000 – $17,475) and $2,525, ($20,000 – $17,475), respectively. (See Figure 5-6.)

Figures 5-5 and 5-6 provide a comprehensive illustration of joint cost allocation employing the net realizable value method.

EXAMPLE 5

The Baxter Company manufactures ice-cream-pop sticks and tongue depressors by a joint process. The scrap wood is turned into toothpicks and is classified as a by-product. The policy of the

Product	Sales value		Separable costs		Net realizable value	Fractional part of total net realizable value		Joint costs to be allocated		Allocated joint costs	Gross profit
Lube	$28,000	–	$8,000	=	$20,000	$\frac{$20,000}{$40,000}$ = 1/2	×	$34,500	=	$17,250	10,750 ($28,000–$17,250)
Maxi	20,000	–	-0-	=	$20,000	$\frac{$20,000}{$40,000}$ = 1/2	×	34,500	=	17,250	2,750 ($20,000–17,250)
					$40,000			$34,500			

FIG. 5-5. *Joint cost allocation—Net realizable value method.*

Product	Sales value		Separable costs		Net realizable value	Fractional part of total net realizable value		Joint costs to be allocated		Allocated joint costs
Lube	$28,000	–	$8,000	=	$20,000	$\frac{$20,000}{$40,000}$ = 1/2	×	$34,950	=	$17,475
Maxi	20,000	–	-0-	=	20,000	$\frac{$20,000}{$40,000}$ = 1/2	×	34,950	=	17,475
					$40,000					$34,950

FIG. 5-6. *Joint cost allocation—Net realizable value method.*

company is to reduce the joint costs by the expected revenue of the toothpicks manufactured.

During the second quarter of 20X1, the company incurred $37,000 of joint costs to manufacture 40,000 boxes of ice-cream-pop sticks and 80,000 boxes of tongue depressors. Five thousand boxes of toothpicks were also produced. A box of toothpicks sells for $.20. The ice-cream-pop stick boxes sell for $.50 per box after $2,000 of additional costs for packaging and selling. The tongue depressors sell for $.75 per box after the additional cost of $3,000 for packaging and selling. The toothpick boxes do not require any additional costs.

There was no beginning inventory, and the inventory is valued at allocated costs with the exception of the toothpicks. These are valued at the sales price. The company uses the net realizable value method to allocate costs.

We find the value of the inventory on hand consisting of 38,000 boxes of ice-cream-pop sticks, 75,000 boxes of tongue depressors, and 4,500 boxes of the toothpicks were sold.

The company reduces its joint costs by the expected sales revenue of the by-product, toothpicks:

Joint costs	$37,000
Expected sales value of by-product (5,000 × .20)	1,000
Joint costs to be allocated	$36,000

(See Figure 5-7 for calculations.)

Baxter Company
Allocation of Joint Costs
Net Realizable Value Method
for the 2nd Quarter, 20X1

Product	Sales value	Separable costs		Net realizable value	Fractional part of joint cost		Total joint cost		Allocated joint cost
Tongue depressors	$60,000 –	$3,000	=	$57,000	$\frac{19^a}{25}$	×	$36,000	=	$27,360
Ice-cream-pop sticks	20,000 –	2,000	=	18,000	$\frac{6^b}{25}$	×	36,000	=	8,640
				$75,000					$36,000

[a] $\frac{\$57,000}{\$75,000}$ [b] $\frac{\$18,000}{\$75,000}$

Total Costs

		Tongue depressors	Ice-cream-pop sticks
(a)	Separate costs	3,000	2,000
(b)	Joint costs	27,360	8,640
(c)	Total costs (a+b)	30,360	10,640
(d)	Total number of boxes produced	80,000	40,000
(e)	Cost per box (c/d)	$.3795	$.266

Inventory

	Number of boxes		Cost per box		Total value in inventory
Tongue depressors	5,000	×	$.3795	=	$1,897.50
Ice-cream-pop sticks	2,000	×	.266	=	532.00
Toothpicks					-0-

FIG. 5-7.

Note: The by-product (toothpicks) should have no inventory value, because the expected sales value ($1,000) is treated as a reduction of the manufacturing joint costs. There are two cost-accounting alternatives here: The company should either reduce the cost of goods sold for the value of the by-product or reduce the work-in-process account. In the latter case, the inventory values of the major products are directly reduced.

CHAPTER PERSPECTIVE

Joint products are two or more products produced from the same manufacturing process. Joint costs may be allocated to joint products under different methods, including relative sales value and volume. By-products have little value to the main product. There are various ways to handle the value of the by-product, including reducing the cost of the main product and treating it as "other revenue." The methods selected to determine the cost of a joint product and by-product should be logical and realistic given the particular circumstances of a company's manufacturing process.

Cost Allocation

INTRODUCTION AND MAIN POINTS

One important aspect of cost analysis deals with the problem of allocating costs to various parts (segments) of the organization. The segment can be products, divisions, departments, or sales territories. Cost allocation (assignment) is necessary to provide useful data for the following purposes: (1) product costing and establishment of selling price; (2) evaluation of managerial performance and control; and (3) making special decisions.

In this chapter, you will learn:
- How to allocate costs to business segments.
- Cost allocation guidelines.
- The criteria in selecting a good allocation basis.
- What allocation techniques may be used.
- Cautions to be exercised with cost allocations.
- How to allocate service department costs to production departments.
- Common bases of cost allocation.
- Segmental reporting.
- Contribution approach to cost allocation.
- Distribution cost analysis and allocation.
- Cost analysis and allocation to products.
- Cost allocation to territories.

ASPECTS OF COST ALLOCATION

There are basically three aspects of cost allocation: (1) Choosing the object of costing. A *cost objective* is an activity for which a separate measure of cost is needed. Examples are departments, products, processes, jobs, contracts, customers, and sales territories. (2) Choosing and accumulating the costs that relate to the object of costing. Examples are manufacturing expenses, selling and administrative expenses, joint costs, common costs, service department costs, and fixed costs. (3) Choosing a method of matching (2) with (1). For example, a cost-allocation base for allocating manufacturing costs would typically be labor hours, machine-hours, or production units.

The allocation of revenues and variable costs typically are straightforward because they are directly traceable to a specific segment of activity. *Direct costs* are directly chargeable to the product or territory. *Semidirect costs* (e.g., advertising) cover several products. *Indirect costs* are not directly identified and must be logically allocated to the cost objective, such as allocating rent based on square footage in a department.

COST-ALLOCATION GUIDELINES

Cost accumulation determines actual cost by program, cost center, or account number for accounting and planning purposes. These accumulated costs must then be assigned to applicable business segments, such as departments, products, services, or territories.

Cost allocation assigns a common cost to two or more departments, products, services, or territories. The costs are allocated in proportion to the relative responsibility for their incurrence. For example, K Mart, a large retail concern, allocates corporate headquarters' costs to stores so that each store manager is aware that these costs exist and must be covered by the individual stores for the company as a whole to be profitable.

Allocation methods are arbitrary, and some allocation plans make more sense than others. Possible allocation fundamentals include units produced, direct-labor cost, direct-labor hours, machine-hours, number of employees, floor space, and replacement cost of equipment.

An allocation base typically remains unchanged for a long time period, because it represents a major policy. It is reviewed infrequently or when an inequity becomes evident.

The allocation base should be straightforward because complexity results in added computational costs and time that may outweigh the benefits. Clarity is needed so that you can easily understand the allocation formulas and rationale.

The following are criteria in choosing proper allocation bases:

Benefits Obtained. Costs may be allocated based on benefits received. For example, corporate advertising may be allocated based on divisional sales. The higher the sales, the more the benefit received from the advertising. Heating can be allocated to user departments based on space occupied.

Equity. Costs may be allocated based on fairness. "Fairness" may be in terms of input expended, resources used, and time spent. The "equity basis" is often used in government contracting to come up with a mutually agreeable price.

Cause-Effect Relationship. Costs may be allocated based on services provided. It is easy to formulate this relationship when dealing with direct manufacturing costs (e.g., direct material, direct labor). Relationships aid in relating the cost objective to the cost incurred. For example, input-output relationships (e.g., direct-labor hours to quantity produced) may reflect a cause/effect basis.

Ability to Bear. Costs may be allocated based on the cost objective's ability to bear. An example is allocating corporate executive salaries based on divisional profitability. It assumes that a more profitable division can absorb—or bear—more costs.

In deciding on an allocation basis, consider what is commonly done by others in your industry.

Allocation Approaches

The National Association of Accountants favors the allocation of *centralized* (general corporate) costs *only* if they satisfy one or more of the following four criteria:[1]

1. The costs can be influenced by a division manager's actions, even if indirectly;
2. The costs reflect the amount of resources that headquarters gives as divisional support;
3. The allocated costs enhance comparability of the division's performance with that of an independent firm that incurs such costs directly; or
4. The costs are the basis for pricing decisions.

Allocation techniques favored by the Cost Accounting Standards Board (CASB) are:

1. Activity measured by the cause of the pool of cost, such as labor hours, machine-hours, or space occupied.
2. Measure of the function's output, such as number of purchase orders processed.
3. Measure of activity based on service received, such as number of employees served by personnel.

Some firms use "sales dollars" to allocate costs. However, sales is typically a poor allocation base because sales vary each period, while allocated costs are *fixed* in nature. The use of a *variable base* to allocate costs may result in inequity between departments because the costs being allocated to one department largely depend on what occurs in another department. For instance, less selling in one department moves more allocated costs to another productive department. *Recommendation:* Sales dollars should be used as a basis of allocation only when a direct casual relationship exists between sales dollars and the allocated service-department costs.

Fringe benefits should be allocated based on the *percentage of related total salary*. A refinement may be to allocate some fringe-related costs (e.g., pension plan, payroll taxes) based on salaries, with others (e.g., dental insurance) based on the number of employees.

Cautions with Cost Allocation

Arbitrary cost allocations may lead to wrong decisions. However, arbitrary cost allocations may be used under the following circumstances:

▬ The arbitrary allocation is done so that employees will act in a certain desired way according to upper management preferences. For example, central R & D costs may be charged to a division so the manager becomes interested in helping central research efforts.

▬ A retainer fee should be charged for essential services such as legal or internal auditing so the user department is motivated to use the important service even though it may not feel it necessary. If the manager is being charged for the service, why not use it?

Allocation of Service Department Costs to Production Departments

There are two basic types of departments in a manufacturing company: production departments and service departments. A *production department* (such as assembly or machining) is where the production or conversion occurs. A *service department* (such as engineering and maintenance) provides support to production departments.

Before developing departmental overhead rates for product costing, service department costs must first be assigned to production departments.

In allocating service department costs, the two general approaches that may be used are:

Single-Rate Method. Departmental costs are accumulated into a single-cost pool. There is no distinction between variable costs and fixed costs.

Dual-Rate Method. Departmental costs are accumulated into two or more cost pools. One pool may be the fixed costs, while the other pool may be the variable costs.

Service costs (e.g., computer services, accounting and legal, printing, management consulting) preferably should be allocated based on *usage*, such as through a competitive hourly rate charged by outsiders.

Other than product costing, the reasons to allocate service-department costs include:

▪ Control and aid in efficiency evaluation.

▪ Superior income and asset measurement for external parties.

▪ Remind production department managers of the existence of indirect costs they have to absorb. Users benefit from service-department costs and should have to pay for them! Without allocation, there is an understatement in the full costs of the operating center. Managers being charged for service-department costs will make sure that managers in the service departments are properly controlling those costs.

▪ Motivate department managers to use services wisely. If the service-department costs were not allocated, production managers would perhaps overuse what they consider to be "free" services. If a service is underused, allocating the costs for such services prompts managers to utilize the service.

▪ Accomplish a basis for cost justification or reimbursement. An example of cost justification is to derive an "equitable" price, such as when a defense contractor wants to obtain cost reimbursement.

Note: Although most service departments are cost centers generating no revenue, a few may in fact obtain some revenues (e.g., the cafeteria). In such a case, the revenues should be netted against the costs, and the *net* cost should be allocated to other departments. In this way, the other departments do not have to absorb costs the service department has been reimbursed for.

Once the service department costs are known, the next step is to allocate the service department costs to the production departments. There are three basic methods of doing so:

1. The direct method;
2. The step method;
3. The reciprocal method.

Direct Method. The direct method allocates the costs of each service directly to production departments, with no intermediate allocation to other service departments. No consideration is given to services performed by one service department for another. This is perhaps the most widely used method, because it is simple and easy to use.

The Crevier Company's factory has two service departments, General Plant (GP) and Engineering (E), and two production departments, Machining and Assembly. Cost data about each of the departments and information on the actual distribution of services are as follows:

	Service Departments		Production Departments	
	General Plant (GP)	Engineering (E)	A Machining	B Assembly
Overhead costs before allocation	$20,000	$10,000	$30,000	$40,000
Direct-labor hours* by General Plant (GP)	15,000	20,000	60,000	40,000
Engineering hours by Engineering (E)	5,000	4,000	50,000	30,000

*Direct-labor hours are the employee hours spent in producing goods. Engineering hours are the time spent by engineers in performing engineering activities.

Using the direct method yields:

	Service Departments		Production Departments	
	GP	E	A	B
Overhead costs	$20,000	$10,000	$30,000	$40,000
Reallocation:				
GP (0, 0, 60%, 40%)*	($20,000)		12,000[a]	8,000[b]
E (0, 0, 5/8, 3/8)#		($10,000)	6,250[c]	3,750[d]
			$48,250	$51,750

[a]($20,000 × 60%) [b]($20,000 × 40%) [c]($10,000 × 5/8) [d]($10,000 × 3/8)
*Base is (60,000 + 40,000 = 100,000); 60,000/100,000 = .6; 40,000/100,000 = .4
#Base is (50,000 + 30,000 = 80,000); 50,000/80,000 = 5/8; 30,000/80,000 = 3/8

Step Method. This is a method of allocating services rendered by service departments to other departments using an allocation sequence; it is also called the "step-down method," and the "sequential method." The sequence begins with the department that renders services to the greatest number of other service departments and continues in step-by-step fashion, ending with the allocation of costs to service departments that provide the least amount of service. After a given service department's costs have been allocated, it does not receive any further charges from other service departments.

Using the same data from the previous example, the step allocation method yields:

| | Service Departments | | Production Departments | |
	GP	E	A	B
Overhead costs	$20,000	$10,000	$30,000	$40,000
Reallocation:				
GP (0, 1/6, 1/2, 1/3)*	($20,000)	3,333[a]	10,000[b]	6,667[c]
E (0, 0, 5/8, 3/8)#		($13,333)	8,333[d]	5,000[e]
			$48,333	$51,667

---

[a]($20,000 × 1/6) [b](20,000 × 1/2) [c]($20,000 × 1/3) [d]($13,333 × 5/8) [e]($13,333 × 3/8)
*Base is (20,000 + 60,000 + 40,000 = 120,000); 20,000/120,000 = 1/6; 60,000/120,000 = 1/2; 40,000/120,000 = 1/3;
#Base is (50,000 + 30,000 = 80,000); 50,000/80,000 = 5/8; 30,000/80,000 = 3/8

Reciprocal Method. The reciprocal allocation method, also known as the "reciprocal service method," the "matrix method," and the "simultaneous allocation method," is a method of allocating service department costs to production departments, where reciprocal services are allowed between service departments. The method sets up simultaneous equations to determine the allocable cost of each service department.

Using the same data, set up the following equations:

$$GP = \$20,000 + 50/85 \ E$$
$$E = \$10,000 + 1/6 \ GP$$

Substituting E from the second equation into the first:

$$GP = \$20,000 + 50/85 \ (\$10,000 + 1/6 \ GP)$$

Solving for GP gives GP = $28,695. Substituting GP = $28,695 into the second equation and solving for E gives E = $14,782.

Using these solved values, the reciprocal method yields:

| | Service Departments | | Production Departments | |
	GP	E	A	B
Overhead costs	$20,000	$10,000	$30,000	$40,000
Reallocation:				
GP (0, 1/6, 1/2, 1/3)	($28,695)	4,782[a]	14,348[b]	9,565[c]
E (50/85, 0, 30/85, 5/85)	8,695	($14,782)	5,217	870
(based on solution to above equation)	0	0	$49,565	$50,435

---

[a]($28,695 × 1/6) [b]($28,695 × 1/2) [c]($28,695 × 1/3)

Variable Costs vs. Fixed Costs

Generally, variable costs should be charged to user departments using the activity base for the incurrence of the cost involved. For example, variable costs of the maintenance department should be charged to production departments based on machine-hours. Departments responsible for the incurrence of service costs must bear them in proportion to actual usage of services.

The fixed costs of service departments constitute the cost of having long-run service capacity available. An equitable allocation basis for the consuming departments is predetermined, "lump-sum amounts." *Predetermined lump-sums* represent amounts to be charged to consuming departments determined in advance and are the same each period. Usually, the lump-sum amount charged to a department is based either on the department's peak-period or long-term average servicing needs. Budgeted fixed costs, not actual fixed costs, should be allocated. Budgeted service-department costs are allocated to production departments at the beginning of the period in order to derive the production department's predetermined overhead application rate.

During the accounting period, actual service-department costs are allocated to production departments. At the end of the reporting period a comparison can be made between budgeted costs and actual costs. The allocation of service-department costs to production departments is an imposed form of transfer pricing.

Companies often have "multistage allocations," where service departments serve each other and production departments. Complex interrelationships may arise. In a simple relationship, management is "costing" a product requiring two hours of machine time in product Department C. Department C utilizes Department A's services, which in turn needs the services of Department B. Part of B's cost may be allocated to A and a part of A's cost to C, so that A and B costs are proportionately included in the cost of product Z. This relationship is depicted in Exhibit 6-1. With this approach, the unit cost of a department's output includes direct labor of that department, part of the costs of departments furnishing the services, and part of the untraceable costs of the entire factory. Of course, the output may be in either volume of the product or in service. (See Exhibit 6-1.)

Exhibit 6-1

Cost-Allocation Sequence

When it is impractical to distinguish between variable costs and fixed costs of a service department, departmental costs should be allocated to consuming departments according to the base reflecting the optimal measure of benefits received. In general, all service department costs incurred to perform specific services to operating departments should be allocated. The allocated costs are used in determining overhead rates and measuring profitability.

Cost Pools and Allocation Bases

A cost pool is *homogeneous* when the activity whose costs are included have a cause-effect relationship to the cost objective, as other activities whose costs are included in the cost pool. These cost pools require allocation to the user departments. Exhibit 6-2 presents corporate headquarters cost pools.

Exhibit 6-2
Corporate Headquarters Cost Pools

Department	Allocation Basis
Payroll	Number of employees or dollar salaries
Personnel	Number of employees
Purchasing	Dollar amount of purchases
Accounts Payable	Number of vendor invoices paid
Internal Audit	Audit time reports
Central Cost and Budget	Dollar of factory cost and selling expenses
Traffic	Number of freight bills
Central Stenographic	Hours spent or number of pages typed
Marketing	Sales
Laundry	Pounds of laundry or number of items processed
Cafeteria	Number of employees
Medical Facilities	Number of employees or hours spent
Custodial Services	Square footage occupied (building and grounds)
Engineering	Periodic evaluation of services rendered or direct-labor hours
Production Planning and Control	Periodic evaluation of services performed or direct labor hours
Receiving and Shipping	Volume handled, number of requisition and issue slips, or square footage occupied
Factory Administration	Labor hours
Bookkeeping	Number of sales invoices or lines per invoice for each product
Accounting	Volume of transactions or labor hours
Tax	Dollars of tax paid
Legal	Research hours for particular case

Tabulating	Number of punched cards processed
Property	Cost of fixed assets
Credit	Number of accounts in division
Billing	Number of invoices
Accounts Receivable	Number of customer accounts or number of postings to customer accounts
Treasury	Identifiable assets

Exhibit 6-3 presents cost items and the basis for their allocation.

Exhibit 6-3
Common Bases of Cost Allocation

Cost	Allocation Basis
Plant management (including area management and general supervisor)	Number of plants or number of hourly employees
Heat and light (energy)	Square footage
Depreciation on building	Square footage
Maintenance and repairs in building	Square footage
Rent	Square footage
Property taxes	Square footage
Insurance	Square footage
Taxes and insurance on equipment	Book value of equipment
Laboratory	Number of jobs performed or time spent on jobs
Power	Horsepower of equipment
Inspection	Number of units inspected
Maintenance and repairs for machinery and equipment	Machine-hours or value of equipment
Plant superintendent	Direct labor dollars
Credit and collection	Sales value of products
Administrative expenses	Sales value of products or the number of orders received for each product
Corporate executive salaries	Sales
Office space	Square footage
Corporate income taxes	Determinants of taxable income

ABC Company produces inexpensive merchandise. The three production departments are molding, filing, and packing. There are two service departments—administration and maintenance. The direct factory costs of these cost centers follow:

	Service Departments		Production Departments		
	Administration	**Maintenance**	**Molding**	**Filing**	**Packing**
Materials		$500	$4,000	$10,000	$6,000
Salaries	$8,000	4,000	7,000	6,000	9,000
Depreciation	200	800	3,000	2,000	200
Rent	14,000				
Power	1,500				
Other	4,000	700	2,000	3,000	1,000
Total	$27,700	$6,000	$16,000	$21,000	$16,200

Material costs in a cost center are proportional to volume. Salaries are 10% fixed and 90% variable with volume in the production centers, and 100% fixed in the service centers. Depreciation is fixed. Power is 70% fixed and 30% variable. Other costs are 75% fixed and 25% variable in factory administration and 50% fixed and 50% variable in the other cost centers. Six thousand units were manufactured.

The variable cost per unit is computed as follows:

	Administration	**Maintenance**	**Molding**	**Filing**	**Packing**
Materials		$500	$4,000	$10,000	$6,000
Salaries			6,300[a]	5,400[b]	8,100[c]
Power	$450[d]				
Other	1,000[e]	350[f]	1,000[g]	1,500[h]	500[i]
	$1,450	$850	$11,300	$16,900	$14,600
Variable cost					
per unit	$.24	$.14	$1.88	$2.82	$2.43
	($1,450/6,000)	($850/6,000)	($11,300/6,000)	($16,900/6,000)	($14,600/6,000)

[a]($7,000 × 90%) [b]($6,000 × 90%) [c]($9,000 × 90%)

[d]($15,000 × 30%) [e]($4,000 × 25%) [f]($700 × 50%)

[g]($2,000 × 50%) [h]($3,000 × 50%) [i]($1,000 × 50%)

XYZ Company has three divisions operating as profit centers and three central administrative departments operating as service centers. Data for the three profit centers are as follows:

	Western Division	Central Division	Eastern Division	Total
Sales	$3,000,000	$6,000,000	$4,000,000	$13,000,000
Profit Contribution	$400,000	$1,800,000	$1,000,000	$3,200,000
Investment	$2,000,000	$3,000,000	$1,000,000	$6,000,000
Employees	1,000	2,000	1,500	4,500

The operating costs for the administrative departments follow:

Accounting	$400,000
Marketing	200,000
Executive offices	300,000
The allocation bases are:	
Accounting—number of employees	
Marketing—sales	
Executive offices—investment	

The income before tax for each division follows:

	Western Division	Central Division	Eastern Division
Profit contribution	$400,000	$1,800,000	$1,000,000
Allocations:			
Accounting	$88,888	$177,778	$133,333
Marketing	46,154	92,308	61,538
Executive offices	100,000	150,000	50,000
Total	$235,042	$420,086	$244,871
Income before tax	$164,958	$1,379,914	$755,129

SEGMENTAL REPORTING AND THE CONTRIBUTION APPROACH TO COST ALLOCATION

A *segment* is any part or activity of the entity about which the manager seeks to obtain cost data. Proper cost allocation is crucial for segmental reporting purposes. *Segmental reporting* is the process of reporting activities of various segments of an organization, such as divisions, product lines, or sales territories. Segmental information is useful for many purposes. Some product lines may be profitable while others are not. Sales territories may have a poor sales mix and are not taking advantage of opportunities. Salespersons may be doing a good job while others are not. Some production divisions may not be properly utilizing their resources. These are just some examples of the usefulness of segmental reporting. Segmental reports may be prepared for activity at different levels of the business and in varying formats, depending on the needs of the manager.

The *contribution approach* is valuable for segmental reporting because it emphasizes the cost-behavior patterns and the controllability of costs that are generally useful for evaluating performance and making decisions. Specifically, the contribution approach to cost allocation is based on the following factors:

1. Fixed costs are much less controllable than variable costs.
2. Distinguish between direct fixed costs and common fixed costs. *Direct fixed costs* can be identified directly with a particular segment of the organization, whereas *common fixed costs* are those costs that cannot be identified directly with a particular segment.
3. Common fixed costs should be clearly identified as *unallocated* in the contribution income statement by segments. Any attempt to allocate these types of costs on some arbitrary basis to the segments of the organization would destroy the value of responsibility accounting and lead to unfair evaluation of performance and misleading managerial decisions.

Figure 6-1 on the following page presents a contribution-margin income statement by division with a further breakdown into product lines.

DISTRIBUTION COST ANALYSIS

Distribution cost analysis aids in planning a company's sales effort. Distribution costs relate to distributing the product to the customer. These costs include storing, handling, packaging, advertising and promotion, selling, transportation (shipping costs to the customer and paying for the delivery of returned goods), and market research. Some companies include credit and administrative costs.

Distribution costs may be analyzed by product, department, branch, territory, class of customer, distribution outlet, and method of sale. Distribution costs are typically controlled by the sales and marketing department.

Distribution cost standards may be either:

1. Generally applicable to overall distribution functions as a whole or by major division or
2. Units that measure individual performance.

Standards that may be used for distribution costs include cost per sales order, cost per customer account, cost per call, cost per

	Entire company	Divisional breakdown		Breakdown of Division Y					
		X	Y	Unallocable	P+1	P+2	P+3	P+4
Sales	$1,200	$300	$900		$300	$100	$200	$300
Variable manufacturing cost of sales	700	200	500		100	50	100	250
Manufacturing contribution margin	$500	$100	$400		$200	$50	$100	$50
Variable selling and administrative costs	200	50	150		40	40	40	30
Contribution margin	$300	$50	$250		$160	$10	$60	$20
Controllable fixed costs by segment managers	180	40	140	$40*	30	5	50	15
Contribution controllable by segment managers	$120	$10	$110	$(40)	$130	$5	$10	$5
Fixed costs controllable by others	70	6	64	20	20	15	5	4
Segmental contribution	$50	$4	$46	$(60)	$110	$(10)	$5	$1
Unallocated costs	23							
Net income	$27							

*Only those costs logically traceable to a product line should be allocated.

P+Product

FIG. 6-1. *Contribution margin income statement by segments.*

mile traveled, cost per day, cost per dollar of gross profit, selling expense as a percent of net sales, and selling expense per unit sold.

Unlike manufacturing, where there typically is only one standard cost for a product, many standard costs exist for distribution of the same item. For example, cost per call may vary by territory. Even in one territory, the standard cost to sell may vary depending on the class of customers. Standards vary because of different distribution channels, products, departments, territories, and customer classes. The conditions in each are not the same.

Distribution-cost data may be analyzed in terms of number of new customers obtained, number of miles or days the salespeople travel, number of sales demonstrations, number of miles of trucking, volume of goods handled in warehouse, and number of shipments handled.

Allocating distribution expenses may be based on the credit terms associated with sales such as:
- cash sales,
- credit sales, and
- installment sales.

Distribution costs may be analyzed by size of order. Costs are segregated by variability factors. Some costs will be recognized as fixed for all order sizes, while other costs may vary depending on volume (e.g., money volume, physical volume).

When distribution costs are to be prorated and determined based on products or territories, the predetermined distribution-cost rate should be based on estimated sales by products or territories. You must establish standards for the activities of obtaining orders and filling orders.

When distribution costs are determined based on customers, costs should be allocated based on the amount of services received by each customer. This information will also help in determining which customers are entitled to price concessions and discounts.

While many distribution costs may be allocated based on sales, some distribution costs vary with factors other than sales volume, such as weight.

Marketing costs may be evaluated based on distribution methods such as direct selling to retailers and wholesalers as well as mail order sales.

Allocation of Costs to Products
In allocating distribution costs to products, some guidelines that may be used are:

■ Actual costs may be allocated based on actual activity.

■ Budgeted costs may be allocated based on budgeted activity. Budgeted costs may be used because distribution costs for product lines are typically fixed and do not significantly change from actual costs. At the end of the year, the variance between budgeted and actual may be allocated to the product lines.

■ Sales-effort costs (e.g., advertising samples) may be allocated on planned activity, while sales-service costs may be allocated based on actual activity. For example, when salespeople are required to report their time by product line, their salaries and related expenses should be allocated on this basis.

Recommendation: The above approaches usually will provide better product-line costs than the generally used method of allocating total distribution costs on actual sales dollars or units.

Exhibit 6-4 presents different distribution costs and how they may be allocated to product lines.

Exhibit 6-4
Distribution Costs and Allocation Bases to Products

Distribution Cost	Allocation Basis
Warehousing	Units or tonnage handled
Sales-service costs	Orders and invoices for each product
Direct-selling costs (salesperson's salaries, commissions, and bonuses as well as sales or branch office expenses)	Sales value of product
Samples	Specific cost of each product sample
General corporate advertising	Sales value of products
Direct product advertising, newspaper, magazine, and direct mail	Directly to product being advertised
Shipping department sales and supplies	Sales value of each product or relative weight of product sales
Delivery expenses	Size of product weighted by quantity sold

Sales-office expense may be assigned by dollar of sale groupings (e.g., sales less than $10,000, sales between $10,000 and $20,000, etc.). Sales-office expense includes the cost of taking an order, entering the order, billings, and accounting for the sale.

In evaluating a product line, factors to be taken into account are its profitability, growth rate, capital employed, and competition. Accurate cost information aids in determining whether to stop production of unprofitable products or substantially raise their selling prices.

The purpose of allocating departmental overhead costs to products is similar to the purpose of allocating service-department costs to production departments. A "fair share" of departmental overhead should be assigned to each product manufactured in the department.

An economic decision to allocate resources may have to be made, such as the allocation of capacity among products. This is especially important in the case of introducing a new product line.

When specific products have associated with them a greater portion of indirect costs, it may be preferable to allocate indirect costs to product lines. This approach may be feasible in pricing, and helpful in decisions about whether to continue producing a product based on profit margins.

Caution: Be careful in allocating a cost to a specific product because an inappropriate allocation may make a profitable product look bad, and vice versa. Bad allocation decisions may keep alive poor products or kill good ones, or just simply waste money.

Exhibit 6-5 shows the contribution of a company's product lines to the total.

Exhibit 6-5
Contribution by Products

	Entire Company	**Cameras**	**Film**
Projected Sales	$100,000	$60,000	$40,000
Variable costs			
Goods sold	$30,000	$10,000	$20,000
Marketing	$5,000	$4,000	$1,000
Total variable costs	$35,000	$14,000	$21,000
Contribution margin	$65,000	$46,000	$19,000
Direct fixed costs			
Production	$4,000	$2,000	$2,000
Marketing	$3,000	$2,000	$1,000
Total direct fixed costs	$7,000	$4,000	$3,000
Profit contribution	$58,000	$42,000	$16,000
Common fixed costs			
Production	$10,000		
Marketing	$8,000		
Administrative and general	$5,000		
Total common costs	$23,000		
Income before tax	$35,000		

You should determine if the company is making money on a particular account. Customer classes may be analyzed in terms of geographic location, type of agent (i.e., wholesaler, retailer), call frequency, annual volume of business, order size, and credit rating.

An illustrative profit and loss statement by customer class is presented in Exhibit 6-6.

Exhibit 6-6
Profit and Loss Statement by Customer Class

	Total Sales		Retail Sales		Mail Order Sales	
	Amount	% of Net Sales	Amount	% of Net Sales	Amount	% of Net Sales
Gross Sales						
Less: Sales Discount and Returns						
Net Sales						
Less: Cost of Sales						
Gross Profit						
Less: Direct Customer Distribution Costs						
Profit After Direct Distribution Costs						
Indirect Customer Distribution Costs						
Net Profit After Distribution Costs						

Allocation of Costs to Territories

Distribution costs should be analyzed by territories since each territory may have its own particular characteristics. For example, the cost to sell in a populated area such as California is different from selling in an area such as North Dakota.

In allocating costs by territory, the following guidelines exist:

Cost	Allocation Base
Salesperson's wages and expenses	Hours spent in each territory
Billing and office expenses	Number of billing items or direct charge
Advertising	Territory covered by media
Transportation	Direct or based on mileage
Credit and collection	Number of customer accounts or sales dollars in territory

Exhibit 6-7
Contribution by Sales Territory *

	Company		Eastern		Central		Western	
	Amount	%	Amount	%	Amount	%	Amount	%
Net sales	6,000	100	3,000	100	2,000	100	1,000	100
Variable cost of sales								
Production	1,000	17	300	10	500	25	200	20
Marketing	500	8	400	13	50	3	50	5
Total variable cost of sales	1,500	25	700	23	550	28	250	25
Contribution margin	4,500	75	2,300	77	1,450	72	750	75
District territory costs								
Advertising and promotion	600	10	300	10	200	10	100	10
District sales office	400	7	200	7	100	5	100	10
Travel and entertainment	800	13	400	13	350	18	50	5
Total direct territory costs	1,800	30	900	30	650	33	250	25
Territory contribution	2,700	45	1,400	47	800	39	750	75
Common fixed costs								
Production	600	10						
Marketing	400	7						
General and administrative	200	3						
Total common fixed costs	1,200	20						
Net income	1,500	25						

*000 omitted

Exhibit 6-7 reveals the contribution of a company's sales territories to overall profits.

CHAPTER PERSPECTIVE

Costs may be allocated to divisions, products, contracts, customers, territories, or any other logical cost objective. Many allocation methods may be used, such as benefits received, equity, and cause-effect. Proper allocation is needed to derive accurate cost figures for product costing, pricing, control, and decision-making purposes.

In appraising the distribution effort, consideration should be given to the number of calls on existing and new customers, number of deliveries, and number of samples distributed.

ENDNOTES

1*National Association of Accountants,* Statement of Management Accounting No. 4B. *"Allocation of Service and Administrative Costs,"* June 13, 1985, paragraph 20.

Activity-Based Costing and Activity-Based Management

INTRODUCTION AND MAIN POINTS

Many companies use a traditional cost system, such as job-order costing or process costing, or some hybrid of the two. This traditional system may provide distorted product cost information. Companies selling multiple products are making critical decisions—about product pricing, making bids, or product mix—based on inaccurate cost data. In all likelihood, the problem is not with assigning the costs of direct labor or direct materials. These prime costs are traceable to individual products, and most conventional cost systems are designed to ensure that this tracing takes place.

The assignment of overhead costs to individual products is another matter. Traditional methods of assigning overhead costs to products—using a single predetermined overhead rate based on a single activity measure—can distort product costs.

After studying the material in this chapter:

■ You will be able to explain the problems associated with traditional overhead costing methods.

■ You will be able to describe how activity-based costing can enhance product costing methods.

■ You will be able to illustrate the two-step procedure involved in activity-based costing.

■ You will be able to associate different cost drivers associated with different cost pools.

■ You will be able to explain what *activity-based management* (ABM) is.

OVERHEAD COSTING: A SINGLE-PRODUCT SITUATION

The accuracy of overhead cost assignment becomes an issue only when multiple products are manufactured in a single facility. If only a single product is produced, all overhead costs are caused by it and traceable to it. The overhead cost per unit is simply total overhead for the year divided by the number of hours or units produced, which was discussed in detail in the previous chapters.

The cost calculation for a single-product setting is illustrated in Table 7-1. There is no question that the cost of manufacturing the product illustrated in Table 7-1 is $28.00 per unit. All manufacturing costs were incurred specifically to make this product. Thus, one way to ensure product-costing accuracy is to focus on producing one product. For this reason, some multiple-product firms choose to dedicate plants to the manufacture of a single product.

Table 7-1
Unit-Cost Computation: Single Product

	Manufacturing costs	Units produced	Unit cost
Direct materials	$800,000	50,000	$16.00
Direct labor	200,000	50,000	4.00
Factory overhead	400,000	50,000	8.00
Total	$1,400,000	150,000	28.00

By focusing on only one or two products, small manufacturers are able to calculate the cost of manufacturing the high-volume products more accurately and price them more effectively.

OVERHEAD COSTING: A MULTIPLE-PRODUCT SITUATION

In a multiple-product situation, manufacturing overhead costs are caused jointly by all products. The problem now becomes one of trying to identify the amount of overhead caused or consumed by each. This is accomplished by searching for *cost drivers,* or activity measures that cause costs to be incurred.

In a traditional setting, it is normally assumed that overhead consumption is highly correlated with the volume of production activity, measured in terms of direct-labor hours, machine-hours, or direct-labor dollars. These volume-related cost drivers are used to assign overhead to products. Volume-related cost drivers use either *plant-wide* or *departmental* rates, which were discussed in the previous chapter.

To illustrate the limitations of this traditional approach, assume that Delta Manufacturing Company has a plant that produces two high-quality fertilizer products: Nitro-X and Nitro-Y. Product costing data are given in Table 7-2. Because the quantity of Nitro-Y produced is five times greater than that of Nitro-X, Nitro-X can be labeled a low-volume product and Nitro-Y a high-volume product.

For simplicity, only four types of factory-overhead costs are assumed: setup, quality control, power, and maintenance. These overhead costs are allocated to the two production departments using the *direct* method.

Table 7-2
Product-Costing Data

	Nitro-X	Nitro-Y	Total
Units produced per year	10,000	50,000	60,000
Production runs	20	30	50
Inspection hours	800	1,200	2,000
Kilowatt-hours	5,000	25,000	30,000
Prime costs (direct materials and direct labor)	$50,000	$250,000	$300,000

Departmental Data	Department 1	Department 2	Total
Direct-labor hours			
Nitro-X	4,000	16,000	20,000
Nitro-Y	76,000	24,000	100,000
Total	80,000	40,000	120,000
Machine-hours:			
Nitro-X	4,000	6,000	10,000
Nitro-Y	16,000	34,000	50,000
Total	20,000	40,000	60,000
Overhead costs:			
Setup costs	$48,000	$48,000	$96,000
Quality control	37,000	37,000	74,000
Power	14,000	70,000	84,000
Maintenance	13,000	65,000	78,000
Total	$112,000	$220,000	$332,000

Assume that the four service centers do not interact. Setup costs are allocated based on the number of production runs handled by each department. Quality-control costs are allocated by the number of inspection hours used by each department. Power costs are allocated in proportion to the kilowatt-hours used. Maintenance costs are allocated in proportion to the machine-hours used.

Plant-Wide Overhead Rate

A common method of assigning overhead to products is to compute a plant-wide rate, using a volume-related cost driver. This approach assumes that all overhead cost variation can be explained by one cost driver.

Assume that machine-hours is chosen. Dividing the total overhead by the total machine-hours yields the following overhead rate:

$$\text{Plant-wide rate} = \$332,000/60,000$$
$$= \$5.53/\text{machine-hour}$$

Using this rate and other information from Table 7-2, the unit cost for each product can be calculated, as given in Table 7-3.

Table 7-3
Unit-Cost Computation: Plant-Wide Rate

Nitro-X

Prime costs	$50,000
Overhead cost $5.53 × 10,000	55,300
	105,300
Unit cost $105,300/10,000 units	$10.53

Nitro-Y

Prime costs	$250,000
Overhead cost $5.53 × 50,000	276,500
	526,500
Unit cost $526,500/50,000 units	$10.53

Departmental Rates

Based on the distribution of labor hours and machine-hours in Table 7-2, Department 1 is labor intensive and Department 2 machine oriented. The overhead costs of Department 1 are about half those of Department 2. Based on these observations, it is obvious that departmental overhead rates reflect the consumption of overhead better than a plant-wide rate. Product costs are more accurate using departmental rates rather than a plant-wide rate.

This approach yields the following departmental rates, using direct-labor hours for Department 1 and machine-hours for Department 2:

$$\text{Department 1 rate} = \$112,000/80,000$$
$$= \$1.40/\text{labor hour}$$
$$\text{Department 2 rate} = \$220,000/40,000$$
$$= \$5.50/\text{machine-hour}$$

Using these rates and the data from Table 7-2, the computation of the unit costs for each product is shown in Table 7-4.

Table 7-4
Unit-Cost Computation: Department Rates

Nitro-X

Prime costs	$50,000
Overhead costs	
Department 1: $1.40 × 4,000 = $5,600	
Department 2: $5.50 × 6,000 = 33,000	38,600
	88,600
Unit cost $88,600/10,000 units	$8.86

Nitro-Y

Prime costs	$250,000
Overhead costs	
Department 1: $1.40 × 76,000 = $106,400	
Department 2: $5.50 × 34,000 = 187,000	293,400
	543,400
Unit cost $543,400/50,000 units	$10.87

Plant-Wide Rate Versus Departmental Rates

Using a single, plant-wide overhead rate based on machine-hours gave the same overhead application and cost per unit for Nitro-X and Nitro-Y—i.e., $10.53. But this would not be an accurate measurement of the underlying relationship, because Nitro-X made light use of overhead-incurring factors while Nitro-Y made heavy use of such services. When products are *heterogeneous,* receiving uneven attention and effort as they move through various departments, departmental rates are necessary to achieve more accurate product costs.

Problems with Costing Accuracy

The accuracy of the overhead cost assignment can be challenged regardless of whether the plant-wide or departmental rates are used. The main problem with either procedure is the assumption that machine-hours or direct-labor hours drive or cause all overhead costs.

From Table 7-2, we know that Nitro-Y—with five times the volume of Nitro-X—uses five times the machine-hours and direct-labor hours. If a plant-wide rate is used, Nitro-Y will receive five times more overhead cost. But does that make sense? Is all overhead driven by volume? Use of a single driver—especially one that is volume related—is not proper.

Examination of the data in Table 7-2 suggests that a significant portion of overhead costs is not driven or caused by volume. For example, setup costs are probably related to the number of setups and quality-control costs are related to the number of hours of inspection. Notice that Nitro-Y has only 1.5 times as many setups as Nitro-X (30/20) and only 1.5 times as many inspection hours (1,200/800). Use of a volume-related cost driver (machine-hours or labor hours) and a plant-wide rate assigns five times more overhead to the Nitro-Y than to Nitro-X. For quality control and setup costs, Nitro-Y is overcosted and Nitro-X is undercosted.

The problems worsen when departmental rates are used. Nitro-Y consumes 19 times as many direct-labor hours (76,000/4,000) as Nitro-X and 5.7 times as many machine-hours (34,000/6,000). Nitro-Y receives 19 times more overhead from Department 1 and 5.7 times more overhead from Department 2.

As Table 7-4 shows, with departmental rates the unit cost of the Nitro-X decreases to $8.86, and the unit cost of Nitro-Y increases to $10.87. This change emphasizes the failure of volume-based cost drivers to accurately reflect each product's consumption of setup and quality-control costs.

Why Volume-Related Cost Drivers Fail

At least two major factors impair the ability of a volume-related cost driver to assign overhead costs accurately: (1) the proportion of non-volume-related overhead costs to total overhead costs; and (2) the degree of product diversity.

Non-volume-related Overhead Costs. In our example, there are four overhead activities: quality control, setup, maintenance, and power. Maintenance and power are volume related. Quality control and setup are less dependent on volume. As a result, volume-based cost drivers cannot assign these costs accurately to products.

Use of volume-based cost drivers to assign non-volume-related overhead costs creates distorted product costs. The severity of this distortion depends on what proportion of total overhead costs these non-volume-related costs represent. In our example, setup costs and quality-control costs represent a substantial share—51%—of total overhead ($170,000/$332,000). This suggests that some care should be exercised in assigning these costs. If non-volume-related overhead costs are only a small percentage of total overhead costs, the distortion of product costs is quite small. In such a case, the use of volume-based cost drivers may be acceptable.

Product Diversity. When products consume overhead activities in different proportions, a firm has product diversity.

To illustrate, the proportion of all overhead activities consumed by both Nitro-X and Nitro-Y is computed and displayed in Table 7-5. The proportion of each activity consumed by a product is called the consumption ratio. As you can see from the table, the consumption ratios for these two products differ from the non-volume-related categories to the volume-related costs.

Table 7-5
Product Diversity: Proportion of Consumption

Overhead activity	Nitro-X	Nitro-Y	Consumption measure
Setup	.40(1)	.60(1)	Production runs
Quality control	.40(2)	.60(2)	Inspection-hours
Power	.17(3)	.83(3)	Kilowatt-hours
Maintenance	.17(4)	.83(4)	Machine-hours

(1) 20/50 (Nitro-X) and 30/50 (Nitro-Y)
(2) 800/2,000 (Nitro-X) and 1,200/2,000 (Nitro-Y)
(3) 5,000/30,000 (Nitro-X) and 25,000/30,000 (Nitro-Y)
(4) 10,000/60,000 (Nitro-X) and 50,000/60,000 (Nitro-Y)

Since the non-volume-related overhead costs are a significant proportion of total overhead and their consumption ratio differs from that of the volume-based cost driver, product costs can be distorted if a volume-based cost driver is used. The solution to this costing problem is to use an *activity-based costing* approach.

ACTIVITY-BASED PRODUCT COSTING

An activity-based cost system is one that traces costs first to activities and then to products. Traditional product costing also involves two stages, but in the first stage costs are traced to departments, not to activities. In both traditional and activity-based costing, the second stage consists of tracing costs to the product. The principle difference between the two methods is the number of cost drivers used. Activity-based costing uses a much larger number of cost drivers than the one or two volume-based cost drivers typical in a conventional system. In fact, the approach separates overhead costs into overhead cost pools, where each cost pool is associated with a different cost driver. Then a predetermined overhead rate is computed for each cost pool and each cost driver. As a result, this method has enhanced accuracy.

First-Stage Procedure

In the first stage of activity-based costing, overhead costs are divided into homogeneous cost pools. A *homogeneous cost pool* is a collection of overhead costs for which cost variations can be explained by a single cost driver. Overhead activities are homogeneous whenever they have the same consumption ratios for all products. Once a pool is defined, the cost per unit of the cost driver is computed for that pool. This is called the *pool rate*. Computing the pool rate completes the first state. The first stage produces two outcomes: (1) a set of homogeneous cost pools and (2) a pool rate.

In Table 7-5, quality-control costs and setup costs can be combined into one homogeneous cost pool, and maintenance and power costs into a second. For the first cost pool, the number of production runs or inspection hours could be the cost driver. Since the two cost drivers are perfectly correlated, they will assign the same amount of overhead to both products. For the second pool, machine-hours or kilowatt-hours could be selected as the cost driver.

Assume that the number of production runs and machine-hours is the cost driver chosen. Using data from Table 7-2, the first-stage outcomes are illustrated in Table 7-6.

Table 7-6
Activity-Based Costing: First-Stage Procedure

Pool 1:

Setup costs	$96,000
Quality-control costs	74,000
Total costs	$170,000
Production runs	50
Pool rate (cost per run) $170,000/50	$3,400

Pool 2:

Power cost	$84,000
Maintenance	78,000
Total costs	$162,000
Machine-hours	60,000
Pool rate (cost per machine-hour) $162,000/60,000	$2.70

Second-Stage Procedure

In the second stage, the costs of each overhead pool are traced to products. This is done using the pool rate computed in the first stage and the measure of the amount of resources consumed by each product. This measure is simply the quantity of the cost driver used by each product. In our example, that would be the number of production runs and machine-hours used by each product. The overhead assigned from each cost pool to each product is computed as follows:

Applied overhead = Pool rate × Cost driver units used

To illustrate, consider the assignment of costs from the first overhead pool to Nitro-X. From Table 7-6, the rate for this pool is $3,400 per production run. From Table 7-2, Nitro-X uses 20 production runs. The overhead assigned from the first cost pool is $68,000 ($3,400 × 20 runs). Similar assignments would be made for the other cost pool and for the other product (for both cost pools).

The total overhead cost per unit of product is obtained by first tracing the overhead costs from the pools to the individual products. This total is then divided by the number of units produced. The result is the unit overhead cost. Adding the per-unit overhead cost to the per-unit prime cost yields the *manufacturing cost per unit*. In Table 7-7, the manufacturing cost per unit is computed using activity-based costing.

Table 7-7
Activity-Based Costing: Second-Stage Procedure Unit Costs

Nitro-X

Overhead:		
Pool 1: $3,400 × 20	$68,000	
Pool 2: $2.70 × 10,000	27,000	
Total overhead costs		$95,000
Prime costs		50,000
Total manufacturing costs		$145,000
Units produced		10,000
Unit cost		$14.50

Nitro-Y

Overhead:		
Pool 1: $3,400 × 30	$102,000	
Pool 2: $2.70 × 50,000	135,000	

Total overhead costs	$237,000
Prime costs	250,000
Total manufacturing costs	$487,000
Units produced	50,000
Unit cost	$9.74

Comparison of Product Costs

In Table 7-8, the unit cost from activity-based costing is compared with the unit costs produced by conventional costing using either a plant-wide or departmental rate. This comparison clearly illustrates the effects of using only volume-based cost drivers to assign overhead costs. The activity-based cost reflects the correct pattern of overhead consumption and is the most accurate of the three costs shown in Table 7-8. Activity-based product costing reveals that the conventional method undercosts the Nitro-X significantly—by at least 37.7% = ($14.50 − 10.53)/$10.53—and overcosts the Nitro-Y by at least 8.1% = ($10.53 − $9.74)/$9.74.

Table 7-8
Comparison of Unit Costs

	Nitro-X	Nitro-Y	Source
Conventional:			
Plant-wide rate	10.53	10.53	Table 7-3
Department rates	8.86	10.87	Table 7-4
Activity-based cost	$14.50	$9.74	Table 7-7

Note: Using only volume-based cost drivers can lead to one product subsidizing another. This subsidy could create the appearance that one group of products is highly profitable and adversely impacts the pricing and competitiveness of another group of products. In a highly competitive environment, accurate cost information is critical for sound planning and decision making.

The Choice of Cost Drivers

At least two major factors should be considered in selecting cost drivers: (1) the cost of measurement and (2) the degree of correlation between the cost driver and the actual consumption of overhead.

The Cost of Measurement. In an activity-based cost system, a large number of cost drivers can be selected and used. It is preferable to select cost drivers that use information that is readily available. Information that is not available in the existing system must be produced, which will increase the cost of the firm's information system. A homogeneous cost pool could offer a number of possible cost drivers. For this situation, any cost driver that can be used with existing information should be chosen. This choice minimizes the costs of measurement.

For instance, quality-control costs and setup costs were placed in the same cost pool, giving the choice of using either inspection-hours or number of production runs as the cost driver. If the quantities of both cost drivers used by the two products are already being produced by the company's information system, which is chosen is unimportant. Assume that inspection-hours by product are not tracked but data for production runs are available. In this case, production runs should be chosen as the cost driver, avoiding the need to produce any additional information.

Indirect Measures and the Degree of Correlation. The existing information structure can be exploited in another way to minimize the costs of obtaining cost-driver quantities. It is possible to replace a cost driver that directly measures the consumption of an activity with a cost driver that indirectly measures that consumption. For example, inspection-hours could be replaced by the actual number of inspections associated with each product; this number is more likely to be known. This replacement only works if hours used per inspection are reasonably stable for each product. *Regression analysis* (covered in Chapter 10) can be utilized to determine the degree of correlation.

A list of potential cost drivers is given in Table 7-9.

Table 7-9
Cost Drivers

Manufacturing:

Number of setups	Direct-labor hours
Weight of material	Number of vendors
Number of units reworked	Machine-hours
Number of orders placed	Number of labor transactions
Number of orders received	Number of units scrapped
Number of inspections	Number of parts
Number of material handling operations	Square footage

Nonmanufacturing:

> Number of hospital beds occupied
> Number of takeoffs and landings for an airline
> Number of rooms occupied in a hotel

Cost drivers that indirectly measure the consumption of an activity usually measure the number of transactions associated with that activity. It is possible to replace a cost driver that directly measures consumption with one that indirectly measures it, without loss of accuracy, provided that the quantities of activity consumed per transaction are stable for each product. The indirect cost driver has a high correlation and can be used.

Hewlett-Packard Illustration of Multiple Cost Pools

Hewlett-Packard Company's Personal Office Computer Division uses two overhead application rates. One rate is based on direct labor and assigns overhead costs associated with production. The second rate is based on material cost and assigns overhead cost associated with procurement. Table 7-10 illustrates these systems. Overhead costs are initially categorized into three cost pools. Then the overhead costs associated with overall manufacturing support functions are allocated between the production-cost pool and the procurement-cost pool. This allocation is based on the number of employees and the estimated percentage of time spent on these two types of activities.

Northeastern Metal, Inc. has established the overhead cost pools and cost drivers as seen in Figure 7-1.

Overhead cost pool	Budgeted overhead cost	Cost driver	Predicted level for cost driver	Predetermined overhead rate
Machine setups	$100,000	Number of setups	100	$1,000 per setup
Material handling	100,000	Weight of raw material	50,000 lbs	$2 per lb
Waste control	50,000	Weight of hazardous chemicals used	10,000 lbs	$5 per lb
Inspection	75,000	Number of inspections	1,000	$75 per inspection
Other overhead costs	$200,000 $525,000	Machine-hours	20,000	$10 per machine-hour

FIG. 7-1. *Northeastern Metal Inc.—Overhead Cost Pools and Cost Drivers.*

Table 7-10
Multiple Overhead Cost Pools—Hewlett-Packard Company:
Personal Office Computer Division

SUPPORT MANUFACTURING OVERHEAD
Includes costs that support the entire manufacturing process but cannot be associated directly with either production or procurement (e.g., production engineering, quality assurance, and central electronic data processing)

PRODUCTION MANUFACTURING OVERHEAD	PROCUREMENT MANUFACTURING OVERHEAD
Includes such costs as production supervision, indirect labor, depreciation, and operating costs associated with production, assembly, and testing and shipping	Includes such costs as purchasing, receiving, inspection of raw materials, material handling, production planning and control, and subcontracting
Applied on the basis of DIRECT LABOR	Applied on the basis of DIRECT MATERIAL

Source: Patell, J. "Cost Accounting, Process Control and Product Design: A Case Study of the Hewlett-Packard Personal Office Computer Division," *Accounting Review*, October, 1987.

Job Number 3941 consists of 2,000 special-purpose machine tools with the following requirements:

Machine setups	2 setups
Raw material required	10,000 pounds
Waste materials required	2,000 pounds
Inspections	10 inspections
Machine-hours	500 machine-hours

The overhead assigned to Job Number 3941 is computed below:

Overhead cost pool	Predetermined overhead rate	Level of cost driver	Assigned overhead cost
Machine setups	$1,000 per setup	2 setups	$2,000
Material handling	$2 per pound	10,000 pounds	20,000
Waste control	$5 per pound	2,000 pounds	10,000
Inspection	$75 per inspection	10 inspections	750
Other overhead costs	$10 per machine-hour	500 machine-hours	5,000
Total			$37,750

The total overhead cost assigned to Job Number 3941 is $37,750 or $18.88 per tool. Compare this with the overhead cost that is assigned to the job if the firm uses a single predetermined overhead rate based on machine-hours:

$$\frac{\text{Total budgeted overhead cost}}{\text{Total predicted machine-hours}} = \frac{\$525,000}{20,000}$$

$$= \$26.25 \text{ per machine-hour}$$

Under this approach, the total overhead cost assigned to Job Number 3941 is $13,125 ($26.25 per machine-hour × 500 machine-hours). This is only $6.56 per tool, which is about one-third of the overhead cost per tool computed when multiple cost drivers are used.

The reason for this wide discrepancy is that these special-purpose tools require a relatively large number of machine setups, a sizable amount of waste materials, and several inspections. They are relatively costly in terms of driving overhead costs. Use of a single predetermined overhead rate obscures that fact.

Misestimating the overhead cost per unit to the extent illustrated above can have serious adverse consequences for the firm;

for example, it can lead to poor decisions about pricing, product mix, or contract bidding. The cost analyst needs to carefully weigh such considerations in designing a product costing system. A costing system using multiple cost drivers is more costly to implement and use, but it may save millions of dollars through improved decisions.

ACTIVITY-BASED MANAGEMENT

Activity-based management (ABM) is now one of the most important ways to be competitive. It is a systemwide, integrated approach that focuses management's attention on activities with the goal of improving customer value, reducing costs, and the resulting profit. The basic premise of ABM is: *Products consume activities; activities consume resources.* To be competitive, you must know both (1) the activities that go into manufacturing the products or providing the services, and (2) the cost of those activities. To cut down a product's costs, you will likely have to change the activities the product consumes. An attitude such as "I want across-the-board-cuts—everyone reduce costs by 10%" rarely obtains the desired results.

In order to achieve desired cost reductions, you must first identify the activities that a product or service consumes, then you must figure out how to rework those activities to improve productivity and efficiency. *Process value analysis* is used to try to determine why activities are performed and how well they are performed. *Activity-based costing,* discussed in this chapter, is a tool used in activity-based management.

Process Value Analysis

Process value analysis is the process of identifying, describing, and evaluating the activities a company performs. It produces the following four outcomes:

1. What activities are done.
2. How many people perform the activities.
3. The time and resources required to perform the activities.
4. An assessment of the value of the activities to the company, including a recommendation to select and keep only those that add value.

Understanding What Causes Costs

Effective cost control requires managers to understand how producing a product requires activities and how activities, in turn, generate costs. Consider the activities of a manufacturer facing a financial crisis. In a system of managing by the members, each department is told to reduce costs in an amount equal to its share of the budget cut. The usual response by department heads is to reduce the number of people and supplies, as these are the only cost items that they can control in the short run. Asking everyone to work harder produces only temporary gains, however, as the pace cannot be sustained in the long run.

Under ABM, the manufacturer reduces costs by studying what activities it conducts and develops plans to eliminate nonvalue-added activities and to improve the efficiency of value-added activities. Eliminating activities that do not create customer value is a very effective way to cut costs. For example, spending $100 to train all employees to avoid common mistakes will repay itself many times over by reducing customer ill will caused by those mistakes.

Value-added and Nonvalue-added Activities

A *value-added activity* is an activity that increases the product's service to the customer. For instance, purchasing the raw materials to make a product is a value-added activity. Without the purchase of raw materials, the organization would be unable to make the product. Sanding and varnishing a wooden chair are value-added activities because customers don't want splinters. Value-added activities are evaluated by how they contribute to the final product's service, quality, and cost.

Good management involves finding and, if possible, eliminating nonvalue-added activities. *Nonvalue-added activities* are activities that, when eliminated, reduce costs without reducing the product's potential to the customer. In many organizations, poor facility layout may require the work in process to be moved around or temporarily stored during production. For example, a midwest steel company that we studied had more than 100 miles of railroad track to move things back and forth in a poorly designed facility. Moving work around a factory, an office, or a store is unlikely to add value for the customer. Waiting, inspecting, and storing are other examples of nonvalue-added activities.

Organizations must change the process that makes nonvalue-added activities necessary. Elimination of nonvalue-added activities requires organizations to improve the process so that the out activities are no longer required. Organizations strive to reduce or eliminate nonvalue-added end activities because, by doing so, they permanently reduce the costs they must incur to produce goods or services without affecting the value to the customer.

Although managers should pay particular attention to nonvalue-added activities, they should also carefully evaluate the need for value-added activities. For example, in wine production, classifying storage as a value-added activity assumes the only way to make good-tasting wine is to allow it to age in storage. Think of the advantage that someone could have if he or she discovered a way to produce wine that tastes as good as *conventionally* aged wine but does not require long storage periods.

Activity Drivers and Categories

Activity output is measured by activity drivers. An activity driver is a factor (activity) that causes (drives) costs. We can simply identify activity output measures by classifying activities into four general categories: (1) unit level, (2) batch level, (3) product level, and (4) facility level. Classifying activities into these general categories is useful because the costs of activities associated with the different levels respond to different types of activity drivers. Table 7-11 describes what they perform, examples, output measures, and examples of possible cost drivers.

Table 7-11
Activity Categories and Drivers

	Unit-level activities	Batch-level activities	Product-level (Product- and customer-sustaining) activities	Facility-level (Capacity-sustaining) activities
Types of activities	Performed each time a unit is produced	Performed each time a batch is produced	Performed as needed to support a product	Sustain a factory's general manufacturing process
Examples	Direct materials, direct labor, assembly, energy to run machines	Quality inspections, machine setups, production scheduling, material handling	Engineering changes, maintenance of equipment, customer records and files, marketing the product	Plant management, plant security, landscaping, maintaining grounds, heating and lighting, property taxes, rent, plant depreciation

Output measures	Unit-level drivers	Batch-level drivers	Product-level drivers	Difficult to define
Examples	Units of product, direct-labor hours, machine-hours	Number of batches, number of production orders, inspection-hours	Number of products, number of changing orders	Plant size (square feet), number of security personnel

The Value Chain of the Business Functions

The value chain concept of the business functions is used throughout the book to demonstrate how to use cost/managerial accounting to add value to organizations (see Figure 7-2). The *value chain* describes the linked set of activities that increase time usefulness (or value) of the products or services of an organization (value-added activities). Activities are evaluated by how they contribute to the final product's service, quality, and cost. In general, the business functions include the following:

▬ **Research and development:** The generation and development of ideas related to new products, services, or processes.

▬ **Design:** The detailed planning and engineering of products, services, or processes.

▬ **Production:** The aggregation and assembly of resources to produce a product or deliver a service.

▬ **Marketing:** The process that (a) informs potential customers about the attributes of products or services, and (b) leads to the purchase of those products or services.

▬ **Distribution:** The mechanism established to deliver products or services to customers.

▬ **Customer service:** The product or service support activities provided to customers.

A *strategy and administration* function spans all the business activities described. Human resource management, tax planning, legal matters, and the like, for example, potentially affect every step of the value chain. Cost and managerial accounting is a major means of helping managers (a) to run each of the business functions, and (b) to coordinate their activities within the framework of the entire organization.

Strategic Cost Analysis

Companies can identify strategic advantages in the marketplace by analyzing the value chain and the information about the costs

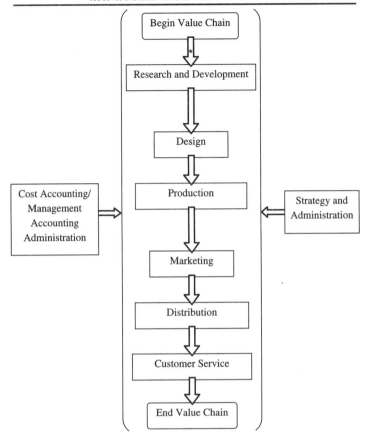

FIG. 7-2. *The value chain and cost/management accounting.*

of activities. A company that eliminates nonvalue-added activities reduces costs without reducing the value of the product to customers. With reduced costs, the company can reduce the price it charges customers, thus giving the company a cost advantage over its competitors, or the company can use the resources saved from eliminating nonvalue-added activities to provide greater service to customers. *Strategic cost analysis* is the use of cost data to develop and identify superior strategies that will produce a sustainable competitive advantage. The idea here is simple: Look for activities that are not on the value chain. If the company can safely eliminate nonvalue-added activities, then it should do so. By identifying and cutting them, you will save the company money and make it more competitive.

Global Strategies
Another approach to gaining a cost advantage is to identify where on the value chain your company has a strategic advantage. Many computer software companies, for example, are looking at foreign markets as a way to capitalize on their investment in research and development. The reservoir of intellectual capital gives these firms an advantage over local competitors who have not yet developed this expertise. These competitors would face research and development costs already incurred by established companies, making it difficult for the newcomers to charge competitive prices and still make a profit.

CHAPTER PERSPECTIVE
This chapter discussed in detail how activity-based costing provides more accurate product cost figures for product costing and pricing, using multiple overhead cost pools and cost drivers. Conventional cost systems are not able to accurately assign the costs of non-volume-related overhead activities. Assigning overhead using only volume-based drivers or a single driver can distort product costs. Two cases were provided to illustrate the use of the activity-based costing system *versus* the traditional system using a single driver such as machine-hours or direct-labor hours. Activity-based costing may provide more accurate information about product costs. It helps managers make better decisions about product design, pricing, marketing, and mix, and encourages continual operating improvements. Activity-based management (ABM), of which ABC is a tool, was discussed.

ACTIVITY-BASED COSTING (ABC) SOFTWARE
Activity-Based Costing (ABC) helps in determining what a product or process should cost, areas of possible cost reduction, and value-added versus nonvalue-added aspects. Numerous PC/network software packages are available for implementing ABC analysis. They are designed for ABC that cost accountants and financial officers can use to aid in accumulating cost information and perform "what-if" testing. Packages are separated into two categories: those developed by independent vendors, and those supported or developed by a Big Six CPA firm.

Price Waterhouse's *ACTIVA* is a comprehensive ABC, profitability, and performance-management software tool. Its features and capabilities include budgeting and planning, product costing and pricing, cost management and analysis, decision support, process improvement, activity-based management (ABM), and variance determination and evaluation. Lead Software's *Activity Analyzer* assigns activities to cost objects and calculates by activity costs and profitability. Profitability may be determined by product, service, customer, and territory, Sapling Software's *Net Prophet* combines ABC, ABM, process-view analysis, budgeting, capacity planning, and constraint checking.

Software from Big Six CPA Firms

1. *The Profit Manager Series,* KPMG Peat Marwick—(800) 537-0047 or (313) 983-0321
2. *ACTIVA,* Price Waterhouse—(314) 425-0500
3. *ABCost Manager,* Coopers & Lybrand—(312) 701-5783
4. *TR/ACM,* Deloitte & Touche—(415) 247-4621 or (617) 261-8615

Software from Independent Vendors

1. *Activity Analyzer,* Lead Software, Inc.—(708) 351-5155
2. *CMS-PC,* ICMS, Inc.—(800) 955-2233 or (817) 633-2873
3. *EasyABC Plus* and *EasyABC Quick,* ABC Technologies, Inc.—(503) 626-4895
4. *Profile ABC,* Applied Computer Services, Inc.—(203) 849-9557
5. *The Cost Blueprint,* ProAct Corporation—(800) 892-4158
6. *NetProphet,* Sapling Software—(416) 678-1661
7. *QUOTE-A-PROFIT,* Manufacturing Management Systems, Inc.—(216) 428-4068
8. *CASSO,* Automation Consulting—(313) 229-2099

REFERENCES

Campbell, R., "Steeling Time with ABC or TOC," *Management Accounting,* January 1995.

Chaffman, Beth M. and Faye Borthick, "Activity-Based Costing in a Service Organization," *CMA Magazine,* December/January 1991.

Collins, Frank, "Improving Performance with Cost-Drivers," *Journal of Accountancy,* June, 1990.

Cooper, Robin and Robert S. Kaplan, *The Design of Cost Management Systems,* (Englewood Cliffs, N.J.: Prentice-Hall, Inc.), 1991.

—————————, "Measuring Costs Right: Make the Right Decisions," *Harvard Business Review,* September/October, 1988.

Cooper, Robin, "The Two-Stage Procedure in Cost Accounting—Part One," *Journal of Cost Management for the Manufacturing Industry,* Vol. 1, No. 2, Summer 1987.

_____, "The Two-Stage Procedure in Cost Accounting—Part Two," *Journal of Cost Management for the Manufacturing Industry,* Vol. 1, No. 3, Fall 1987.

_____, "The Rise of Activity Costing—Part One," *Journal of Cost Management for the Manufacturing Industry,* Vol. 2, No. 2, Summer 1988.

_____, "The Rise of Activity Costing—Part Three," *Journal of Cost Management for the Manufacturing Industry,* Vol. 2, No. 4, Winter 1989.

Ness, J. and T. Cucuzza, "Tapping the Full Potential of ABC," *Harvard Business Review,* July/August 1995.

Raffish, Norm, "How Much Does That Product Really Cost," *Management Accounting,* March 1991.

Reeve, James, "Projects, Models, and Systems—Where Is ABM Headed?" *Journal of Cost Management,* Summer 1996.

Shank, John K. and Vijay Govindarajan, "Transaction-Based Costing for the Complex Product Line: A Field Study," *Journal of Cost Management for the Manufacturing Industry,* Vol. 2, No. 2 (Summer 1988).

Sweeney, Robert B. and James W. Mays, "ABM Lifts Bank's Bottom Line," *Management Accounting,* March 1997.

Just-In-Time Manufacturing and Cost Management

INTRODUCTION AND MAIN POINTS

The problem of inventory control occurs in almost every organization. It exists whenever products are held to meet some expected future demand. In most industries, cost of inventory represents the largest liquid asset under the control of management. It is very important to develop a production and inventory planning system that minimizes both purchasing and carrying costs.

Effective purchasing and management of materials is a high priority in most manufacturing firms. Cost of materials, as a proportion of total product cost, has continued to rise significantly during the last few years and is a concern of top management.

The Japanese have demonstrated the ability to effectively manage their production systems. Much of their success has been attributed to what is known as the *Just-In-Time (JIT)* approach to production and inventory control, which has generated a great deal of interest among practitioners. The "Kanban" system has been a focal point of interest, with its dramatic impact on the inventory performance and productivity of the Japanese auto industry.

After studying the material in this chapter:

━ You will be able to compare JIT with traditional manufacturing.

━ You will know the benefits of JIT.

━ You will be able to explain the impacts of JIT on cost accounting and cost management.

━ You will recognize how JIT manufacturing improves product-costing accuracy.

━ You will be familiar with some successful applications of JIT in U.S. manufacturing firms.

WHAT IS JUST-IN-TIME (JIT)?

Just-In-Time (JIT) is a demand-pull system. Demand for customer output (not plans for using input resources) triggers production. Production activities are "pulled," not "pushed," into action. JIT production, in its purest sense, is buying and producing in very small quantities "just in time" for use. The basic idea has its roots in Japan's densely populated industrial areas and its lack of resources, both of which have produced frugal personal habits among the Japanese people. The idea was developed into a formal management system by Toyota in order to meet the precise demands of customers for various vehicle models and colors with minimum delivery delays.

As a philosophy, JIT targets inventory as an evil that obscures problems that should be solved. By contributing significantly to costs, say JIT proponents, large inventories keep a company from being as competitive or profitable as it otherwise might be. Practically speaking, JIT has the *elimination of waste* as its principal goal, and the principal measure of success is how much or how little inventory there is. Virtually anything that achieves this end can be considered a JIT innovation.

The little inventory that exists in a JIT system must be of good quality. This requirement has led to JIT purchasing practices uniquely able to deliver high-quality materials.

JIT systems integrate five functions of the production process—sourcing, storage, transportation, operations, and quality control—into one controlled manufacturing process. In manufacturing, JIT means that a company produces only the quantity needed for delivery to dealers or customers. In purchasing, it means suppliers deliver subassemblies just in time to be assembled into finished goods. In delivery, it requires selecting a transportation mode that will deliver purchased components and materials in small-lot sizes at the loading dock of the manufacturing facilities just in time to support the manufacturing process.

JIT COMPARED WITH TRADITIONAL MANUFACTURING

JIT manufacturing is a demand-pull, rather than the traditional "push" approach. The philosophy underlying JIT manufacturing is to produce a product when it is needed and only in the quantities demanded by customers. Demand "pulls" products through the manufacturing process. Each operation produces only what is necessary to satisfy the demand of the succeeding operation. No production takes place until a signal from a succeeding process indicates a need to produce. Parts and materials arrive just in time to be used in production. To illustrate the differences between pull and push systems of material control, we use the example of a fast-food restaurant:

> At McDonald's, the customer orders a hamburger, the server gets one from the rack, the hamburger maker keeps an eye on the rack and makes new hamburgers when the number gets too low. The manager orders more ground beef when the maker's inventory gets too low. In effect, the customer's purchase triggers the pull of materials through the system.... In a push system, the caterer estimates how many steaks are likely to be ordered in any given week. He/she reckons how long it takes to broil a steak: he/she can figure out roughly how many meals are needed in a certain week.... (See reference [3]).

Reduced Inventories. The primary goal of JIT is to reduce inventories to insignificant or zero levels. In traditional manufacturing, inventories result whenever production exceeds demand. Inventories are needed as a buffer when production does not meet expected demand.

Manufacturing Cells and Multifunction Labor. In traditional manufacturing, products are moved from one group of identical machines to another. Typically, machines with identical functions are located together in an area referred to as a department or process. Workers who specialize in the operation of a specific machine are located in each department. JIT replaces this traditional pattern with a pattern of manufacturing cells or work centers. Robots supplement people to do many routine operations.

Manufacturing cells contain machines that are grouped in families, usually in a semicircle. The machines are arranged so that they can be used to perform a variety of operations in sequence. Each cell is set up to produce a particular product or product family. Products move from one machine to another from start to finish. Workers are assigned to cells and are trained to operate all machines within the cell. Labor in a JIT environment is multifunction labor, not specialized labor. Each manufacturing cell is basically a minifactory or a factory within a factory. A comparison of the physical layout of JIT with the traditional system is shown in Figure 8-1.

Traditional Manufacturing

Department A   Department B   Department C

<P1> X   X   <P1> Y   Y   <P1> Z   Z
<P2>   <P2>   <P2>

Each product passes through departments that specialize in one process. Departments process multiple products.

JIT Manufacturing

Product 1 (P1)   Product 2 (P2)
Manufacturing Cell 1   Manufacturing Cell 2

          Y   Y
<P1> X   Z   <P2> X   Z

Notice that each product passes through its own cell. All machines necessary to process each product are placed within the cell. Each cell is dedicated to the production of one product or one subassembly.

           Symbols:
           X = Machine A   P1 = Product 1
           Y = Machine B   P2 = Product 2
           Z = Machine C

FIG. 8-1. *Physical layout—traditional vs. JIT manufacturing.*

Total Quality Control. JIT involves a stronger emphasis on quality control. A defective part brings production to a grinding halt. Poor quality simply cannot be tolerated in a stockless manufacturing environment. In other words, JIT cannot be implemented without a commitment to *total quality control (TQC)*. TQC is an endless quest for perfect quality. This approach to quality is opposed to the traditional concept of *acceptable quality level (AQL)*. AQL allows defects to occur provided they are within a predetermined level.

Decentralization of Services. JIT requires easy and quick access to support services, which means that centralized service departments must be scaled down and their personnel assigned to work directly to support production. For example, with respect to raw materials, JIT calls for multiple stock points, each one near where the material will be used. There is no need for a central warehouse location.

Suppliers as Outside Partners. The most important aspects of the JIT purchasing concept focus on (1) new ways of dealing with suppliers, and (2) a clear-cut recognition of the appropriate purchasing role in developing corporate strategy. Suppliers should be viewed as "outside partners" who can contribute to the long-run welfare of the buying firm rather than as outside adversaries.

Better Cost Management. Cost management differs from cost accounting in that it refers to the management of cost, whether or not the cost has direct impact on inventory or the financial statements. The JIT philosophy simplifies the cost-accounting procedure and helps managers manage and control their costs, which will be discussed in detail later in the chapter.

JIT recognizes that with simplification comes better management, better quality, better service, and better cost. Traditional cost-accounting systems have a tendency to be very complex, with many transactions and reporting of data. Simplification of this process transforms a cost *accounting* system into a cost *management* system that can be used to support management's needs for better decisions about product design, pricing, marketing, and mix, and to encourage continual operating improvements.

The major differences between JIT manufacturing and traditional manufacturing are summarized in Table 8-1.

Table 8-1
Comparison of JIT and Traditional Manufacturing

JIT	Traditional
1. Pull system	1. Push system
2. Insignificant or zero inventories	2. Significant inventories
3. Manufacturing cells	3. "Process" structure
4. Multifunction labor	4. Specialized labor
5. Total quality control (TQC)	5. Acceptable quality level (AQL)
6. Decentralized services	6. Centralized services
7. Simple cost accounting	7. Complex cost accounting

Benefits of JIT

The potential benefits of JIT are numerous. First, JIT practice reduces inventory levels, which means lower investments in inventories. Since the system requires only the smallest quantity of materials needed immediately, it substantially reduces the overall inventory level. In many Japanese companies that use the JIT concept, inventory levels have been reduced to a point at which the annual working-capital turnover ratio is much higher than that experienced by U.S. counterparts. For instance, Toyota reported inventory-turnover ratios of 41 to 63, while comparable U.S. companies reported inventory-turnover ratios of 5 to 8.

Since purchasing under JIT requires a significantly shorter delivery lead time, lead-time reliability is greatly improved. Reduced lead time and increased reliability also contribute to a significant reduction in the safety-stock requirements. Safety stock is extra units of inventory carried as protection against possible stock outs.

Reduced lead times and setup times increase scheduling flexibility. The cumulative lead time, which includes both purchasing and production lead times, is reduced. Thus, the firm schedule within the production planning horizon is reduced. This results in a longer "look-ahead" time that can be used to meet shifts in market demand. The smaller lot-size production made possible by reduced setup time also adds flexibility.

Improved quality levels have been reported by many companies. When the order quantity is small, sources of quality problems are quickly identifiable, and can be corrected immediately. In many cases, employee quality consciousness also tends to improve, producing an improvement in quality at the production source.

The costs of purchased materials may be reduced through more extensive value analysis and cooperative supplier-development activities.

Other financial benefits of JIT include:
1. Lower investments in factory space for inventories and production
2. Less obsolescence risk in inventories
3. Reduction in scrap and rework
4. Decline in paperwork
5. Reduction in direct material costs through quantity purchases

EXAMPLES OF JIT IMPLEMENTATION IN THE U.S.

The following are examples of the many implementations of JIT in the U.S.:

▬ The Oldsmobile division of General Motors (GM) has implemented a JIT project that permits immediate electronic communication between Oldsmobile and 70 of its principal suppliers, who provide 700 to 800 parts representing around 85% of the parts needed for the new GM-20 cars.

■ PTC Components, a supplier to GM, has assisted GM in its use of stockless production by sending one truck a week to deliver timing chains to several of GM's engine plants rather than accumulate a truckload to ship to each plant.

■ Ford introduced JIT production at its heavy-duty truck plant in Kentucky, which forced Firestone to switch its tire searching point from Mansfield to Dayton, Ohio. By combining computerized ordering and halving inventory, Firestone has been able to reduce its own finished-goods inventory. In addition, its production planning is no longer guesswork.

■ Each day a truck from Harley-Davidson Motor Co. transports 160 motorcycle seats and assorted accessories 800 miles to Harley's assembly plant in York, Pennsylvania, as a part of their advanced "Materials as Needed" (MAN) program—its version of JIT.

■ The Hoover Company has used JIT techniques in its two plants at North Canton, Ohio, for a number of years for production scheduling and material flow control of 360 different models and 29,000 part numbers.

■ Some plants of Du Pont used JIT and had an inventory savings of 30 cents on the dollar for their first year.

■ The Vancouver division of Hewlett-Packard reported the following benefits two years after the adoption of the JIT method:

Work-in-process inventory dollars	down 82%
Space used	down 40%
Scrap/rework	
Production time:	down 30%
Impact printers	down 7 days to 2 days
Thermal printers	down 7 days to 3 hours
Labor efficiency	up 50%
Shipments	up 20%

Note: The implementation experiences listed above do not suggest a quick or across-the-board adoption of this concept. In many companies (particularly U.S. firms), the JIT purchasing concept simply may not be practical or feasible. In others, it may not be applicable to all product lines. However, many progressive companies are either investigating or implementing some form of the system.

JIT COSTING SYSTEM

The cost-accounting system of a company that adopts JIT is quite simple compared to job-order or processing costing. Under JIT, raw materials and work-in-process (WIP) accounts are typically combined into one account called "resources in process" or "raw and in-process" (RIP). Under JIT, the materials arrive at the receiving area and are whisked immediately to the factory area.

The stores-control account vanishes. The journal entries that accompany JIT costing are remarkably simple, as the following example shows:

Raw and in-process (RIP) inventory	45,000	
Accounts payable or cash		45,000
To record purchases		
Finished goods	40,000	
RIP inventory		40,000
To record raw materials in completed units		

As can be seen, there are no stores-control and WIP accounts under JIT.

In summary, JIT costing can be characterized as follows:
1. There are fewer inventory accounts.
2. There are no work orders. Thus, there is no need for detailed tracing or actual raw materials.
3. With JIT, activities can be eliminated on the premise that they do not add value. Prime targets for elimination are storage areas for WIP inventory and material-handling facilities.
4. Direct-labor costs and factory-overhead costs are not tracked to specific orders. Direct labor is now regarded as just another part of factory overhead. Furthermore, factory overhead is accounted for as follows: Virtually all of the factory overhead incurred each month, now including direct labor, flows through to cost of goods sold in the same month. Tracking overhead through WIP and finished-goods inventory provides no useful information. Therefore, it makes sense to treat manufacturing overhead as an expense charged directly to cost of goods sold.

PRODUCT-COSTING ACCURACY AND COST MANAGEMENT WITH JIT

The costs of many activities previously classified as indirect costs have been transferred to the direct cost in the JIT environment.

For example, under JIT workers on the production line will do plant maintenance and setups, while under traditional systems these activities were done by other workers classified as indirect labor. Table 8-2 compares the traceability of some manufacturing costs under the traditional system with their traceability in the JIT environments.

Table 8-2
Traceability of Product Cost in
Traditional Versus JIT Manufacturing

	Traditional	JIT
Direct labor	Direct	Direct
Direct materials	Direct	Direct
Material handling	Indirect	Direct
Repairs and maintenance	Indirect	Direct
Energy	Indirect	Direct
Operating supplies	Indirect	Direct
Supervision	Indirect	Direct
Insurance and taxes	Indirect	Indirect
Building depreciation	Indirect	Indirect
Equipment depreciation	Indirect	Direct
Building occupancy	Indirect	Indirect
Product-support services	Indirect	Indirect

We can see that JIT manufacturing increases direct traceability in many manufacturing costs, thus enhancing the accuracy of product costing. *Note:* JIT does not convert all indirect costs into direct costs. Even with JIT installed, some overhead activities remain common to the work centers. Nonetheless, JIT, coupled with activity-based accounting (ABA), gives rise to a tremendous improvement in product-costing accuracy over the traditional approach.

In traditional purchasing environments, many firms place great emphasis on purchase-price variances. Favorable purchase-price variances can sometimes be achieved by buying larger quantities to take advantage of price discounts or by buying lower-quality materials. In JIT, the emphasis is on quality, availability, and the total cost of operations, and not just on the purchase price of materials.

In many traditional plants, much of the internal accounting effort is devoted to setting labor and overhead standards and in calculating and reporting variances from these standards. Firms using JIT report reduced emphasis on the use of labor and over-head variances. Even firms retaining variance analysis stress that a change in *focus* is appropriate in a JIT plant. The emphasis is on the analysis at the plant level, with focus on *trends* that may be occurring in the manufacturing process rather than the absolute magnitude of individual variances.

Furthermore, traditional performance measures (such as labor efficiency and machine utilization) that are commonplace in many cost-accounting systems are not appropriate within the JIT philosophy of cost management. They are all inappropriate for the following reasons:

(a) They all promote building inventory beyond what is needed in the immediate time frame.

(b) Emphasizing performance to standard gives priority to output, at the expense of quality.

(c) Direct labor in the majority of manufacturers accounts for only 5 to 15% of total product cost.

(d) Using machine utilization is inappropriate because it encourages results in building inventory ahead of needs.

Table 8-3 lists typical performance measures under the traditional and JIT systems.

Table 8-3
Performance Measures in Traditional Vs. JIT Systems

Traditional	JIT
Direct-labor efficiency	Total head-count productivity
Direct-labor utilization	Return on assets
Direct-labor productivity	Days of inventory
Machine utilization	Group incentives
	Lead time by product
	Response time to customer feedback
	Number of customer complaints
	Cost of quality
	Setup reduction

CHAPTER PERSPECTIVE

This chapter discussed the basic concepts underlying the Just-In-Time (JIT) system. JIT was compared with the traditional system. Its tangible benefits were addressed. Examples of JIT implementation in the U.S. were also presented.

JIT is having an effect on product costing. Under JIT manufacturing, many indirect costs are converted to direct costs. This conversion reduces the need to use multiple cost drivers to assign overhead costs to products, thus enhancing product-costing accuracy. JIT simplifies the cost-accounting procedure. This simplification will transform a cost *accounting* system into a cost *management* system that can be used to support management's needs for better decisions about product design, pricing, marketing, and mix, and to encourage continual operating improvements.

REFERENCES

DeLuizio, M.C., "The Tools of Just-in-Time," *Journal of Cost Management,* Vol. 7, No. 2, 1993.

Foster, George and Charles Horngren, "JIT: Cost Accounting and Cost Measurement Issues," *Management Accounting,* June 1987, pp. 19–25.

_____ , "Cost Accounting and Cost Management in a JIT Environment," *Journal of Cost Management,* Winter 1988, pp. 4–14.

Guo, M.H., "Inventory Accounting and Just-in-Time Production: A Taiwanese Experience," *Advances in International Accounting,* Vol. 6, No. 1, 1994.

Hunt, R., L. Garrett, and C.M. Mertz, "Direct Labor Cost Not Always Relevant at H-P," *Management Accounting,* February 1985, p. 61.

Karmarkar, Uday, "Getting Control of Just-in-Time," *Harvard Business Review,* September-October 1989, pp. 122–131.

McIlhattan, Robert D., "How Cost Management Systems Can Support the JIT Philosophy," *Management Accounting,* September 1987, pp. 2–26.

Analysis of Cost Behavior and Cost Estimation I

INTRODUCTION AND MAIN POINTS

Not all costs behave in the same way. There are certain costs that vary in proportion to changes in volume or activity, such as labor hours and machine-hours. There are other costs that do not change even though volume changes. An understanding of cost behavior is helpful:

1. For break-even and cost-volume-profit analysis.
2. To appraise divisional performance.
3. For flexible budgeting.
4. To make short-term choice decisions.
5. To make transfer pricing decisions.

After studying the material in this chapter:

▬ You will be able to define and give examples of variable costs, fixed costs, and mixed costs.

▬ You will be able to distinguish between committed and discretionary fixed costs.

▬ You will be able to separate mixed costs into their variable and fixed portions, using *engineering analysis* and *account analysis.*

▬ You will be able to explain the advantages and disadvantages of the high-low method for developing a *cost-volume formula.*

▬ You will be able to develop a formula using the high-low method.

A FURTHER LOOK AT COSTS BY BEHAVIOR

As we discussed in Chapter 2, costs may be viewed as variable, fixed, or mixed (semivariable), depending on how a cost will react or respond to changes in the level of activity. This classification is made within a specified range of activity, called the *relevant range.* The relevant range is the volume zone within which the behavior of variable costs, fixed costs, and selling prices can be predicted with reasonable accuracy.

Variable Costs. As previously discussed, variable costs vary in total with changes in volume or level of activity. Examples of variable costs include the costs of direct materials, direct labor, and sales commissions. The following factory overhead items fall in the variable-cost category:

Variable Factory Overhead

Supplies	Receiving Costs
Fuel and power	Overtime premium
Spoilage and defective work	

Fixed Costs. As previously discussed, fixed costs do not change in total regardless of the volume of level or activity. Examples include advertising expense, salaries, and depreciation. The following factory overhead items also fall in the fixed-cost category:

Fixed Factory Overhead

Property taxes	Rent on factory building
Depreciation	Indirect labor
Insurance	Patent amortization

Mixed (Semivariable) Costs. As previously discussed, mixed costs contain both a fixed element and a variable one. Salespersons' compensation, including salary and commission, is an example. The following factory overhead items may be considered mixed costs:

Mixed Factory Overhead

Supervision	Maintenance and repairs
Inspection	Compensation insurance
Service-department costs	Employer's payroll taxes
Utilities	Rental of delivery truck
Fringe benefits	Quality costs
Cleanup costs	

Note that factory overhead, taken as a whole, would be a perfect example of mixed costs. Figure 9-1 displays how each of these three types of costs vary with changes in volume.

TYPES OF FIXED COSTS—COMMITTED AND DISCRETIONARY

Strictly speaking, there is no such thing as a fixed cost. In the long run, all costs are variable. However, some fixed costs, called *discre-*

tionary (or *managed* or *programmed*) fixed costs, change. It is important to note that these costs change because of managerial decisions, not because of changes in volume. Examples of discretionary types of fixed costs are advertising, training, and research and development. Another type of fixed costs, called *committed fixed costs*, are those costs that do not change and are the result of previously made commitments. Fixed costs such as rent, depreciation, insurance, and executive salaries are types of committed fixed costs, since management has committed itself for a long period of time regarding the company's production facilities and manpower requirements.

ANALYSIS OF MIXED (SEMIVARIABLE) COSTS

As we saw earlier, many costs are mixed. For managerial purposes—cost-volume-profit analysis, performance evaluation, flexible budgeting, and short-term decision making—mixed costs need to be separated into variable and fixed components. Since mixed costs contain both fixed and variable elements, the analysis takes the following mathematical form, which is called a *cost-volume formula* (also known as the *flexible budget formula* or *cost function*):

$$y = a + bx$$

where y = the mixed cost to be broken up; x = any given measure of activity such as direct-labor hours, machine-hours, or production volume; a = the fixed cost component; and b = the variable rate per unit of x.

Figure 9-1 shows patterns in cost behavior.

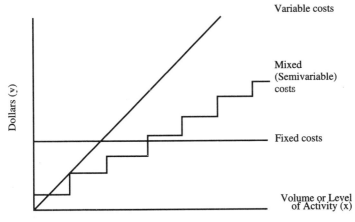

FIG. 9-1. *Cost behavior patterns.*

Separating the mixed cost into its fixed and variable components is the same thing as estimating the parameter values a and b in the cost-volume formula. There are several methods available for this purpose, including engineering analysis, account analysis, the high-low method, and the least-squares method (regression analysis). The first three are discussed in this chapter.

Engineering Analysis

Engineering analysis measures cost behavior according to what costs *should* be, not by what costs *have been*. It entails a systematic review of materials, labor, support services, and facilities needed for product and services. Engineers use time and motion studies and similar engineering methods to estimate what costs should be from engineers' specifications of the inputs required to manufacture a unit of output or to perform a particular service. This can be used for existing products or for new products similar to what has been produced before. Disadvantages of this method are that it is prohibitively costly and often not timely. Furthermore, it is difficult to estimate indirect costs. The engineering method is most useful when costs involved are variable costs, where there is a clear input/output relation.

Account Analysis

Account analysis selects a volume-related cost driver, and classifies each account from the accounting records as a variable or fixed cost. The cost accountant then looks at each cost account balance and estimates either the variable cost per unit of cost driver activity or the periodic fixed cost. Account analysis requires a detailed examination of the data, presumably by cost accountants and managers who are familiar with the activities of the company, and the way the company's activities affect costs. Because account analysis is judgmental, different analysts are likely to provide different estimates of cost behavior.

EXAMPLE 1

The cafeteria department of Los Al Health Center reported the following costs for October 20X1:

Monthly Cost	October 20X1 Amount
Food and beverages	$9,350
Hourly wages and benefits	18,900
Supervisor's salary	4,000
Equipment depreciation and rental	6,105
Supplies	2,760
Total cafeteria costs	$41,115

The cafeteria served 11,520 meals during the month. Using an account analysis to classify costs, we can determine the cost function. Note that in this example, the supervisor's salary ($4,000 per month) and the equipment depreciation and rental ($6,105 per month) are fixed, while the remainder ($31,010) varies with the cost drive, i.e., the number of meals served. Dividing the variable costs by the number of meals served yields $2.692 and the department's cost-volume formula is $10,105 + $2.692 per meal.

The High-Low Method

The high-low method, as the name indicates, uses two extreme data points to determine the values of a (the fixed-cost portion) and b (the variable rate) in the equation $y = a + bx$. The extreme data points are the highest representative x-y pair and the lowest representative x-y pair. The activity level x, rather than the mixed cost item y, governs their selection.

The high-low method can be explained, step by step, as follows:

Step 1: Select the highest pair and the lowest pair
Step 2: Compute the variable rate, b, using the formula:

$$\text{Variable rate} = \frac{\text{Difference in cost y}}{\text{Difference in activity x}}$$

Step 3: Compute the fixed cost portion as:

Fixed cost portion = Total mixed cost – Variable cost

Flexible Manufacturing Company decides to relate total factory overhead costs to direct-labor hours (DLH) to develop a cost-volume formula in the form of $y = a + bx$. Twelve monthly observations are collected. They are given in Table 9-1 and plotted as shown in Figure 9-2.

Table 9-1

Month	Direct-labor hours (x) (000 omitted)	Factory overhead (y) (000 omitted)
January	9 hours	$15
February	19	20
March	11	14
April	14	16
May	23	25
June	12	20
July	12	20
August	22	23
September	7	14
October	13	22
November	15	18
December	17	18
Total	174 hours	$225

FIG. 9-2. *Scatter diagram.*

The high-low points selected from the monthly observations are

	x	y	
High	23 hours	$25	(May pair)
Low	7	14	(September pair)
Difference	16 hours	$11	

Thus:

Variable rate b $= \dfrac{\text{Difference in y}}{\text{Difference in x}} = \dfrac{\$11}{16 \text{ hours}} = \$0.6875$ per DLH

The fixed-cost portion is computed as:

	High	Low
Factory overhead (y)	$25	$14
Variable expense		
(0.6875/DLH)	(15.8125)	(4.8125)
	$9.1875	$9.1875

Therefore, the cost-volume formula for factory overhead is $9.1875 fixed plus $0.6875 per DLH.

The high-low method is simple and easy to use. It has the disadvantage of using two extreme data points, which may not be representative of normal conditions. The method may yield unreliable estimates of a and b in our formula. In such a case, it would be wise to drop them and choose two other points that are more representative of normal situations. Be sure to check the scatter diagram for this possibility.

CHAPTER PERSPECTIVE

Cost analysts investigate cost behavior for cost-volume-profit analysis, for appraisal of managerial performance, for flexible budgeting, and to make short-term choice decisions. We have looked at three types of cost behavior—variable, fixed, and mixed. We illustrated three simple methods of separating mixed costs into their variable and fixed components.

Analysis of Cost Behavior and Cost Estimation II

INTRODUCTION AND MAIN POINTS

One popular method for estimating the cost-volume formula is *regression analysis*. Regression analysis is a statistical procedure for mathematically estimating the average relationship between the dependent variable and the independent variable(s). The estimation method used for this purpose is the *least-squares method.*

There are two types of regressions. One is simple regression and the other is multiple regression. *Simple regression* involves one independent variable—e.g., DLH or machine-hours alone—whereas *multiple regression* involves two or more activity variables.

To discuss the least-squares method, we will assume a simple linear regression. This means that we will maintain the $y = a + bx$ relationship.

After studying the material in this chapter:

▬ You will be able to explain the advantages and disadvantages of the least-squares method.

▬ You will be able to develop a cost-volume formula using the least-squares method.

▬ You will be able to utilize a spreadsheet program, such as Excel, to develop the *cost-volume* formula.

▬ You will be able to briefly explain various regression statistics such as the coefficient of determination and t-value.

▬ You will understand the need for multiple regression analysis.

▬ You will be able to explain the difference between the contribution income statement and the traditional income statement and their uses.

THE LEAST-SQUARES METHOD (REGRESSION ANALYSIS)

Unlike the high-low method, the regression method includes all observed data and attempts to find a line of best fit to estimate the variable rate and the fixed-cost portion. To find this line, a technique called the least-squares method is used.

To explain the least-squares method, we define the error as the difference between the observed value and the estimated one of some mixed cost and denote it with u.

Symbolically,

$$u = y - y'$$

where y = observed value of a semivariable expense:

y' = estimated value based on $y' = a + bx$.

The least-squares criterion requires that the line of best fit be such that the sum of the squares of the errors (or the vertical distance in Figure 10-1 from the observed data points to the line) is a minimum, i.e.:

$$\text{minimum: } \sum u^2 = \sum(y - y')^2$$

Using differential calculus, we obtain the following equations, called normal equations:

$$\sum y = na + b\sum x$$

$$\sum xy = a\sum x + b\sum x^2$$

Solving the equations for b and a yields:

$$b = \frac{n\sum xy - (\sum x)(\sum y)}{n\sum x^2 - (\sum x)^2}$$

$$a = \overline{y} - b\overline{x}$$

where $\overline{y} = \sum y/n$ and $\overline{x} = \sum x/n$.

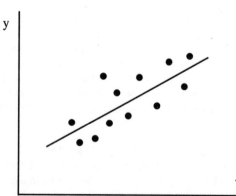

FIG. 10-1. *y and y'*.

EXAMPLE 1

To illustrate the computations of b and a, we will refer to the data in Table 10-1. All the sums required are computed and shown below.

Table 10-1

DHL (x)	Factory Overhead (y)	xy	x^2	y^2
9 hours	$15	135	81	225
19	20	380	361	400
11	14	154	121	196
14	16	224	196	256
23	25	575	529	625
12	20	240	144	400
12	20	240	144	400
22	23	506	484	529
7	14	98	49	196
13	22	286	169	484
15	18	270	225	324
17	18	306	289	324
174 hours	$225	3,414	2,792	4,359

From the table above:

$$\Sigma x = 174 \qquad \Sigma y = 225 \qquad \Sigma xy = 3,414 \qquad \Sigma x^2 = 2,792$$

$$\overline{x} = \Sigma x/n = 174/12 = 14.5 \qquad \overline{y} = \Sigma y/n = 225/12 = 18.75$$

Substituting these values into the formula for b first:

$$b = \frac{n\Sigma xy - (\Sigma x)(\Sigma y)}{n\Sigma x2 - (\Sigma x)^2} = \frac{(12)(3,414) - (174)(225)}{(12)(2,792) - (174)^2} = \frac{1,818}{3,228} = 0.5632$$

$$a = \overline{y} - b\overline{x} = 18.75 - (0.5632)(14.5) = 18.75 - 8.1664 = 10.5836$$

The cost-volume formula then is:

$$y' = \$10.5836 + \$0.5632 \, x;$$

or $10.5836 fixed, plus $0.5632 per DLH.

Note: Σy^2 is not used here but rather is computed for future use.

EXAMPLE 2

Assume that $10 is to be expended in advertising for next year; the projected sales for the next year would be computed as follows:

$$y' = 10.5836 + 0.5632\ x$$
$$= 10.5836 + 0.5632\ (10)$$
$$= \$16.2156$$

REGRESSION STATISTICS

Unlike the high-low method, regression analysis is a statistical method. It uses a variety of statistics to tell about the accuracy and reliability of the regression results. They include:

1. Correlation coefficient (r) and coefficient of determination (r^2)
2. Standard error of the estimate (S_e)
3. Standard error of the regression coefficient (S_b) and t-statistic

Correlation Coefficient (r) and Coefficient of Determination (r^2)

The correlation coefficient, r, measures the degree of correlation between y and x. The range of values it takes on is between -1 and $+1$. More widely used, however, is the coefficient of determination, designated r^2. Simply put, r^2 tells us how good the estimated regression is. In other words, it is a measure of "goodness of fit" in the regression. Therefore, the higher the r^2, the more confidence we have in our estimated cost formula.

More specifically, the coefficient of determination represents the proportion of the total variation in y that is explained by the regression equation. It has the range of values between 0 and 1.

EXAMPLE 3

The statement "Factory overhead is a function of machine-hours with $r^2 = 70\%$" can be interpreted as "70% of the total variation of factory overhead is explained by the regression equation or the change in machine-hours and the remaining 30% is accounted for by something other than machine-hours."

The coefficient of determination is computed as

$$r^2 = 1 - \frac{\Sigma(y - y')^2}{\Sigma(y - \overline{y})^2}$$

In a simple regression situation, however, there is a shortcut method available:

$$r^2 = \frac{[n\Sigma xy - (\Sigma x)(\Sigma y)]^2}{[n\Sigma x^2 - (\Sigma x)^2]\ [n\Sigma y^2 - (\Sigma y)^2]}$$

Comparing this formula with the one for b, we see that the only additional information we need to compute r^2 is Σy^2.

EXAMPLE 4

From the table prepared in Example 1, $\Sigma y^2 = 4,359$. Using the shortcut method for r^2,

$$r^2 = \frac{(1,818)^2}{(3,228)[(12)(4,359) - (225)^2]} = \frac{3,305,124}{(3,228)(52,308 - 50,625)} = \frac{3,305,124}{(3,228)(1,683)}$$

$$= \frac{3,305,124}{5,432,724} = 0.6084 = 60.84\%$$

This means that about 60.84% of the total variation in total factory overhead is explained by DLH and the remaining 39.16% is still unexplained. A relatively low r^2 indicates that there is a lot of room for improvement in our estimated cost-volume formula $(y' = \$10.5836 + \$0.5632x)$. Machine-hours or a combination of DLH and machine-hours might improve r^2.

Standard Error of the Estimate (S_e)

The standard error of the estimate, designated S_e, is defined as the standard deviation of the regression. It is computed as

$$S_e \frac{\sqrt{\Sigma(y - y')^2}}{n - 2} = \frac{\sqrt{\Sigma y^2 - a\Sigma y - b\Sigma xy}}{n - 2}$$

This formula can be used to gain some idea of the accuracy of our predictions.

EXAMPLE 5

Going back to our example data, S_e is calculated as

$$S_e = \sqrt{\frac{4,359 - (10.5836)(225) - (0.5632)(3,414)}{12 - 2}} = \sqrt{\frac{54.9252}{10}} = 2.3436$$

If the cost analyst wants to be 95% confident in his/her prediction, the confidence interval would be the estimated cost $(y') \pm t \times S_e$. As a rule of thumb, we use $t = 2$.

EXAMPLE 6

From Example 2,
$$y' = \$16.2156$$
Therefore, the range for the prediction, given an advertising expense of $10, would be:
$$\$16.2156 \pm 2(2.3436)$$
$$= \$16.2156 \pm 4.6872, \text{ which means}$$
$$\$11.5284 - \$20.9028$$

Standard Error of the Regression Coefficient (S_b) and the t-Statistic

The standard error of the regression coefficient, designated S_b, and the t-statistic are closely related. S_b is calculated as:

$$S_b = \frac{S_e}{\sqrt{\sum(x - \bar{x})^2}}$$

or, in shortcut form:

$$S_b = \frac{S_e}{\sqrt{\sum x^2 - \bar{x}\sum x}}$$

S_b gives an estimate of the range where the true value of the b coefficient will "actually" be. The t-statistic tells you how reliable an independent variable x is in explaining the dependent variable y. It is determined by dividing the estimated regression coefficient, b, by its standard error, S_b. Thus, the t-statistic measures how many standard errors the coefficient is away from zero. Generally, any t value greater than +2 or less than −2 is acceptable. The higher the t value, the greater the confidence in the coefficient as the predictor.

EXAMPLE 7

The S_b for our example is:

$$S_b = \frac{2.3436}{\sqrt{2{,}792 - (14.5)(174)}}$$

$$= \frac{2.3436}{\sqrt{2{,}792 - 2{,}523}} = \frac{2.3436}{\sqrt{269}} = .143$$

Thus, t-statistic = b/S_b = .5632/.143 = 3.94. Since t = 3.94 > 2, we can conclude that the b coefficient is reliable.

USE OF A SPREADSHEET PROGRAM FOR REGRESSION

We can use an electronic spreadsheet program such as Excel in order to develop a model and estimate most of the statistics we discussed thus far. Figure 10-2 shows the Excel regression output for Example 1.

SUMMARY OUTPUT

Regression Statistics

Multiple R	0.7799829
R Square	0.6083733 (R^2)
Adjusted R Square	0.5692106
Standard Error	2.3436222 (S_e)
Observations	12

ANOVA

	df	SS	MS	F	Significance F
Regression	1	85.32434944	85.324349	15.5345178	0.00276865
Residual	10	54.92565056	5.4925651		
Total	11	140.25			

	Coefficients	Standard Error (Sb)	t Stat	P-value*	Lower 95%	Upper 95%
Intercept	10.583643	2.17960878	4.8557536	0.00066562	5.72717128	15.440115
Advertising	0.563197	0.142893168	3.9413853	0.00276865	0.24481115	0.8815829

*The P-value for X variable (advertising here in this example) = .00277 indicates that we have a 0.277% chance that the true value of the X variable coefficient is equal to 0, implying a high level of accuracy about the estimated value of 0.563197.

The result shows:

$Y' = 10.58364 + 0.563197\ X$

    (1) R-squared (R^2) = .608373 = 60.84%
    (2) Standard error of the estimate (S_e) = 2.343622
    (3) Standard error of the coefficient (S_b) = 0.142893
    (4) t-value = 3.94

All of the above are the same as the ones manually obtained.

FIG. 10-2. *Excel regression output.*

MULTIPLE REGRESSION

The least-squares method provides an opportunity for the cost analyst to consider more than one independent variable. In case a simple regression is not good enough to provide a satisfactory cost-volume formula (as indicated typically by a low r^2), the cost analyst should use multiple regression. Presented below is an example of multiple regression and a spreadsheet printout (Figure 10-3).

EXAMPLE 8
Assume the following data:

Factory overhead costs (y)	Direct-labor hours (x_1)	Machine-hours (x_2)
$3,200	26	50
2,001	15	35
2,700	18	40
3,135	21	45
2,964	20	40

First, we present two simple regression results (one variable at a time):

Simple regression 1 Simple regression 2
$y = a + b x_1$ $y = a + b x_2$

(See Figure 10-3 for simple and multiple regression results.)

USE OF DUMMY VARIABLES

In many cost analyses, an independent variable may be discrete or categorical. For example, in estimating heating and fuel bills, the season will make a big difference. To control this effect, a dummy variable can be included in the regression model. This variable will have a value equal to 1 during the winter months and 0 during all the other months.

A dummy variable can also be used to account for jumps or shifts in fixed costs. This situation is well illustrated by the data given below

Month	Factory overhead costs (y)	Direct-labor hours (x_1)	Shift dummy (x_2)
1	$2234	105	1
2	2055	89	1
3	2245	99	1
4	2110	85	1

5	2377	118	1
6	2078	89	1
7	2044	101	0
8	2032	112	0
9	2134	107	0
10	2090	100	0
11	2078	109	0
12	2007	93	0

A simple regression of overhead versus DLH gives (Figure 10-3):

$$Y' = 1614.85 + 5.06 X_1 \qquad R^2 = 22.42\%, S_e = 100.33$$
$$(2.98)$$

The explanatory power of the model is extremely low, and the coefficient of DLH is barely statistically significant (i.e., $t = 5.06/2.98 = 1.7 < 2$). The data suggests that there might be a decrease around the end of the sixth month. To test this hypothesis, we define a dummy variable, X_2, as a shift or jump, where

$$X_2 = \begin{cases} 1 \text{ if } t = 1,2,...,6 \\ 0 \text{ if } t = 7,8,...12 \end{cases}$$

Rerunning the regression with the shift variable leads to the following printout (Figure 10-3):

$$Y' = 1258.13 + 7.78 X_1 + 166.95 X_2 \qquad R^2 = 80.40\%, S_e = 53.15$$
$$(1.66) \qquad (32.35)$$

The explanatory power of the model is quite good, and both the DLH shift variables are highly significant (t-values are 4.68 and 5.16, respectively).

COST PREDICTION

1. If we wished to predict costs for the first six months of the following year, the predicted equation is:

$$Y' = 1258.13 + 7.78 X_1 + 166.95 X_2$$
$$= 1258.13 + 7.78 X_1 + 166.95 (1)$$
$$= 1425.08 + 7.78 X_1$$

2. If we wished to predict costs for the second six months of the following year, the predicted model becomes:

$$Y' = 1258.13 + 7.78 X_1 + 166.95 X_2$$
$$= 1258.13 + 7.78 X_1 + 166.95 (0)$$
$$= 1258.13 + 7.78 X_1$$

SUMMARY OUTPUT

Regression Statistics

Multiple R	0.473539
R Square	0.22424
Adjusted R Square	0.146664
Standard Error	100.3256
Observations	12

ANOVA

	df	SS	MS	F	Significance F
Regression	1	29094.34	29094.34	2.890577	0.119937
Residual	10	100652.3	10065.23		
Total	11	129746.7			

	Coefficients	Standard Error	t Stat	P-value	Lower 95%	Upper 95%
Intercept	1614.845	300.6753	5.370727	0.000314	944.8983	2284.791
DLH	5.058711	2.975415	1.70017	0.119937	−1.57093	11.68835

FIG. 10-3. *Simple regression (OH vs. DLH).*

SUMMARY OUTPUT

Regression Statistics

Multiple R	0.89667
R Square	0.804018
Adjusted R Square	0.760466
Standard Error	53.15389
Observations	12

ANOVA

	df	SS	MS	F	Significance F
Regression	2	104318.6	52159.32	18.46128	0.000653
Residual	9	25428.02	2825.336		
Total	11	129746.7			

	Coefficients	Standard Error	t Stat	P-value	Lower 95%	Upper 95%
Intercept	1258.128	173.6558	7.244951	4.84E-05	865.2906	1650.964
Dummy	166.9477	32.35462	5.159933	0.000595	93.75638	240.139

FIG. 10-4. *Multiple regression (OH vs. DLH and dummy).*

THE CONTRIBUTION INCOME STATEMENT

The traditional (absorption) income statement for external reporting shows the functional classification of costs—that is, manufacturing costs vs. nonmanufacturing expenses (or operating expenses). An alternative type of income statement, known as the contribution income statement, organizes the costs by behavior rather than by function. It shows the relationship of variable costs and fixed costs, regardless of the functions a given cost item is associated with.

The contribution approach to income determination provides data that are useful for managerial planning and decision making. For example, the contribution approach is useful:

1. For breakeven and cost-volume-profit analysis,
2. In evaluating the performance of the division and its manager, and
3. For short-term and non-routine decisions.

However, the contribution income statement is not acceptable for income-tax or external-reporting purposes, because it ignores fixed overhead as a product cost.

The statement highlights the concept of contribution margin, which is the difference between sales and variable costs. The traditional format, on the other hand, emphasizes the concept of gross margin, which is the difference between sales and cost of goods sold. These two concepts are independent; they have nothing to do with each other. Gross margin is available to cover nonmanufacturing expenses, whereas contribution margin is available to cover fixed costs. The concept of contribution margin has numerous applications for internal management; these will be examined in Chapter 15.

Factory overhead cost (y)	Direct-labor hours (x_1)	Machine-hours (x_2)
3200	26	50
2001	15	35
2700	18	40
3135	21	45
2964	20	40

```
          Simple regression 1: y = a + b x₁
```

$$\text{Simple regression 1: } y = a + b\,x_1$$

```
               Regression Output


     Constant                          700
     Std. Err. of Y Est.          270.7224
     r²                           0.767950
     No. of Observations                 5
     Degrees of Freedom                  3

     X Coefficient(s)        105
     Std. Err. of Coeff. 33.32363
     t-value             3.150916*
```

$y' = 700 + 105\ x_1$ with $r^2 = 0.767950 = 76.80\%$

```
           Simple regression 2: y = a + b x₂
```

$$\text{Simple regression 2: } y = a + b\,x_2$$

```
               Regression Output

     Constant                      -324.153
     Std. Err. of Y Est.           275.8156
     r²                            0.759137
     No. of Observations                  5
     Degrees of Freedom                   3

     X Coefficient(s)      74.38461
     Std. Err. of Coeff. 24.19063
     t-value             3.074935*
```

$y' = -324.15 + 74.38\ x_2$ with $r^2 = 0.759137 = 75.91\%$

```
        Multiple regression: y = a + b x₁ + c x₂
```

$$\text{Multiple regression: } y = a + b\,x_1 + c\,x_2$$

```
               Regression Output

     Constant                         254.5
     Std. Err. of Y Est.           326.5095
     r²                            0.774974
     No. of Observations                  5
     Degrees of Freedom                   2
```

```
X Coefficient(s)          63.75        30.25
Std. Err. of Coeff.   169.9209     121.0729
t-value                0.375174*    0.249849
```

$y' = 254.5 + 63.75\ x_1 + 30.25\ x_2$ with $r^2 = 0.774974 = 77.50\%$

*(calculated independently)

Summary and Conclusion

As can be seen, there was only a slight increase in r^2 from 76.8% in simple regression 1 and 75.91% in simple regression 2 to 77.50%. Apparently, the extra independent variable added little new explanatory power. Furthermore, t-values for both independent variables came out to be much less than 2 (approximately 0.38 and 0.25, respectively), which means both variables together in the same regression equation were not statistically significant. All this indicates that either simple regression was good enough for the purpose of developing the cost-volume formula. Between the two simple regression results, however, simple regression 1 appears to be superior to simple regression 2 for two reasons: (1) It has higher r^2 and t-values; and (2) simple regression 2 gives a negative fixed cost (-324.153), which is suspect.

FIG. 10-5. *Simple and multiple regression results for cost-volume formula.*

A comparison is made between the traditional format and the contribution format below:

Traditional Format

Sales		$15,000
Less: Cost of goods sold		7,000
Gross Margin		$8,000
Less: Operating expenses		
Selling	$2,100	
Administrative	1,500	3,600
Net Income		$4,400

Contribution Format

Sales		$15,000
Less: Variable expenses		
Manufacturing	$4,000	
Selling	1,600	
Administrative	500	6,100
Contribution margin		$8,900
Less: Fixed expenses		
Manufacturing	$3,000	
Selling	500	
Administrative	1,000	4,500
Net Income		$4,400

CHAPTER PERSPECTIVE

We have discussed two additional methods of separating a mixed cost into its variable and fixed components. Heavy emphasis was placed on the use of simple and multiple regression.

Managerial accountants prepare the income statement in a contribution format, which organizes costs by behavior rather than by the functions of manufacturing, sales, and administration. The contribution income statement is widely used as an internal planning and decision-making tool.

Cost-Volume-Profit and Break-Even Analysis I

INTRODUCTION AND MAIN POINTS

Cost-volume-profit (CVP) analysis, together with cost behavior information, helps cost analysts and managerial accountants perform many useful analyses. CVP analysis deals with how profit and costs change with a change in volume. More specifically, it looks at the effects on profits of changes in such factors as variable costs, fixed costs, selling prices, volume, and mix of products sold. By studying the relationships of costs, sales, and net income, management is better able to cope with many planning decisions. *Break-even analysis,* a branch of CVP analysis, determines the break-even sales. Break-even point—the financial crossover point where revenues exactly match costs—does not show up in corporate earnings reports, but managerial accountants find it an extremely useful measurement.

After studying the material in this chapter:

■ You will be familiar with various contribution margin concepts.

■ You will be able to compute the sales necessary to break even or to achieve a target income.

■ You will be able to prepare break-even and profit-volume charts.

■ You will be able to perform a variety of "what-if" analyses using the contribution approach.

■ You will be able to define and explain margin of safety and cash break-even point.

QUESTIONS ANSWERED BY CVP ANALYSIS

CVP analysis tries to answer the following questions:

    (a) What sales volume is required to break even?

    (b) What sales volume is necessary to earn a desired profit?

    (c) What profit can be expected on a given sales volume?

    (d) How would changes in selling price, variable costs, fixed costs, and output affect profits?

    (e) How would a change in the mix of products sold affect the break-even and target income volume and profit potential?

CONTRIBUTION MARGIN (CM)

For accurate CVP analysis, a distinction must be made between costs as either variable or fixed. Mixed costs must be separated into their variable and fixed components.

In order to compute the break-even point and perform various CVP analyses, note the following important concepts.

1. Contribution Margin (CM). The contribution margin is the excess of sales (S) over the variable costs (VC) of the product or service. It is the amount of money available to cover fixed costs (FC) and to generate profit. Symbolically, $CM = S - VC$.
2. Unit CM. The unit CM is the excess of the unit selling price (p) over the unit variable cost (v). Symbolically, unit $CM = p - v$.
3. CM Ratio. The CM ratio is the contribution margin as a percentage of sales—i.e.:

$$CM \text{ ratio} = \frac{CM}{S} = \frac{S-VC}{S} = 1 - \frac{VC}{S}$$

The CM ratio can also be computed using per-unit data as follows:

$$CM \text{ ratio} = \frac{Unit\ CM}{p} = \frac{p-v}{p} = 1 - \frac{v}{p}$$

Note that the CM ratio is 1 minus the variable-cost ratio. For example, if variable costs account for 70% of the price, the CM ratio is 30%.

To illustrate the various concepts of CM, we present the following data for Porter Toy Store:

EXAMPLE 1

	Total	Per unit	Percentage
Sales (1,500 units)	$37,500	$25	100%
Less: Variable costs	15,000	10	40
Contribution margin	$22,500	$15	60%
Less: Fixed costs	15,000		
Net income	$7,500		

From the data listed above, CM, unit CM, and the CM ratio are computed as:

$$CM = S - VC = \$37{,}500 - \$15{,}000 = \$22{,}500$$
$$Unit\ CM = p - v = \$25 - \$10 = \$15$$
$$CM\ ratio = \frac{CM}{S} = \frac{\$22{,}500}{\$37{,}500} = 60\%, \text{ or } \frac{Unit\ CM}{P} = \frac{\$15}{\$25} = 0.6 = 60\%$$

BREAK-EVEN ANALYSIS

The break-even point represents the level of sales revenue that equals the total of the variable and fixed costs for a given volume of output at a particular capacity use rate. For example, you might want to ask the break-even occupancy rate (or vacancy rate) for a hotel or the break-even load rate for an airliner. Generally, the lower the break-even point, the higher the profit and the less the operating risk, other things being equal. The break-even point also provides managerial accountants with insights into profit planning. It can be computed using the following formulas:

$$Break\text{-}even\ point\ in\ units = \frac{Fixed\ costs}{Unit\ CM}$$

$$Break\text{-}even\ point\ in\ dollars = \frac{Fixed\ costs}{CM\ ratio}$$

EXAMPLE 2

Using the same data given in Example 1, where unit CM = $25 - $10 = $15, and CM ratio = 60%, we get:

Break-even point in units = $15,000/$15 = 1,000 units
Break-even point in dollars = $15,000/0.6 = $25,000

Or, alternatively:

1,000 units × $25 = $25,000

GRAPHICAL APPROACH IN A SPREADSHEET FORMAT

The graphical approach to obtaining the break-even point is based on the so-called *break-even (B-E) chart*, as shown in Figure 11-1. Sales revenue, variable costs, and fixed costs are plotted on the vertical axis, while volume, x, is plotted on the horizontal axis. The break-even point is the point where the total sales revenue line intersects the total cost line. The chart can also effectively report profit potentials over a wide range of activity and therefore be used as a tool for discussion and presentation. The profit-volume (P-V) chart, as shown in Figure 11-2, focuses directly on how profits vary with changes in volume.

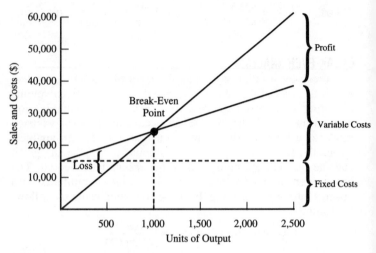

FIG. 11-1. *Break-even chart.*

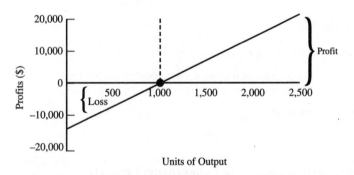

FIG. 11-2. *Profit-volume (P-V) chart.*

Profits are plotted on the vertical axis, while units of output are shown on the horizontal axis. The P-V chart provides a quick condensed comparison of how alternatives on pricing, variable costs, and fixed costs may affect net income as volume changes. The P-V chart can be easily constructed from the B-E chart. Note that the slope of the chart is the unit CM.

DETERMINATION OF TARGET INCOME VOLUME

Besides determining the break-even point, CVP analysis determines the sales required to attain a particular income level or target net income. The formula is:

$$\text{Target income sales volume} \quad = \quad \frac{\text{Fixed costs plus target income}}{\text{Unit CM}}$$

EXAMPLE 3

Using the same data given in Example 1, assume that Porter Toy Store wishes to attain a target income of $15,000 before tax.

Then, the target income volume required would be:

$$\frac{\$15,000 + \$15,000}{\$25 - \$10} \quad = \quad \frac{\$30,000}{\$15} \quad = \quad 2,000 \text{ units}$$

CASH BREAK-EVEN POINT

If a company has a minimum of available cash or the opportunity cost of holding excess cash is too high, management may want to know the volume of sales that will cover all cash expenses during a period. This is known as the *cash break-even point*. Not all fixed operating costs involve cash payments. For example, depreciation expenses are noncash fixed charges. To find the cash break-even point, the noncash charges must be subtracted from fixed costs. Therefore, the cash break-even point is lower than the usual break-even point. The formula is:

$$\text{Cash break-even point} \quad = \quad \frac{\text{Fixed costs} - \text{depreciation}}{\text{Unit CM}}$$

EXAMPLE 4

Assume from Example 1 that the total fixed costs of $15,000 include depreciation of $1,500. Then the cash break-even point is:

$$\frac{\$15,000 - \$1,500}{\$25 - \$10} \quad = \quad \frac{\$13,500}{\$15} \quad = \quad 900$$

Porter Toy Store has to sell 900 units to cover only the fixed costs involving cash payments of $13,500 and to break even.

IMPACT OF INCOME TAXES

If target income is given on an after-tax basis, the target income volume formula becomes:

$$\text{Target income volume} = \frac{\text{Fixed costs} + [\text{Target after-tax income}/(1\text{-tax rate})]}{\text{Unit CM}}$$

EXAMPLE 5

Assume that Porter Toy Store wants to achieve an after-tax income of \$6,000. The tax rate is 40%. Then:

$$\text{Target income volume} = \frac{\$15,000 + [\$6,000/(1 - 0.4)]}{\$15}$$

$$= \frac{\$15,000 + \$10,000}{\$15} = 1,667 \text{ units}$$

MARGIN OF SAFETY

The margin of safety is a measure of difference between the actual sales level and the break-even sales. It is the amount by which sales revenue may drop before losses begin, and is expressed as a percentage of expected sales:

$$\text{Margin of safety} = \frac{\text{Expected sales} - \text{Break-even sales}}{\text{Expected sales}}$$

The margin of safety is often used as a measure of operating risk. The larger the ratio, the safer the situation, since there is less risk of reaching the break-even point.

EXAMPLE 6

Assume Porter Toy Store projects sales of \$35,000 with a break-even sales level of \$25,000. The projected margin of safety is:

$$\frac{\$35,000 - \$25,000}{\$35,000} = 28.57\%$$

SOME APPLICATIONS OF CVP ANALYSIS AND WHAT-IF ANALYSIS

The concepts of contribution margin and the contribution income statement have many applications in profit planning and short-term decision making. Many "what-if" scenarios can be evaluated using them as planning tools, especially utilizing a spreadsheet program such as Excel. Some applications are illustrated in the following examples.

EXAMPLE 7

Recall that Porter Toy Store has a CM of 60% and fixed costs of $15,000 per period. Assume that the company expects sales to go up by $10,000 for the next period. How much will income increase?

Using the CM concepts, we can quickly compute the impact of a change in sales on profits. The formulas for computing the impact are:

Change in net income = Dollar change in sales × CM ratio

Thus:

Increase in net income = $10,000 × 60% = 6,000

The income will go up by $6,000, assuming there is no change in fixed costs.

If we are given a change in unit sales instead of dollars, the formula becomes:

Change in net income = Change in unit sales × Unit CM

EXAMPLE 8

Assume that the company expects sales to go up by 400 units. How much will income increase? From Example 1, the company's unit CM is $15. Again, assuming there is no change in fixed costs, the income will increase by $6,000:

$$400 \text{ units} \times \$15 = \$6,000$$

EXAMPLE 9

What net income is expected on sales of $47,500?

The answer is the difference between the CM and the fixed costs:

CM:	$47,500 × 60%	$28,500
Less: Fixed costs		15,000
Net income		$13,500

EXAMPLE 10

The store is considering increasing the advertising budget by $5,000, which would increase sales revenue by $8,000.

Should the advertising budget be increased?

The answer is no, since the increase in the CM is less than the increased cost:

Increase in CM:	$8,000 × 60%	$4,800
Increase in advertising		5,000
Decrease in net income		$ (200)

EXAMPLE 11

Consider the original data. Assume again that Porter Toy Store is currently selling 1,500 units per period. In an effort to increase sales, management is considering cutting its unit price by $5 and increasing the advertising budget by $1,000. If these two steps are taken, management feels that unit sales will go up by 60%. Should the two steps be taken?

A $5 reduction in the selling price will cause the unit CM to decrease from $15 to $10. Thus,

Proposed CM: 2,400 units × $10	$24,000
Present CM: 1,500 units × $15	22,500
Increase in CM	$1,500
Increase in advertising outlay	1,000
Increase in net income	$ 500

The answer, therefore, is yes. Alternatively, the same answer can be obtained by developing income statements in a contribution format:

	(A) Present (1,500 units)	(B) Proposed (2,400 units)	(B – A) Difference
Sales			
Less: Variable	$37,500 (@$25)	$48,000 (@$20)	$10,500
cost	15,000	24,000	9,000
CM	$22,500	$24,000	$1,500
Less: Fixed costs	15,000	16,000	1,000
Net income	$7,500	$8,000	$ 500

SALES MIX ANALYSIS

Break-even and cost-volume-profit analysis requires some additional computations and assumptions when a company produces and sells more than one product. In multiproduct firms, sales mix is an important factor in calculating an overall company break-even point.

Different selling prices and different variable costs result in different unit CM and CM ratios. As a result, the break-even points and cost-volume-profit relationships vary with the relative proportions of the products sold, called the *sales mix*. In break-even and CVP analysis, it is necessary to predetermine the sales mix and then compute a weighted average unit CM. It is also necessary to assume that the sales mix does not change for a specified period. The break-even formula for the company as a whole is:

$$\text{Break-even sales in units (or in dollars)} = \frac{\text{Fixed costs}}{\text{Weighted average unit CM}}$$
$$\text{(or CM ratio)}$$

EXAMPLE 12

Assume that Knibex, Inc., produces cutlery sets out of high-quality wood and steel. The company makes a deluxe cutlery set and a standard set that have the following unit CM data:

	Deluxe	Standard
Selling price	$15	$10
Variable cost per unit	12	5
Unit CM	$ 3	$ 5
Sales mix	60%	40%
Fixed costs	$76,000	

The weighted average unit CM = ($3)(0.6) + ($5)(0.4) = $3.80. Therefore, the company's break-even point in units is

$$\$76,000/\$3.80 = 20,000 \text{ units,}$$

which is divided as follows:

A: 20,000 units × 60%	=	12,000 units
B: 20,000 units × 40%	=	8,000
		20,000 units

Note: An alternative is to build a package containing three deluxe models and two economy models (3:2 ratio). By defining the product as a package, the multiple-product problem is converted into a single-product one. Then use the following three steps as follows:

Step 1: Compute the package CM as follows:

	Deluxe	Standard	
Selling price	$15	$10	
Variable cost per unit	12	5	
Unit CM	$3	$5	
Sales mix	3	2	
Package CM	$9	$10	= $19 package total

Step 2: Determine the number of packages that need to be sold to break even as follows:

$76,000/$19 per package = 4,000 packages

Step 3: Multiply this number by their respective mix units:

Deluxe:	4,000 packages × 3 units	= 12,000 units
Economy:	4,000 packages × 2 units	= 8,000 units
		20,000 units

EXAMPLE 13

Assume that Dante, Inc., is a producer of recreational equipment. It expects to produce and sell three types of sleeping bags—the Economy, the Regular, and the Backpacker. Information on the bags is given as follows:

Budgeted

	Economy	Regular	Backpacker	Total
Sales	$30,000	$60,000	$10,000	$100,000
Sales mix	30%	60%	10%	100%
Less: VC	24,000	40,000	5,000	69,000
CM	$6,000	$20,000	$5,000	$31,000
CM ratio	20%	33 1/3%	50%	31%
Fixed costs				$18,600
Net income				$12,400

The CM ratio for Dante, Inc., is $31,000/$100,000 = 31%. Therefore, the break-even point in dollars is

$18,600/0.31 = $60,000

which will be split in the mix ratio of 3:6:1 to give us the following break-even points for the individual products:

Economy:	$60,000 × 30%	=	$18,000
Regular:	$60,000 × 60%	=	36,000
Backpacker:	$60,000 × 10%	=	6,000
			$60,000

One of the most important assumptions underlying CVP analysis in a multiproduct firm is that the sales mix will not change during the planning period. But if the sales mix changes, the break-even point will also change.

EXAMPLE 14

Assume that total sales from Example 13 was achieved at $10,000 but that an actual mix came out differently from the budgeted mix (i.e., for Regular, 60% to 30%, and for Backpacker, 10% to 40%).

	Actual			
	Economy	Regular	Backpacker	Total
Sales	$30,000	$30,000	$40,000	$100,000
Sales mix	30%	30%	40%	100%
Less: VC	24,000	20,000*	20,000**	64,000
CM	$6,000	$10,000	$20,000	$36,000
CM ratio	20%	33 1/3%	50%	36%
Fixed costs				$18,600
Net income				$17,400

*$20,000 = $30,000 × (100% − 33 1/3%) = $30,000 × 66 2/3%
**$20,000 = $40,000 × (100% − 50%) = $40,000 × 50%

Note: The shift in sales mix toward the more profitable Backpacker line has caused the CM ratio for the company as a whole to go up from 31% to 36%.

The new break-even point will be:

$$\$51,667 = \$18,600/0.36$$

The break-even dollar volume has decreased from $60,000 to $51,667. The improvement in the mix caused net income to go up. It is also important to note that, generally, the shift of emphasis from low-margin products to high-margin ones will increase the overall profits of the company.

CVP ANALYSIS WITH STEP-FUNCTION COSTS

The introduction of step-function costs is somewhat more difficult than it might first appear. Ideally, we would like to be able to assume that, for any given relevant range, we could simply add together the step-function costs and the fixed costs to give us the total applicable fixed costs. We could then utilize the formula as described above. Unfortunately, the process is not quite that simple, as the following example illustrates.

EXAMPLE 15

Amco Magazine Company publishes a monthly magazine. The company has fixed costs of $100,000 a month, variable costs per magazine of $.80, and charges $1.80 per magazine. In addition, the company also has supervisory costs. These costs behave as follows:

Volume	Costs
0–50,000	$10,000
50,001–100,000	20,000
100,001–150,000	30,000

Amco's monthly break-even volume (number of magazines) can be calculated, step by step, as follows:

First, if we attempt to solve the break-even formula at the first level of fixed costs, we have the following equation:

$$x = FC/(p-v)$$
$$= (\$100,000 + 10,000)/(\$1.80 - \$.80)$$
$$= \$110,000/\$1$$
$$= 110,000 \text{ units}$$

The problem with this solution is that, while the break-even volume is 110,000 magazines, the relevant range for the step-function costs was only 0–50,000 magazines. Thus, a break-even of greater than 50,000 magazines is invalid and we must move to the next step on the step function, which gives us the following equation:

$$x = FC/(p-v)$$
$$= (\$100,000 + 20,000)/(\$1.80 - \$.80)$$
$$= \$120,000/\$1$$
$$= 120,000 \text{ units}$$

This solution is also invalid. Only when we get to the third level do we encounter a valid solution, as follows:

$$x = FC/(p-v)$$
$$= (\$100,000 + 30,000)/(\$1.80 - \$.80)$$
$$= \$130,000/\$1$$
$$= 130,000 \text{ units}$$

The conclusion we must draw is that the incorporation of step-function costs in the CVP formula requires a trial-and-error process to reach the break-even volume.

From a profit-seeking perspective, a 150,000-unit level is most profitable.

	50,000	100,000	150,000
CM(@1)	$ 50,000	$100,000	$150,000
FC	100,000	120,000	130,000
NI	($50,000)	($20,000)	$ 20,000

CHAPTER PERSPECTIVE

Cost-volume-profit analysis is useful as a frame of reference, as a vehicle for expressing overall managerial performance, and as a planning device via break-even techniques and "what-if" scenarios. The following points highlight the analytical usefulness of CVP analysis as a tool for profit planning:

1. A change in either the selling price or the variable cost per unit alters CM or the CM ratio and the break-even point.
2. As sales exceed the break-even point, a higher-unit CM or CM ratio will result in greater profits than a small-unit CM or CM ratio.
3. The lower the break-even sales, the less risky the business and the safer the investment, other things being equal.
4. A large margin of safety means lower operating risk, since a large decrease in sales can occur before losses are experienced.
5. Using the contribution income statement model and a spreadsheet program such as Excel, a variety of "what-if" planning and decision scenarios can be evaluated.
6. In a multiproduct firm, sales mix is often more important than overall market share. The emphasis on high-margin products tends to maximize overall profits of the firm.

Cost-Volume-Profit and Break-Even Analysis II

INTRODUCTION AND MAIN POINTS

This chapter takes a further look at cost-volume-profit analysis. Specifically, we will cover the following topics:

1. Cost-volume-profit analysis as applied to non-profit organizations.
2. Cost-volume-profit analysis under conditions of uncertainty.
3. Operating leverage, financial leverage, and total leverage.

After studying the material in this chapter:

■■■ You will be able to apply the CVP technique to nonprofit organizations.

■■■ You will be able to understand how statistics can help in the face of uncertainty about sales.

■■■ You will be able to make probabilistic statements about break-even sales, such as "what is the chance of breaking even?"

■■■ You will be able to explain the relationship between break-even sales and operating leverage.

■■■ You will be able to calculate the degrees of operating leverage, financial leverage, and total leverage.

COST-VOLUME-REVENUE ANALYSIS AND NONPROFIT ORGANIZATIONS

Cost-volume-profit (CVP) analysis and break-even analysis is not limited to profit firms. CVP is appropriately called cost-volume-revenue (CVR) analysis, as it pertains to nonprofit organizations. The CVR model not only calculates the break-even service level, but helps answer a variety of "what-if" decision questions.

LMC, Inc., a Los Angeles county agency that helps rehabilitate mentally ill patients has a $1,200,000 lump-sum annual budget appropriation. On top of this, the agency charges each patient $600 a month for board and care. All of the appropriation and revenue must be spent. The variable costs for rehabilitation activity average $700 per patient per month. The agency's annual fixed costs are $800,000. The agency manager wishes to know how many patients can be served. Let x = number of patients to be served.

$$
\begin{aligned}
\text{Revenue} &= \text{Total expenses} \\
\text{Lump sum appropriation} + \$600\,(12)\,x &= \text{Variable expenses} + \text{Fixed costs} \\
\$1,200,000 + \$7,200\,x &= \$8,400\,x + \$800,000 \\
(\$7,200 - \$8,400)\,x &= \$800,000 - \$1,200,000 \\
-\$1,200\,x &= -\$400,000 \\
x &= \$400,000/\$1,200 \\
x &= 333 \text{ patients}
\end{aligned}
$$

We investigate the following two "what-if" scenarios:

1. Suppose the manager of the agency is concerned that the total budget for the coming year will be cut by 10% to the amount of $1,080,000. All other things remain unchanged. The manager wants to know how this budget cut affects the next year's service level.

$$
\begin{aligned}
\$1,080,000 + \$7,200\,x &= \$8,400\,x + \$800,000 \\
(\$7,200 - \$8,400)\,x &= \$800,000 - \$1,080,000 \\
-\$1,200\,x &= -\$280,000 \\
x &= \$280,000/\$1,200 \\
x &= 233 \text{ patients}
\end{aligned}
$$

2. The manager does not reduce the number of patients served, despite a budget cut of 10%. All other things remain unchanged. How much more does he/she have to charge patients for board and care? In this case, x = board-and-care charge per year:

$$
\begin{aligned}
\$1,080,000 + 333\,x &= \$8,400\,(333) + \$800,000 \\
333\,x &= \$2,797,200 + \$800,000 - \$1,080,000 \\
333\,x &= \$2,517,200 \\
x &= \$2,517,200/333 \text{ patients} \\
x &= \$7,559
\end{aligned}
$$

The monthly board-and-care charge must be increased to $630 ($7,559/12 months).

ASSUMPTIONS UNDERLYING BREAK-EVEN AND CVP ANALYSIS

The basic break-even and CVP models are subject to a number of limiting assumptions. They are:

   (a) The selling price per unit is constant throughout the entire relevant range of activity.

   (b) All costs are classified as fixed or variable.

   (c) The variable cost per unit is constant.

   (d) There is only one product or a constant sales mix.

   (e) Inventories do not change significantly from period to period.

   (f) Volume is the only factor affecting variable costs.

COST-VOLUME-PROFIT ANALYSIS UNDER CONDITIONS OF UNCERTAINTY

The CVP analysis discussed so far assumed that all variables determining profit or contribution margin—the selling price, variable costs, sales volume, and fixed costs—are known with certainty. This is not a realistic assumption. If one or more of these variables are subject to uncertainty, the managerial accountant should analyze the potential impact of this uncertainty. This additional analysis is required in evaluating alternative courses of action and in developing contingency plans. If management must choose between two products, expected profitability and risk should be considered before a choice is made. For example, if both products have the same expected profits, management might want to select the less risky product (less variation in profits).

One way of handling the conditions of uncertainty is to use what-if analysis, which has been discussed in previous chapters.

Statistical Method

Another approach to dealing with uncertainty is to use a statistical (probability) model. Let us suppose that sales volume is subject to uncertainty and, in fact, *normally distributed*.

Note: The normal distribution is one of the most widely used probability distributions. It is bell-shaped and its shape is completely summarized by two statistics—the mean and the standard deviation. For the definition of these terms, refer to Chapter 19.

With the *normality* assumption, utilize the standard statistical method to summarize the effect of the uncertainty in sales volume on a dependent variable such as profit or contribution margin. Also, we can answer the following planning questions:

   1. What is the probability of breaking even?

   2. What is the chance that profits from the proposal would be at least a certain amount?

   3. What are the chances that the proposal would cause the company to lose as much as a specified amount?

Any uncertainty in sales volume affects the total contribution margin (CM) and profit (p). The expected contribution margin, E(CM), is the unit CM times the expected volume, E(x):

$$
\begin{aligned}
E(CM) &= \text{unit } CM \times E(x) \\
&= (p - v)\, E(x)
\end{aligned}
$$

The expected profit, $E(\pi)$, is the expected contribution margin minus the fixed costs (FC):

$$E(\pi) = E(CM) - FC = (p - v)\, E(x) - FC$$

Because of the uncertainty in sales volume, the expected contribution margin and profit are also uncertain. The standard deviation of the expected contribution margin and profit is equal to the unit CM times the standard deviation of the sales volume. In equation form,

$$\sigma_\pi = (p - v)\, \sigma_x$$

where σ_π = standard deviation of expected profits and σ_x = standard deviation of sales volume.

Rodeo Corporation has annual fixed costs of \$1,500,000 and variable costs of \$4.50 per unit. The selling price per unit is stable at \$7.50, but the annual sales volume is uncertain and normally distributed, with mean expected sales of 600,000 units and a standard deviation of 309,278 units. Management expects this pattern to continue in the future. The normal distribution of profits is illustrated in Figure 12-1.

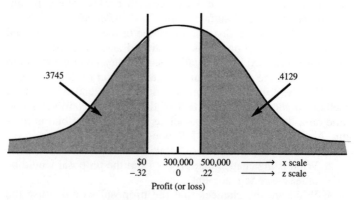

FIG. 12-1. *Probability distribution of profits.*

The expected contribution is $1,800,000:

$$E(CM) = (\$7.50 - \$4.50) \times 600,000 \text{ units}$$
$$= \$3 \times 600,000 = \$1,800,000$$

The expected profits are $300,000:

$$E(\pi) = \$1,800,000 - \$1,500,000 = \$300,000$$

The standard deviation of the expected profits is $927,834:

$$\sigma_\pi = \$3 \times 309,278 = \$927,834$$

From the results obtained in the preceding example, we will address the following questions:

1. What is the probability of breaking even?
2. What is the probability of obtaining a profit of $500,000 or more?
3. What is the probability of losing as much as $250,000?

In each case, we must determine the standard normal variate, better known as z, which is the number of standard deviations from any profit to the expected (mean) profit.

To determine the probability of at least breaking even, we first determine z, as follows:

$$z = \frac{0 - E(\pi)}{\sigma_\pi} = \frac{\$0 - \$300,000}{\$927,834} = -.32$$

In Table 5 of the Appendix (Normal Distribution), the probability of obtaining a z value of −.32 or less is .3745 (1 − .6255 = .3745), which means there is only a 37.45% chance that the company would lose money or about a 62.55% chance the company will at least break even. *Note:* Here, we are looking for the shaded area in Figure 12-2. Table 5 in the Appendix gives the area of the other side of the curve.

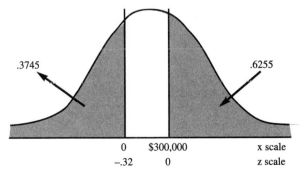

FIG. 12-2. *Probability of losing money.*

To find the probability of obtaining at least a profit of $500,000, we first determine the number of standard deviations $500,000 is from the expected profit:

$$z = \frac{\$500,000 - \$300,000}{\$927,834} = \frac{\$200,000}{\$927,834} = .22$$

From Table 5 we calculate that the chances are only .5871 of earning less than $500,000; thus we conclude that the chances of bettering a $500,000 profit are .4129, or 41.29% (1 − .5871 = .4129).

To find the probability of losing as much as $250,000, again we calculate the value for z:

$$z = \frac{-\$250,000 - \$300,000}{\$927,834} = \frac{-\$550,000}{\$927,834} = -.59$$

Table 5 in the Appendix indicates that there is only a .2776 (1 − .7224 = .2776) chance of losing $250,000 or more.

To summarize:
1. The chance of breaking even is better than 62.55%.
2. The chance of making at least $500,000 is 41.29%.
3. The chance of losing $250,000 or more is approximately 27.76%.

Caution: In the previous example, we have considered sales volume to be subject to uncertainty—random variable. It is also possible to consider fixed costs, variable costs, and selling price as random variables to test the effect of their uncertainty on profits. When one of these four variables—sales volume, price, variable cost, and fixed cost—is allowed to be uncertain, the analysis is accomplished exactly as we illustrated it above. However, if they become random variables simultaneously, the analysis is complicated and best left for a more advanced text in statistics.

LEVERAGE
Leverage is that portion of the fixed costs that represents a risk to the firm. Operating leverage, a measure of operating risk, refers to the fixed operating costs found in the firm's income statement. Financial leverage, a measure of financial risk, refers to financing a portion of the firm's assets, bearing fixed financing charges in hopes of increasing the return to the common stockholders. The higher the financial leverage, the higher the financial risk and the higher the cost of capital. Cost of capital rises because it costs

more to raise funds for a risky business. Total leverage is a measure of total risk.

Operating Leverage

Operating leverage, a measure of operating risk, arises from fixed operating costs. A simple indication of operating leverage is the effect that a change in sales has on earnings. The formula is:

Operating leverage at a given level of sales (x)

$$= \frac{\text{Percentage change in EBIT}}{\text{Percentage change in sales}}$$

$$= \frac{\Delta EBIT/EBIT}{\Delta x/ x} = \frac{(p-v)\,\Delta x/\,(p-v)x - FC}{\Delta x/ x}$$

$$= \frac{(p-v)x}{(p-v)x - FC}$$

where EBIT = earnings before interest and taxes = $(p-v)x - FC$.

The Wayne Company manufactures and sells doors to home builders. The doors are sold for $25 each. Variable costs are $15 per door, and fixed operating costs total $50,000. Assume further that the Wayne Company is currently selling 6,000 doors per year. Its operating leverage is:

$$\frac{(p-v)x}{(p-v)x - FC} = \frac{(\$25 - \$15)(6,000)}{(\$25 - \$15)(6,000) - \$50,000} = \frac{\$60,000}{\$10,000} = 6$$

which means if sales increase (decrease) by 1%, the company can expect its net income to increase (decrease) by six times that amount, or 6%.

Financial Leverage

Financial leverage, a measure of financial risk, arises from fixed financial costs. One way to measure financial leverage is to determine how earnings per share are affected by a change in EBIT (or operating income).

Financial leverage at a given level of sales (x) =

$$\frac{\text{Percentage in change in EPS}}{\text{Percentage in change in EBIT}} = \frac{(p-v)x - FC}{(p-v)x - FC - IC}$$

where EPS is earnings per share and IC is fixed finance charges—i.e., interest expense or preferred stock dividends.

(Preferred stock dividend must be adjusted for taxes—i.e., preferred stock dividend/$(1 - t)$.)

Using the data in the preceding example, the Wayne Company has total financial charges of \$2,000, half in interest expense and half in preferred stock dividend. Assume a corporate tax rate of 40%.

First, the fixed financial charges are:

$$IC = \$1,000 + \frac{\$1,000}{(1 - 0.4)} = \$1,000 + \$1,667 = \$2,667$$

Therefore, Wayne's financial leverage is computed as follows:

$$\frac{(p - v)x - FC}{(p - v)x - FC - IC} = \frac{(\$25 - \$15)(6,000) - \$50,000}{(\$25 - \$15)(6,000) - \$50,000 - \$2,667}$$

$$= \frac{\$7,333}{\$10,000}$$

$$= 1.36$$

which means that if EBIT increases (decreases) by 1%, Wayne can expect its EPS to increase (decrease) by 1.36 times, or by 1.36%.

Total Leverage
Total leverage is a measure of total risk. The way to measure total leverage is to determine how EPS is affected by a change in sales.

$$\text{Total leverage at a given level of sales (x)} = \frac{\text{Percentage in change in EPS}}{\text{Percentage in change in sales}}$$

$$= \text{operating leverage} \times \text{financial leverage}$$

$$= \frac{(p - v)x}{(p - v)x - FC} \times \frac{(p - v)x - FC}{(p - v)x - FC - IC}$$

$$= \frac{(p - v)x}{(p - v)x - FC - IC}$$

From the previous examples, the total leverage for Wayne Company is:

Operating leverage $\times$ financial leverage $= 6 \times 1.36 = 8.16$

or

$$\frac{(p-v)x}{(p-v)x - FC - IC} = \frac{(\$25 - \$15)(6,000)}{(\$25 - \$15)(6,000) - \$50,000 - \$2,667}$$

$$= \frac{\$60,000}{\$7,333}$$

$$= 8.18 \text{ (due to rounding error)}$$

which means that if sales increase (decrease) by 1%, Wayne can expect its EPS to increase (decrease) by 8.18%.

ABSORPTION VERSUS DIRECT COSTING

The most commonly accepted theory of product costing holds that the cost of producing a product includes direct materials, direct labor, and an apportioned share of the factory overhead costs. This method of assigning costs to products, called *absorption (full) costing,* is the method generally required for tax purposes.

Because all costs, including fixed overhead, are applied to production under absorption costing, variations in unit-product cost may result solely from variations in production volume. If fixed costs are $200,000, and 20,000 units are produced, unit fixed cost is $10; if volume is 40,000, unit fixed cost is $5. Because these variations are not controllable at the production manager level and may obscure other significant variations in cost, they can be excluded from product cost through the use of a costing technique referred to as *direct (variable or marginal) costing.*

Under direct costing, all variable manufacturing costs are charged to the product, and all fixed costs, including fixed manufacturing costs, are charged to expense. Thus, all manufacturing costs must first be classified as fixed or variable. Direct materials and direct labor costs are usually completely variable, but factory overhead costs must be separated into variable and fixed portions. All variable costs—direct materials, direct labor, and variable overhead—are assigned to production and become part of the unit costs of the products produced. All fixed costs are assumed to be costs of the period and are charged to expenses.

In summary, the only difference between absorption costing and direct costing is in the treatment of fixed manufacturing costs. Under absorption costing they are treated as product costs, and under direct costing they are treated as period costs.

Absorption and Direct Costing Compared

The differences between direct and absorption costing can be seen from an illustration comparing the income statement that would result from applying each technique to the same data. Assume the following information:

Beginning inventory	-0-	Variable costs (per unit)	
Production (units)	10,000	Direct materials	$2.00
Sales (units)	9,000	Direct labor	1.00
		Factory overhead	0.30
		Total	$3.30

Fixed factory overhead	$ 6,000		
Selling expenses	15,000	Variable selling expenses	
Administrative expenses	12,000	(per unit)	$0.20
Total	$33,000	Selling price (per unit)	$8.00

Income Statement Under Direct Costing. Under direct costing, the year's income statement would be as shown in Figure 12-3.

Sales (9,000 units at $8)		$72,000
Cost of goods sold:		
Variable production costs incurred		
(10,000 units at $3.30)	$33,000	
Less: Inventory (1,000 units at $3.30)	3,300	29,700
Manufacturing margin		$42,300
Variable selling expenses (9,000 units at $0.20)		1,800
Contribution margin		$40,500
Period costs:		
Factory overhead	$ 6,000	
Selling expenses	15,000	
Administrative expenses	12,000	33,000
Net income		$ 7,500

FIG. 12-3. *Income statement under direct costing.*

Note that all of the fixed manufacturing costs are considered costs of the period and are not included in inventories. The fixed factory overhead is treated as a period cost and is deducted, along with the selling and administrative expenses, in the period incurred. That is,

Direct materials	$xx
Direct labor	xx
Variable factory overhead	xx
Product cost	$xx

Income Statement Under Absorption Costing. Figure 12-4 contains the income statement that would be prepared under absorption costing.

Sales (9,000 units at $8)		$72,000
Cost of goods sold:		
Variable costs of production		
(10,000 units at $3.30)	$33,000	
Fixed overhead costs	6,000	
Total costs of producing 10,000 units	$39,000	
Less: Inventory (1,000 units at $3.90)	3,900	35,100
Gross margin		$36,900
Operating expenses:		
Selling ($15,000 fixed plus 9,000 at $0.20 each)	$16,800	
Administrative	12,000	28,800
Net income		$ 8,100

*$3.90 = $3.30 + ($6,000/10,000 units) = $3.30 + $.60

FIG. 12-4. *Income statement under absorption costing.*

Note that the fixed manufacturing costs are included as part of the product cost and that some of these costs are included in the ending inventory. Under absorption costing, the cost to be inventoried includes all manufacturing costs, both variable and fixed. Nonmanufacturing (operating) expenses, i.e., selling and administrative expenses, are treated as period expenses and thus are charged against current revenue:

Direct materials	$xx
Direct labor	xx
Variable factory overhead	xx
Fixed factory overhead	xx
Product cost	$xx

The ending inventory is priced at so-called full cost; that is, the cost of ending inventory includes fixed factory overhead.

Two important facts should be noted:

1. Effects of the two costing methods on net income:
   (a) When production exceeds sales, a larger net income will be reported under absorption costing.
   (b) When sales exceeds production, a larger net income will be reported under direct costing
   (c) When sales and production are equal, net income will be the same under both methods.
2. Reconciliation of the direct and absorption costing net income figures:
   (a) The difference in net income can be reconciled as follows:

Change in inventory	$\times$	Fixed factory overhead rate	$=$	Difference in net income

   (b) The above formula works only if the fixed overhead rate per unit does not change between the periods.

We can prove:

1. Difference in net income: $8,100 - $7,500 = $600. Absorption costing shows a larger net income.
2. Reconciliation of difference in net income:

Change in inventory	$\times$	Fixed factory overhead rate	$=$	Difference in net income
1,000	$\times$	$0.6 (6,000/10,000 units)	$=$	$600

Managerial Use of Direct Costing. Direct costing is used for internal purposes only. It highlights the concept of contribution margin and focuses on the costs by behavior rather than by function. Its managerial uses include: (1) relevant cost analysis, (2) break-even and cost-volume-profit (CVP) analyses, and (3) short-term decision making.

An understanding of cost behavior is extremely useful for managerial planning and decision-making purposes. It allows managerial accountants to perform short-term planning analysis, such as break-even analysis. Cost-volume-profit analysis is useful as a frame of reference, as a vehicle for expressing overall managerial performance, and as a planning device via break-even techniques and what-if scenarios. Breaking down the costs by behavior, which is reflected in a contribution (direct-costing) income statement, facilitates the use of various short-term profit-planning tools on the part of managerial accountants.

Direct costing is, however, not acceptable for external reporting or income-tax reporting. Companies that use direct costing for internal reporting must convert to absorption costing for external reporting.

CHAPTER PERSPECTIVE

We discussed how the traditional CVP analysis can be applied to the nonprofit setting. Illustrations were provided. Furthermore, if one of the variables that enter into the determination of profit is a random variable and normally distributed, we can introduce the standard statistical procedure to summarize the effect of this uncertainty on contribution margin or profit.

Closely related to CVP analysis is the concept of leverage. Leverage is that portion of the fixed costs that represents a risk to the firm. Operating leverage, a measure of operating risk, refers to the fixed operating costs found in the firm's income statement.

Budgeting

INTRODUCTION AND MAIN POINTS

A comprehensive (master) budget is a formal statement of management's expectations regarding sales, expenses, volume, and other financial transactions of the organization for the coming period. Simply put, a budget is a set of pro forma (projected or planned) financial statements. It consists of a pro forma income statement, pro forma balance sheet, and cash budget.

A budget is a tool for both planning and control. At the beginning of the period, the budget is the plan or standard; at the end of the period it serves as a control device to help management measure its performance against the plan so that future performance may be improved. International Paper, a large forest-products company, uses key budgets, including sales and expense projections, as the starting points for developing business strategies.

Prior to development of the budget, certain questions must be asked and certain assumptions must be made. What will the inflation rate be? Where is competition headed? Will suppliers increase prices? Will customer tastes change? You also must explore the financial alternatives available to you. For instance, what will occur if you raise your selling price? What will be the effect if one variable (e.g., advertising) is changed?

It is important to realize that with the aid of computer technology, budgeting can be used as an effective device for evaluation of "what-if" scenarios. Through the use of simulations you should be able to move toward finding the best course of action among various alternatives. If you do not like what you see on the budgeted financial statements with respect to various financial ratios such as liquidity, activity (turnover), leverage, profit margin, and market value ratios, you can always alter your decision and planning set.

In this chapter, you will learn:
▬ What types of budgets there are.
▬ How to prepare sales, production, cost, and cash budgets.
▬ How budgets aid in planning and control.
▬ The preparation of a pro forma balance sheet and pro forma income statement.
▬ How computerized spreadsheets may be used in the budgeting process.
▬ How computer-based models help budgeting and "what-if" analysis.
▬ What zero-base budgeting is.

TYPES OF BUDGETS

Budgets are classified broadly into two categories: the *operating budget,* which reflects the results of operating decisions, and the *financial budget*, which reflects the financial decisions of the firm.

The operating budget consists of:
▬ Sales budget
▬ Production budget
▬ Direct-materials budget
▬ Direct-labor budget
▬ Factory overhead budget
▬ Selling and administrative expense budget
▬ Pro forma income statement

The financial budget consists of:
▬ Cash budget
▬ Pro forma balance sheet

The major steps in preparing the budget are:
1. Preparing a sales forecast.
2. Determining the expected production volume.
3. Estimating manufacturing costs and operating expenses.
4. Determining cash flow and other financial effects.
5. Formulating projected financial statements.

Figure 13-1 shows a simplified diagram of the various parts of the comprehensive (master) budget, the master plan of the company.

COMPREHENSIVE BUDGET

To illustrate how budgets are put together, we will focus on a manufacturing company called the Johnson Company, which produces and markets a single product. We will assume that the company develops the master budget in contribution format for

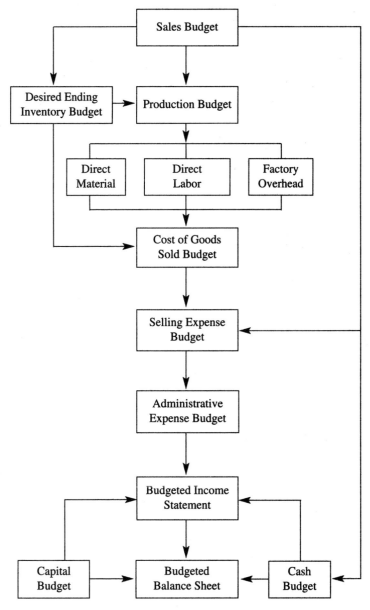

FIG. 13-1. *Comprehensive (master) budget.*

20B on a quarterly basis. We will highlight the variable cost-fixed cost breakdown throughout the illustration.

THE SALES BUDGET

The sales budget is the starting point in preparing the master budget, since estimated sales volume influences nearly all other items appearing in the master budget. Ordinarily, the sales budget indicates the quantity of each product expected to be sold.

After sales volume has been estimated, the sales budget is constructed by multiplying the expected unit selling price. Generally, the sales budget includes a computation of expected cash collections from credit sales, which will be used later for cash budgeting.

EXAMPLE 1

THE JOHNSON COMPANY
Sales Budget
for the Year Ending December 31, 20B

| | Quarter | | | | |
	1	2	3	4	Total
Expected sales in units	800	700	900	800	3,200
Unit sales price	× $80	× $80	× $80	× $80	× $80
Total sales	$64,000	$56,000	$72,000	$64,000	$256,000

Schedule of Expected Cash Collections

		1	2	3	4	Total
Accounts receivable, 12/31/20A		$9,500[*]				$9,500
1st quarter sales	($64,000)	44,800[+]	$17,920[++]			62,720
2d quarter sales	($56,000)		39,200	$15,680		54,880
3d quarter sales	($72,000)			50,400	$20,160	70,560
4th quarter sales	($64,000)				44,800	44,800
Total cash collections		$54,300	$57,120	$66,080	$64,960	$242,460

[*] All of the $9,500 accounts receivable balance is assumed to be collectible in the first quarter.
[+] 70% of a quarter's sales are collected in the quarter of sale.
[++] 28% of a quarter's sales are collected in the quarter following, and the remaining 2% are uncollectible.

THE PRODUCTION BUDGET

After sales are budgeted, the production budget can be determined so proper planning may occur. The number of units expected to be manufactured to meet budgeted sales and inventory requirements are set forth in the production budget. This budget will help you to find out your cash needs. The expected volume of production is determined by subtracting the estimated inventory at the beginning of the period from the sum of the units expected to be sold and the desired inventory at the end of the period. The production budget can be illustrated as follows:

EXAMPLE 2

THE JOHNSON COMPANY
Production Budget
for the Year Ending December 31, 20B

| | Quarter | | | | |
	1	2	3	4	Total
Planned sales (Example 1)	800	700	900	800	3,200
Desired ending inventory*	70	90	80	100+	100
Total needs	870	790	980	900	3,300
Less: Beginning inventory++	80	70	90	80	80
Units to be produced	790	720	890	820	3,220

*10% of the next quarter's expected sales.
+Estimated.
++The same as the previous quarter's ending inventory.

THE DIRECT-MATERIAL BUDGET

When the level of production has been computed, a direct-material budget should be constructed to show how much material will be required for production and how much material must be purchased to meet this production requirement. The purchase will depend on both expected usage of materials and inventory levels. The formula for computation of the purchase is:

Purchase in units = Usage + Desired ending material inventory units
– Beginning inventory units

The direct-material budget is usually accompanied by a computation of expected cash payments for materials.

EXAMPLE 3

THE JOHNSON COMPANY
Direct-Material Budget
for the Year Ending December 31, 20B

	Quarter				
	1	2	3	4	Total
Units to be produced (Example 2)	790	720	890	820	3,220
Material needs per unit (lbs.)	×3	×3	×3	×3	×3
Material needs for production	2,370	2,160	2,670	2,460	9,660
Desired ending inventory of materials*	216	267	246	250[+]	250
Total needs	2,586	2,427	2,916	2,710	9,910
Less: Beginning inventory of materials[++]	237	216	267	246	237
Materials to be purchased	2,349	2,211	2,649	2,464	9,673
Unit price	× $2	× $2	× $2	× $2	× $2
Purchase cost	$4,698	$4,422	$5,298	$4,928	$19,346

Schedule of Expected Cash Disbursements

Accounts payable, 12/31/20A	$2,200				$2,200
1st quarter purchases ($4,698)	2,349	$2,349[**]			4,698
2d quarter purchases ($4,422)		2,211	$2,211		4,422
3d quarter purchases ($5,298)			2,649	$2,649	5,298
4th quarter purchases ($4,928)				2,464	2,464
Total disbursements	$4,549	$4,560	$4,860	$5,113	$19,082

---

*10% of the next quarter's units needed for production.

[+]Estimated.

[++]The same as the prior quarter's ending inventory.

[**]50% of a quarter's purchases are paid for in the quarter of purchase; the remainder are paid for in the following quarter.

THE DIRECT-LABOR BUDGET

The production requirements as set forth in the production budget also provide the starting point for the preparation of the direct-labor budget. To compute direct-labor requirements, expected production volume for each period is multiplied by the number of direct-labor hours required to produce a single unit. The direct-labor hours to meet production requirements is then multiplied by the direct-labor cost per hour to obtain budgeted total direct-labor costs.

EXAMPLE 4

THE JOHNSON COMPANY
Direct-Labor Budget
for the Year Ending December 31, 20B

	Quarter				
	1	2	3	4	Total
Units to be produced					
(Example 2)	790	720	890	820	3,220
Direct-labor hours per unit	× 5	× 5	× 5	× 5	× 5
Total hours	3,950	3,600	4,450	4,100	16,100
Direct-labor cost per hour	× $5	× $5	× $5	× $5	× $5
Total direct-labor cost	$19,750	$18,000	$22,250	$20,500	$80,500

THE FACTORY OVERHEAD BUDGET

The factory overhead budget should provide a schedule of all manufacturing costs other than direct materials and direct labor. Using the contribution approach to budgeting requires the development of a predetermined overhead rate for the variable portion of the factory overhead. In developing the cash budget, we must remember that depreciation does not entail a cash outlay and therefore must be deducted from the total factory overhead in computing cash disbursement for factory overhead.

EXAMPLE 5

To illustrate the factory overhead budget, we will assume that:
■ Total factory overhead budgeted = $6,000 fixed (per quarter), plus $2 per hour of direct labor.
■ Depreciation expenses are $3,250 each quarter.
■ All overhead costs involving cash outlays are paid for in the quarter incurred.

THE JOHNSON COMPANY
Factory Overhead Budget
for the Year Ending December 31, 20B

| | Quarter | | | | |
	1	2	3	4	Total
Budgeted direct-labor hours					
(Example 4)	3,950	3,600	4,450	4,100	16,100
Variable overhead rate	× $2	× $2	× $2	× $2	× $2
Variable overhead budgeted	$7,900	$7,200	$8,900	$8,200	$32,200
Fixed overhead budgeted	6,000	6,000	6,000	6,000	24,000
Total budgeted overhead	$13,900	$13,200	$14,900	$14,200	$56,200
Less: Depreciation	3,250	3,250	3,250	3,250	13,000
Cash disbursement					
for overhead	$10,650	$9,950	$11,650	$10,950	$43,200

THE ENDING INVENTORY BUDGET

The desired ending inventory budget provides us with the information required for the construction of budgeted financial statements. Specifically, it will help compute the cost of goods sold on the budgeted income statement. Secondly, it will give the dollar value of the ending materials and finished-goods inventory to appear on the budgeted balance sheet.

EXAMPLE 6

THE JOHNSON COMPANY
Ending Inventory Budget
for the Year Ending December 31, 20B

	Ending inventory units	Unit cost	Total
Direct materials	250 pounds (Example 3)	$2 (Example 3)	$500
Finished goods	100 units (Example 2)	$41*	$4,100

*The unit variable cost of $41 is computed as follows:

	Unit cost	Units	Total
Direct materials (Example 3)	$2	3 pounds	$6
Direct labor (Example 4)	5	5 hours	25
Variable overhead (Example 5)	2	5 hours	10
Total variable manufacturing cost			$41

THE SELLING AND ADMINISTRATIVE EXPENSE BUDGET

The selling and administrative expense budget lists the operating expenses involved in selling the products and in managing the business. In order to complete the budgeted income statement in contribution format, variable selling and administrative expense per unit must be computed.

EXAMPLE 7

THE JOHNSON COMPANY
Selling and Administrative Expense Budget
for the Year Ending December 31, 20B

| | Quarter | | | | |
	1	2	3	4	Total
Expected sales in units	800	700	900	800	3,200
Variable selling and administrative expense per unit[*]	× $4	× $4	× $4	× $4	× $4
Budgeted variable expense	$3,200	$2,800	$3,600	$3,200	$12,800
Fixed selling and administrative expenses:					
Advertising	1,100	1,100	1,100	1,100	4,400
Insurance	2,800				2,800
Office salaries	8,500	8,500	8,500	8,500	34,000
Rent	350	350	350	350	1,400
Taxes			1,200		1,200
Total budgeted selling and administrative expenses[+]	$15,950	$12,750	$14,750	$13,150	$56,600

---

[*]Includes sales agents' commissions, shipping, and supplies. Variable selling and administrative expense per unit equals total selling and administrative expenses divided by total units.
[+]Paid for in the quarter incurred.

THE CASH BUDGET

The cash budget is prepared for the purpose of cash planning and control. It presents the expected cash inflow and outflow for a designated time period. The cash budget helps management keep cash balances in reasonable relationship to its needs. It aids in avoiding unnecessary idle cash and possible cash shortages. The cash budget usually consists of four major sections:

1. The receipts section, which is the beginning cash balance, cash collections from customers, and other receipts.
2. The disbursements section, which comprises all cash payments made by purpose.
3. The cash surplus or deficit section, which simply shows the difference between the cash receipts section and the cash disbursements section.
4. The financing section, which provides a detailed account of the borrowings and repayments expected during the budgeting period.

EXAMPLE 8

To illustrate, we will make the following assumptions:

▬ The company desires to maintain a $5,000 minimum cash balance at the end of each quarter.

▬ All borrowing and repayment must be in multiples of $500 at an interest rate of 10% per annum. Interest is computed and paid as the principal is repaid. Borrowing takes place at the beginning of each quarter and repayment at the end of each quarter.

THE JOHNSON COMPANY
Cash Budget
For the Year Ending December 31, 20B

		Quarter				Year as
	Example	1	2	3	4	a whole
Cash balance, beginning Quarter 1	Given	$10,000	$9,401*	$5,461	$9,106	$10,000
Add: Receipts: Collection from customers	1	54,300	57,120	66,080	64,960	242,460
Total cash available		$64,300	$66,521	$71,541	$74,066	$252,460
Less: Disbursements:						
Direct materials	3	$4,549	$4,560	$4,860	$5,113	$19,082
Direct labor	4	19,750	18,000	22,250	20,500	80,500
Factory overhead	5	10,650	9,950	11,650	10,950	43,200
Selling and Administrative	7	15,950	12,750	14,750	13,150	56,600
Machinery purchase	Given	—	24,300	—	—	24,300
Income tax	Given	4,000	—	—	—	4,000
Total disbursements		$54,899	$69,560	$53,510	$49,713	$227,682
Cash surplus (deficit)		$9,401	$(3,039)	$18,031	$24,353	$24,778

Financing:				
Borrowing	—	$8,500	—	—	$8,500
Repayment	—	—	($8,500)	—	(8,500)
Interest	—	—	(425)**	—	(425)
Total financing	—	$8,500	($8,925)	—	($425)
Cash balance, ending	$9,401	$5,461	$9,106	$24,353	$24,353

*The beginning cash balances for quarters 2–4 are the ending balances from the prior quarters.
**$425 ($8,500 × 10% × ½).

THE BUDGETED INCOME STATEMENT

The budgeted income statement summarizes the various component projections of revenue and expenses for the budgeting period. However, for control purposes the budget can be divided into quarters or even months, depending on the need.

EXAMPLE 9

THE JOHNSON COMPANY
Budgeted Income Statement
for the Year Ending December 31, 20B

	Example		
Sales (3,200 units @ $80)	1		$256,000
Less: Variable expenses			
Variable cost of goods sold			
(3,200 units @ $41)	6	$131,200	
Variable selling and administrative	7	12,800	144,000
Contribution margin			$112,000
Less: Fixed expenses			
Factory overhead	5	$24,000	
Selling and administration	7	43,800	67,800
Net operating income			$44,200
Less: Interest expense	8		425
Net income before taxes			$43,775
Less: Income taxes	20%*		8,755
Net income			$35,020

*Assumed.

THE BUDGETED BALANCE SHEET

The budgeted balance sheet is developed by beginning with the balance sheet for the year just ended and adjusting it, using all the activities that are expected to take place during the budgeting period. Some of the reasons why the budgeted balance sheet must be prepared are:

▬ It could disclose some unfavorable financial conditions that management might want to avoid.

▬ It serves as a final check on the mathematical accuracy of all the other schedules.

▬ It helps management perform a variety of ratio calculations.

▬ It highlights future resources and obligations.

EXAMPLE 10

To illustrate, we will use the following balance sheet for the year 20A.

THE JOHNSON COMPANY
Balance Sheet
December 31, 20A

Assets		Liabilities and Stockholders' Equity	
Current assets:		Current liabilities:	
Cash	$10,000	Accounts payable	$2,200
Accounts receivable	9,500	Income tax payable	4,000
Material inventory	474	Total current liabilities	$6,200
Finished goods inventory	3,280		
Total current assets	$23,254		
Fixed assets:		Stockholders' equity:	
Land	$50,000	Common stock, no-par	70,000
Building and equipment	100,000	Retained earnings	37,054
Accumulated depreciation	(60,000)	Total stockholder's equity	$107,054
Total fixed assets	$90,000		
		Total liabilities and	
Total assets:	$113,254	stockholders' equity	$113,254

THE JOHNSON COMPANY
Budgeted Balance Sheet
December 31, 20B

Assets			Liabilities and Stockholders' Equity		
Current assets:			Current liabilities:		
Cash	$24,353	(a)	Accounts payable	$2,464	(h)
Accounts receivable	23,040	(b)	Income tax payable	8,755	(i)
			Total current liabilities	$11,219	

Material inventory	500	(c)			
Finished goods inventory	4,100	(d)			
Total current assets	$51,993				
Fixed assets:			Stockholders' equity:		
Land	$50,000	(e)	Common stock, no-par	70,000	(j)
Building and			Retained earnings	72,074	(k)
equipment	124,300	(f)			
Accumulated			Total stockholders'		
depreciation	(73,000)	(g)	equity	$142,074	
Total fixed assets	$101,300				
			Total liabilities and		
Total assets:	$153,293		stockholders' equity	$153,293	

Computations:

(a) From Example 8 (cash budget).

(b) $9,500 (balance sheet 20A) + $256,000 sales (from Example 9) – $242,460 receipts (from Example 8) = $23,040.

(c) and (d) from Example 6 (ending inventory budget).

(e) No change.

(f) $100,000 (balance sheet 20A) + $24,300 (from Example 8) = $124,300.

(g) $60,000 (balance sheet 20A) + $13,000 (from Example 5) = $73,000.

(h) $2,200 (balance sheet 20A) + $19,346 (from Example 3) – $19,082 (from Example 8) = $2,464 (all accounts payable relate to material purchases), or 50% of 4th-quarter purchases = 50% ($4,928) = $2,464.

(i) From Example 9 (budgeted income statement).

(j) No change.

(k) $37,054 + $35,020 net income (from Example 9) = $72,074

THE USE OF COMPUTER SOFTWARE FOR BUDGETING

Profit planning and budgeting can be done using a microcomputer with a powerful spreadsheet program such as Excel. An electronic spreadsheet may be used to efficiently and quickly prepare the budget. Such software makes tedious, mechanical calculations simple. More importantly, if a budgetary figure is changed (e.g., sales), the electronic spreadsheet will change all other budgetary amounts related to it (e.g., cost of sales, selling expenses). Hence, it is easy to make different sales projections and see what the resulting costs and profitability will be. This is referred to as "what-if" analysis.

COMPUTER-BASED MODELS FOR BUDGETING

Besides using spreadsheet programs, many companies are developing computer-based models for financial planning and budgeting, using powerful, yet easy-to-use, financial modeling languages such as Comshare's Interactive Financial Planning System (IFPS). The models help not only in building a budget for profit planning but answer a variety of what-if scenarios. The resultant calculations provide a basis for choice among alternatives under conditions of uncertainty. For example, the financial planning model at Ralston Purina Company tells management that a 1% change in the price of a prime commodity will cause a change in the company's cost models and may result in the need to build a new corporate plan and master budget amounts. At Dow Chemical, 140 separate cost inputs, constantly revised, are inputted into the financial model. Management continually monitors such factors as raw-material costs and prices by country or region.

Interactive Financial Planning System (IFPS)

IFPS is a multipurpose interactive financial modeling system that supports and facilitates building, solving, and asking "what-if" questions of financial models. The output from an IFPS model is in the format of a spreadsheet—that is, a matrix or table in which:

■ The rows represent user-specified variables, such as market share, sales, growth in sales, unit price, gross margin, variable cost, contribution margin, fixed cost, net income, net present value, internal rate of return, and earnings per share.

■ The columns designate a sequence of user-specified time periods, such as month, quarter, year, and total, and percentages or divisions.

■ The entries in the body of the table display the values taken by the model variable over time or by segments of the firm, such as divisions, product lines, sales territories, and departments.

IFPS offers the following key features:

■ Like other special-purpose modeling languages, IFPS is like English. That means that without an extensive knowledge of computer programming, the cost analyst can build financial models and use them for what-if scenarios and managerial decisions.

■ IFPS has a collection of built-in financial functions that perform the calculations, such as net present value (NPV), internal rate of return (IRR), loan amortization schedules, and depreciation alternatives.

■ IFPS also has a collection of built-in mathematical and statistical functions, such as regression and moving-average functions.

■ IFPS supports use of leading and/or lagged variables that are commonly used in financial modeling. For example, cash collections lag behind credit sales of prior periods.

■ IFPS also supports deterministic and probabilistic modeling. It offers a variety of functions for sampling from probability distributions.

■ IFPS is nonprocedural in nature. This means that the relationships, logic, and data used to calculate the various values in the output do not have to be arranged in any particular top-to-bottom order in an IFPS model. IFPS automatically detects and solves a system of two or more linear or nonlinear equations.

■ IFPS has extensive editing capabilities that include adding statements to and deleting statements from a model, making changes in existing statements, and making copies of parts or all of a model.

■ IFPS supports sensitivity analysis by providing the following solution options:

   a. *What-if.* The IFPS lets you specify one or more changes in the relationships, logic, data, and/or parameter values in the existing model and recalculates the model to show the impact of these changes on the performance measures.

   b. *Goal seeking.* In the goal-seeking mode, the IFPS can determine what change would have to take place in the value of a specified variable in a specified time period to achieve a specified value for another variable. For example, the user can ask the system to answer the question, "What would the unit sales price have to be for the project to achieve a target return on investment of 20%?"

   c. *Sensitivity.* This command is employed to determine the effect of a specified variable on one or more other variables. The sensitivity command is similar to the what-if command, but it produces a convenient, model-produced tabular summary for each new alternative value of the specified variable.

   d. *Analyze.* The analyze command examines in detail those variables that have contributed to the value of a specified variable and their values.

   e. *Impact.* The impact command is used to determine the effect on a specified variable of a series of percentage changes in one or more specified variables.

   f. *IFPS/optimum.* The IFPS/optimum routine is employed to answer questions of the "What is the best?" type rather than "What if?"

Financial Planning and Budgeting Software

More and more financial planning and budgeting software—client/server and Windows-based—are clouding the market. A few popular ones are summarized below.

Commander FDC and Commander Budget. Comshare's integrated suite of Windows-based, client/server financial and managerial applications for statutory consolidations, enterprise budgeting, and management reporting are built around a central financial database and share the same core technology. Commander FDC and Commander Budget provide specialized application interfaces to the financial database, which holds historic, actual, budget, and forecast data. Commander FDC is designed for use by finance professionals involved in the monthly closing process. Commander Budget is designed to meet the needs of all business professionals involved in the budgeting process, from cost center managers to budget administrators. With either application, anyone familiar with Excel or Lotus 1-2-3 can easily do reporting and data entry. Additional modules for what-if analysis, exception detection, and executive reporting from the financial database round out Comshare's financial managerial applications.

Cashe. Cashe by Business Matters Incorporated is a new approach to financial forecasting and business modeling for people who make decisions that impact the overall financial position of their organizations. Cashe gives you a disciplined way of capturing and modifying your business assumptions so that financial forecasts can be reviewed, updated, and compared easily. Cashe's power comes from its built-in content and knowledge, which allow you to forecast your business's financial performance accurately without having to worry about formulas or accounting rules. Working on the business information you provide, Cashe's self-adjusting model ensures accuracy by automatically reflecting any changes you make throughout the entire model. Cashe is not intended to replace your spreadsheet but to work with it, allowing you to import and export all your financial models. The result is that with Cashe, you forecast more accurately, more comprehensively, and more often.

QL Financials. QL Financials by Microcompass Systems, Ltd., delivers true client/server financial management with many advanced features in a full Windows environment. It is a fully integrated suite of functionally rich modules, including general ledger, budget management, cash book/treasury management, accounts payable, accounts receivable, sales ordering/invoicing, fixed assets, requisitioning/purchase ordering, inventory management, and system integration. QL is written in Uniface Version 6, the world's leading 4GL development environment, and has been designed to meet the needs of both public and private sectors at departmental and corporate levels. Written to full TICKIT standards, QL offers multicurrency and multilingual functionality in a complete desktop environment.

Computer Software Designed for Budgeting

In addition to specialized budgeting and financial modeling software discussed previously, there are a variety of computer software designed specifically for budgeting and Decision Support Systems (DSS) software. Some are *stand-alone* packages, others are *templates,* and still others are spreadsheet *add-ins.*

Budget Express. Budget Express "understands" the structure of financial worksheets and concepts such as months, quarters, years, totals, and subtotals, speeding up budget and forecast preparation. The program creates column headers for months, automatically totals columns and rows, and calculates quarterly and yearly summaries. And for sophisticated what-if analyses, just specify your goal and Budget Express displays your current and target values as you make changes. (Add-in)

ProPlans. ProPlans creates your financial plan automatically and accurately, and slices months from your annual planning and reporting process. You just enter your forecast data and assumptions into easy-to-follow, comprehensive data-entry screens, and ProPlans automatically creates the detailed financials you need to run your business for the next year—your income statement, balance sheet, cash flow statement, and ratio reports. (Template)

Profit Planner. Profit Planner provides titles and amounts for revenues, cost of sales, expenses, assets, liabilities, and equity in a ready-to-use 1-2-3 template. Financial tables are automatically generated on screen. It presents results in 13 different table formats, including a pro forma earnings statement, balance sheet, and cash flow statement. Profit Planner even compares your earnings statement, balance sheet, and ratios against industry averages, so you're not working in a vacuum. (Template)

Up Your Cash Flow. This program generates cash flow and profit & loss forecasts; detailed sales by product/product line and payroll by employee forecasts, monthly balance sheets, bar graphs, ratio and break-even analyses, and more. (Stand-alone)

Cash Collector. This assists you in reviewing and aging receivables. You always know who owes what; nothing "falls through the cracks." What happens when collection action is required? Simply click through menu-driven screens to automatically generate letters and other professionally written collection documents (all included) that are proven to pull in the payments. (Stand-alone)

Cash Flow Analysis. This software provides projections of cash inflow and cash outflow. You input data into eight categories: sales, cost of sales, general and administrative expense, long-term debt, other cash receipts, inventory build-up/reduction, capital expenditures (acquisition of long-term assets such as store furniture), and income tax. The program allows changes in assumptions and scenarios and provides a complete array of reports. (Stand-alone)

Quicken. This program is a fast, easy-to-use, inexpensive accounting and budgeting program that can help you manage your business, particularly your cash flow. You record bills as postdated transactions when they arrive; the program's *Billminder* feature automatically reminds you when bills are due, then you can print checks for due bills with a few keystrokes. Similarly, you can record invoices and track aged receivables. Together, these features help you maximize cash on hand. (Stand-alone)

CapPLANS. This program evaluates profitability based on Net Preset Value (NPV), Internal Rate of Return (IRR), and payout period. Choose among five depreciation methods, including Modified Accelerated Cost Recovery System (MACRS). Run up to four sensitivity analyses. Project profitability over a 15-year horizon. In addition to a complete report of your analysis, CapPLANS generates a concise, four-page executive summary—great for expediting approval. Add ready-made graphs to illustrate profitability clearly, at a glance. (Template)

Project Evaluation Toolkit. This calculates the dollar value of your project based on six valuation methods, including discounted cash flow and impact on the corporate balance sheet. Assess intangibles such as impact on corporate strategy, investors, or labor relations. Use scenario planning to show the effects of changing start dates, sales forecasts, and other critical variables. (Template)

@Risk. How will a new competitor affect your market share? @Risk calculates the likelihood of changes and events that affect your bottom line. First use @Risk's familiar @ functions to define the risk in your worksheet. Then let @Risk run thousands of what-if tests using one of two proven statistical sampling techniques—Monte Carlo or Latin Hypercube. You get a clear,

colorful graph that tells you the likelihood of every possible bottom-line value. At a glance you'll know if your risk is acceptable, or if you need to make a contingency plan. (Add-in)

CFO Spreadsheet Applications. These ready-to-use spreadsheet templates offer easy ways to make many financial decisions. They are divided into four modules: cash management, tax strategies, capital budgeting, and advanced topics. (Template)

What's Best! If you have limited resources—for example, people, inventory, materials, time, or cash—then What's Best! can tell you how to allocate these resources in order to maximize or minimize a given objective, such as profit or cost. What's Best! uses a proven method—linear programming (LP)—to help you achieve your goals. This product can solve a variety of business problems that cut across every industry at every level of decision making. (Stand-alone)

Inventory Analyst. Inventory Analyst tells precisely how much inventory to order, and when to order it. Choose from four carefully explained ordering methods: economic order quantity (EOQ), fixed order quantity, fixed months requirements, and level load by workdays. Inventory Analysts ensures that you'll always have enough stock to get you through your ordering period.

Just load up to 48 months' worth of inventory history, and Inventory Analyst makes the forecast based on one of three forecasting methods: time series, exponential smoothing, or moving averages. It explains which method is best for you. Inventory Analyst will adjust your forecast for seasonality. (Template)

PrecisionTree. PrecisionTree helps you create decision trees and identify your best course of action using proven decision analysis techniques. You clarify options and rewards, describe uncertainty quantitatively, weigh multiple objectives simultaneously, and define your attitudes about risk in your spreadsheet. PrecisionTree can combine decision analysis with Monte Carlo simulation for risk analysis capabilities. (Excel add-in)

SIMUL8. SIMUL8 is a full-features simulation package. Fully integrated with Excel, it uses easy-to-enter graphics to represent both the objects in your system, such as machines and workers, and the process flows that describe their interaction. It is a powerful tool for many business processes, such as invoice and order flow, hospital process design, and any other situations where flows and processes can be redesigned and optimized. (Stand-alone)

Optima! Optima! is a Windows-based application designed to model and simulate business processes. It layouts the structure of your business (or a process within your business), defines how processes work, then tries various "what-if" scenarios to determine how to improve things. It takes flowcharting to the next level by bringing simulation to the charts you create. The program can be used for Business Process Reengineering (BPR), ISO 9000 Registration, Total Quality Management (TQM), process improvement, and more. (Stand-alone)

ZERO-BASE BUDGETING

Traditional budgeting techniques involve adding or subtracting a given percentage increase or decrease to the preceding period's budget and arriving at a new budget. The prior period's costs are considered to be basic, and the emphasis is usually placed on what upward revisions are to be made for the coming year. The traditional method focuses on inputs rather than outputs related to goal achievement, and as such never calls for the evaluation of corporate activities from a cost/benefit perspective.

Zero-base budgeting (ZBB) can be described as a technique that requires each manager to justify his or her entire budget request in detail from a base of zero, and as such calls for an analysis of the output values of each activity of a particular cost center. Cost estimates are built from scratch. This approach requires that all activities under scrutiny be defined in decision packages (discussed later), which are evaluated and ranked in order of importance at various levels.

ZBB is most applicable in planning service and support expenses rather than direct manufacturing expenses. This technique is best suited to operations and programs over which management has some discretion. For example, it can be used to develop:
- Administrative and general support
- Marketing
- Research
- Engineering
- Manufacturing support
- Capital budgets

It should not be used for:
- Direct labor
- Direct material
- Factory overhead

These are usually budgeted through various methods discussed in previous sections. Figure 13-2 helps our understanding of ZBB by indicating the key differences between ZBB and traditional (incremental) budgeting systems.

Traditional	Zero Base
Starts from existing base	Starts with base zero
Examines cost/benefit for new activities	Examines cost/benefit for all activities
Starts with dollars	Starts with purposes and activities
Does not examine new ways of operating as integral part of process	Explicitly examines new approaches
Results in a nonalternative budget	Results in a choice of several levels of service and cost

FIG. 13-2. *Differences between traditional and zero-base budgeting.*

The Zero-Base Budgeting Process

The various actions involved in implementing ZBB are outlined below.

Setting Objectives and Assumptions. The business objectives and plan assumptions begin the zero-base budgeting process. Plan assumptions serve as input to the various operating departments in preparing their individual budgets. To effectively analyze the operation, lower management will need planning assumptions about inflation rates, salary increases, etc. For example, an annual inflation rate of 5% may be assumed to reflect changing price levels. It is possible that, in beginning phases, a company would want to test ZBB in a specific division before widespread organizational application.

Defining Identifiable Segments. An activity unit is the basic cost element which is the subject of ZBB. An activity unit is usually made up of a group of employees who work toward a common goal.

The decision units need to be established at an organizational level high enough so that the person responsible for the unit has effective control over the activities. Furthermore, it is desirable that decision units be roughly similar in size (in terms of personnel and dollars) to allow for effective comparison.

Decision-Unit Analysis.

1. *Description of Current Practice.* Following the listing of activity objectives, you describe how your department currently operates and the resources used (people/dollars).

2. *Workload and Performance Measurement.* Performance measurements are next developed to examine the productivity and effectiveness of the manager's current approach. For example, a performance measurement for production control is on-time delivery.

3. *Alternatives.* ZBB next requires that you consider alternative ways of operating.

4. *Ranking Analysis.* In this step, you determine which is the most important service provided by your unit. The highest priority is given to the minimum increment of service—the amount of service that the organization must undertake to provide any meaningful service. Additional increments are developed, with each successive increment containing the services that are next in order of priority. There is an analysis, evaluation, and ranking of decision packages on the basis of cost-benefit.

5. *Review and Reallocate Resources.* The increments developed by unit managers provide top-level management with the basic information for resource-allocation decisions. The prioritization of service levels is the key factor in this process. Ranking takes place when the manager meets with all the decision-unit managers to prioritize the unit activities based on group objectives. Once ranking has been performed at various levels, a ranking table is prepared as a record of all the decisions that have been made in ZBB. This ranking table indicates what will and will not be funded and ranks activities in priorities to allow for easy adjustments to be made during the year.

6. *Detailed Budgets Prepared.* Once allocation decisions are made, detailed budgets are prepared. These budgets usually are prepared on the basis of incremental activities indicated on management's ranking table.

7. *Evaluate Performance.* ZBB provides financial data as well as workload and performance measurements that can be monitored periodically. To be effective, ZBB needs to be measured and controlled. An example of a control measure is comparison of actual vs. budgeted costs for each unit.

A decision package is made up for each product that a manager wants his or her department to produce. Assuming 50 possible products (old and new), there will be 50 decision packages.

The decision package indicates the manager's recommended way of accomplishing a given product in terms of dollar cost and time. For example, lowering quality can reduce the cost. Shortening the time period may increase the cost because of overtime. An illustrative decision package for producing a candy bar to be manufactured in the Mixing department follows:

Candy Bar
Decision Package

	Alternative A	$8,000	5 months
	Recommended Way	$10,000	3 months
	Alternative B	$11,000	$3^{1}/_{2}$ months

Each of the decision packages for all 50 products is then submitted to upper management. Upper management evaluates the decision packages coming from all the departments of the company, including that from the Mixing department, then sets a priority ranking of all packages, along with a cutoff. The decision package for the candy bar may be rejected because it does not pass the cutoff. If it is accepted, upper management gives permission to the department manager to produce the product either in the recommended way or in an alternative fashion. An alternative approach may be chosen because it is cheaper.

The advantages of ZBB are:
1. ZBB creates an analytical atmosphere that promotes the reorganization of activities to a more efficient mode.
2. ZBB involves line managers in the budgeting process, and as such fosters support for implementation throughout all company levels.
3. ZBB allows top management to define those service levels required from each business segment.
4. ZBB matches service levels to available resources.

The disadvantages of ZBB are:
1. The cost-benefit relationship probably may be one in which the cost to undertake ZBB outweighs the benefits derived.
2. ZBB is a time-consuming process. However, long intervals may be used for project evaluation (e.g., every three years).
3. ZBB is perceived as an implied threat to existing programs.
4. ZBB requires a good data system to support analysis, and in many cases no such system exists.
5. Managers tend to overlook the goal of ZBB in evaluating activity units, and focus on personnel security and interests.

6. Thrust usually comes from top to bottom, and subordinates see little benefit for themselves.
7. The thought of creating a budget from scratch causes considerable resistance if support groups and training programs are not in place.

CHAPTER PERSPECTIVE

A budget is a detailed quantitative plan outlining the acquisition and use of financial and other resources of an organization over some given time period. It is a tool for planning. If properly constructed, it is used as a control device. We showed, step by step, how to formulate a master budget. The process begins with the development of a sales budget and proceeds through a number of steps that ultimately lead to the cash budget, the budgeted income statement, and the budgeted balance sheet.

A budget helps you direct attention from the present to the future. It assists you in anticipating problems so that you can deal with them effectively, and it reveals whether you can expand. Further, a budget helps you achieve departmental goals by giving you a reference point for control reporting. The budgetary process also assists you in searching for weaknesses, which you can strengthen before they become major problems.

In recent years, spreadsheet software and computer-based models have been used for budgeting in an effort to speed up the budgeting process and allow budget analysts to investigate the effects of changes in budget assumptions. Zero-base budgeting looks at each proposed project every period to see if proper justification exists for it. Proposals are ranked in priority order subject to budget constraints. ZBB is a planning and budgeting tool that uses cost-benefit analysis of projects and functions to improve resource allocation in the organization.

Cost-Center Control Through Standard Costs and Gross Profit Analysis

INTRODUCTION AND MAIN POINTS

The information provided by cost analysts to managers includes standard costs. *Standard costs* are costs that are established in advance to serve as targets to be met and, after the fact, to determine how well those targets were actually met. Standard costing operates on the premise that managers should be held responsible for their performance, the performance of their subordinates, and for all activities within their department. Once standards have been set, managers want to focus attention on deviations from those standards.

Variance analysis based on standard costs and *flexible budgets* is a common tool for control of a *cost center* such as a production department.

After studying the material in this chapter:
■ You will be able to compute the direct materials price and quantity variances and explain their significance.
■ You will be able to calculate the direct-labor rate and efficiency variances and explain their importance.
■ You will be able to compute the variable overhead spending and efficiency variances and discuss their significance.
■ You will be able to prepare a flexible budget and explain its advantage over the static budget format.
■ You will be able to calculate and properly interpret the fixed overhead spending and volume variances.
■ You will be able to distinguish among the two-way, three-way, and four-way variance analysis for factory overhead.
■ You will be able to compute *mix* and *yield variances.*
■ You will be able to explain *gross profit analysis.*

STANDARD COSTS AND VARIANCE ANALYSIS FOR COST CENTERS

One of the most important phases of responsibility accounting is establishing standard costs and evaluating performance by comparing actual costs with the standard costs. The difference between the actual costs and standard costs, called the *variance,* is calculated for individual cost centers. Variance analysis is a key tool for measuring performance of a cost center. The standard cost is based on physical and dollar measures; it is determined by multiplying the standard quantity of an input by its standard price. Two general types of variances can be calculated for most cost items: a *price variance* and a *quantity variance.* The price variance is calculated as follows:

$$\text{Price Variance} = \text{Actual Quantity} \times (\text{Actual Price} - \text{Standard Price})$$
$$= \quad AQ \times (AP - SP)$$
$$= \quad \underset{(1)}{(AQ \times AP)} - \underset{(2)}{(AQ \times SP)}$$

The quantity variance is calculated as follows:

$$\begin{matrix} \text{Quantity} \\ \text{Variance} \end{matrix} = \begin{pmatrix} \text{Actual} & - & \text{Standard} \\ \text{Quantity} & & \text{Quantity} \end{pmatrix} \times \begin{matrix} \text{Standard} \\ \text{Price} \end{matrix}$$
$$= \quad (AQ - SQ) \times SP$$
$$= \quad \underset{(2)}{(AQ \times SP)} - \underset{(3)}{(SQ \times SP)}$$

Figure 14-1 shows a general (3-column) model for variance analysis that incorporates items (1), (2), and (3) from the above equations. It is important to note four things:

1. A price variance and a quantity variance can be calculated for all three variable-cost items—direct materials, direct-labor, and the variable portion of factory overhead. The variance is not called by the same name. A price variance is called a materials price variance in the case of direct materials, a labor-rate variance in the case of direct-labor, and a variable overhead spending variance in the case of variable factory overhead.

2. A cost variance is unfavorable (U) if the actual price (AP) or actual quantity (AQ) exceeds the standard price (SP) or standard quantity (SQ); a variance is favorable (F) if the actual price or actual quantity is less than the standard price or standard quantity.

3. The standard quantity allowed for output—item (3)—is the key concept in variance analysis. This is the standard quantity that should have been used to produce actual output. It is computed by multiplying the actual output by the number of input units allowed.

4. Variances for fixed overhead are of questionable usefulness for control purposes, since these variances are usually beyond the control of the production department.

Figure 14-1 is a model for variance analysis applicable to variable manufacturing costs.

Actual Quantity of Inputs, at Actual Price (AQ × AP) (1)	Actual Quantity of Inputs, at Standard Price (AQ × SP) (2)	Standard Quantity Allowed for Output, at Standard Price (SQ × SP) (3)
	Price Variance (1) − (2)	Quantity Variance (2) − (3)	
	Total Variance	
* Materials-purchase price variance * Labor rate variance * Variable overhead spending variance	* Materials-quantity (usage) variance * Labor efficiency variance * Variable overhead efficiency variance	

FIG. 14-1. *General model for variance analysis of variable manufacturing costs.*

We will now illustrate the variance analysis for each of the variable manufacturing cost items.

MATERIALS VARIANCES

A materials purchase price variance is isolated at the time of purchase of the material. It is computed based on the actual quantity purchased. The purchasing department is responsible for any materials price variance that might occur. The materials-quantity (usage) variance is computed based on the actual quantity used. The production department is responsible for any materials-quantity variance that might occur. Unfavorable price variances may be caused by: inaccurate standard prices, inflationary cost increases, scarcity in raw-material supplies resulting in higher prices, and purchasing department inefficiencies. Unfavorable materials-quantity variances may be the result of poorly trained workers, improperly adjusted machines, or outright waste on the production line. Table 14-1 provides the reasons and responsible parties for unfavorable materials variance.

Table 14-1
Reason and Responsible Party for an Unfavorable
Materials Variance

Reason	Responsible Party
Overstated price paid, failure to take discounts, improper specifications, insufficient quantities, use of a lower-grade material purchased to economize on price, uneconomical size of purchase orders, failure to obtain an adequate supply of a needed variety, purchase at an irregular time, or sudden and unexpected purchase required	Purchasing
Poor mix of materials, poorly trained workers, improperly adjusted machines, substitution of nonstandard materials, poor production scheduling, poor product design or production technique, lack of proper tools or machines, carelessness in not returning excess materials to storeroom, or unexpected volume changes	Production manager
Failure to detect defective goods	Receiving
Inefficient labor, poor supervision, or waste on the production line	Foreman
Inaccurate standard price	Budgeting
Excessive transportation charges or too small a quantity purchased	Traffic management
Insufficient quantity bought because of a lack of funds	Financial

EXAMPLE 1

Dallas Ewing Corporation uses a standard cost system. The standard variable costs for a product are as follows:

Materials: 2 pounds at \$3 per pound
Labor: 1 hour at \$5 per hour
Variable overhead: 1 hour at \$3 per hour

During March, 25,000 pounds of material was purchased for $74,750 and 20,750 pounds of material was used in producing 10,000 units of finished product. Direct-labor costs incurred were $49,896 (10,080 direct-labor hours) and variable overhead costs incurred were $34,776.

Using the general (3-column) model, the materials variances are shown in Figure 14-2.

Actual Quantity of Inputs, at Actual Price (AQ × AP) (1)	Actual Quantity of Inputs, at Standard Price (AQ × SP) (2)	Standard Quantity Allowed for Output, at Standard Price (SQ × SP) (3)
25,000 lb × $2.99 = $74,750	25,000 lb × $3.00 = $75,000	20,000 lb* × $3.00 = $60,000

price variance
$250 (F) (1 − 2)

20,750 lb × $3.00
= $62,250

quantity variance
$2,250 (U) (2 − 3)

_____

*10,000 units actually produced × 2 pounds allowed per unit = 20,000 pounds.

FIG. 14-2. *Materials variances.*

It is important to note that the amount of materials purchased (25,000 pounds) differs from the amount of materials used in production (20,750 pounds). The materials-purchase price variance was computed using 25,000 pounds purchased, whereas the materials-quantity (usage) variance was computed using the 20,750 pounds used in production. A total variance cannot be computed because of the difference.

Alternatively, we can compute the materials variance as follows:

Materials-purchase price variance = AQ (AP − SP)
  = (AQ × AP) − (AQ × SP)
  = (25,000 pounds)($2.99 − $3.00)
  = $74,750 − $75,000
  = $250 (F)

Materials-quantity (usage) variance = (AQ − SQ) SP
  = (20,750 pounds − 20,000 pounds)($3.00)
  = $62,250 − $60,000
  = $2,250 (U)

LABOR VARIANCES

Labor variances are isolated when labor is used for production. They are computed in a manner similar to the materials variances, except that in the 3-column model the terms "efficiency" and "rate" are used in place of the terms "quantity" and "price." The production department is responsible for both the prices paid for labor services and the quantity of labor services used. Therefore, the production department must explain why any labor variances occur. Unfavorable rate variances may be explained by an increase in wages, poor scheduling of production resulting in overtime work, or the use of labor commanding higher wage rates than contemplated. Table 14-2 provides the possible reasons for a labor price variance and the ones responsible. Unfavorable efficiency variances may be explained by poor supervision, poor-quality workers, poor quality of materials requiring more labor time, machine breakdowns, and employee unrest. Table 14-3 provides the cause and responsible entity for an unfavorable labor efficiency variance.

Table 14-2
Reasons for a Labor Price Variance and the Responsible Party

Reason	Responsible Party
Use of overpaid or excessive number of workers	Production manager or union contract
Poor job descriptions or excessive wages	Personnel
Overtime and poor scheduling of production	Production planning

Table 14-3
Cause and Responsible Entity for an Unfavorable Labor Efficiency Variance

Cause	Responsible Entity
Poor-quality workers or poor training	Personnel or Training
Inadequate supervision, inefficient flow of materials, wrong mixture of labor for a given job, inferior tools or idle time from production delays	Foreman
Employee unrest	Personnel or Foreman
Improper functioning of equipment	Maintenance
Insufficient material supply or poor quality	Purchasing

Using the general (3-column) model, the labor variances are shown below in Figure 14-3.

Actual Hours of Inputs, at Actual Rate (AH × AR) (1)	Actual Hours of Inputs, at Standard Rate (AH × SR) (2)	Standard Hours Allowed for Output, at Standard Rate (SH × SR) (3)
$10,080 h × $4.95 = $49,896	10,080 h × $5.00 = $50,400	10,000* h × $5.00 = $50,000

	Rate Variance (1) – (2) $504 (F)	Efficiency Variance (2) – (3) $400 (U)

Total Variance $104 (F)

---

*10,000 units actually produced × 1 hour (h) allowed per unit = 10,000 hours.

Note: The symbols AQ, SQ, AP, and SP have been changed to AH, SH, AR, and SR to reflect the terms "hour" and "rate."

FIG. 14-3. *Labor variances.*

EXAMPLE 2
Using the same data given in Example 1, the labor variances can be calculated as shown in Figure 14-3.

Alternatively, we can calculate the labor variances as follows:

Labor rate variance
= AH (AR – SR)
= (AH × AR) – (AH × SR)
= (10,080 hours)($4.95 – $5.00)
= $49,896 – $50,400
= $504 (F)

Labor efficiency variance
= (AH – SH) SR
= (10,080 hours – 10,000 hours) × $5.00
= $50,400 – $50,000
= $400 (U)

VARIABLE OVERHEAD VARIANCES

The variable overhead variances are computed in a way that is very similar to the way labor variances are computed. The production department is usually responsible for any variable overhead variance that might occur. Unfavorable variable overhead spending variances may be caused by any of a large number of factors: acquiring supplies for a price different from the standard, using more supplies than expected, waste, and theft of supplies. Unfavorable variable overhead efficiency variances might be caused by such factors as: poorly trained workers, poor-quality materials, faulty equipment, work interruptions, poor production scheduling, poor supervision, employee unrest, etc. When variable overhead is applied using direct-labor hours, the efficiency variance will be caused by the same factors that cause the labor-efficiency variance. However, when variable overhead is applied using machine hours, inefficiency in machinery will cause a variable overhead efficiency variance.

EXAMPLE 3

Using the same data given in Example 1, the variable overhead variances can be computed as shown in Figure 14-4.

Actual Hours of Inputs, at Actual Rate (AH × AR) (1)	Actual Hours of Inputs, at Standard Rate (AH × SR) (2)	Standard Hours Allowed for Output, at Standard Rate (SH × SR) (3)
10,080 h × $3.45 = $34,776	10,080 h × $3.00 = $30,240	10,000 h* × $3.00 = $30,000

	Spending variance (1) – (2) $4,536 (U)	Efficiency variance (2) – (3) $240 (U)

Total Variance $4,776 (U)

*10,000 units actually produced × 1 hour (h) allowed per unit = 10,000 hours.

FIG. 14-4. *Variable overhead variances.*

Alternatively, we can compute the variable overhead variances as follows:

Variable overhead spending variance = AH (AR – SR)

$$= (AH \times AR) - (AH \times SR)$$
$$= (10,080 \text{ hours})(\$3.45 - \$3.00)$$
$$= \$34,776 - \$30,240$$
$$= \$4,536 \text{ (U)}$$

Variable overhead efficiency variance = (AH − SH) SR
$$= (10{,}080 \text{ hours} - 10{,}000 \text{ hours}) \times \$3.00$$
$$= \$30{,}240 - \$30{,}000$$
$$= \$240 \text{ (U)}$$

FLEXIBLE BUDGETS AND PERFORMANCE REPORTS

A flexible budget is a tool that is extremely useful in cost control. In contrast to a static budget, the flexible budget is characterized as follows:

1. It is geared toward a range of activity rather than a single level of activity.

2. It is dynamic in nature rather than static. By using the cost-volume formula (or flexible budget formula), a series of budgets can be easily developed for various levels of activity.

The static (fixed) budget is geared for only one level of activity and has problems in cost control. Flexible budgeting distinguishes between fixed and variable costs, thus allowing for a budget that can be automatically adjusted (via changes in variable cost totals) to the particular level of activity actually attained. Thus, variances between actual costs and budgeted costs are adjusted for volume ups and downs before differences due to price and quantity factors are computed.

The primary use of the flexible budget is to accurately measure performance by comparing actual costs for a given output with the budgeted costs for the same level of output.

EXAMPLE 4

To illustrate the difference between the static budget and the flexible budget, assume that the Assembly Department of Mills Industries, Inc., is budgeted to produce 6,000 units during June. Assume further that the company was able to produce only 5,800 units. The budget for direct-labor and variable overhead costs is as follows:

Mills Industries, Inc.
The Direct-Labor and Variable Overhead Budget
Assembly Department for the Month of June

Budgeted production	6,000 units
Actual production	5,800 units
Direct labor	$39,000
Variable overhead costs:	
Indirect labor	6,000
Supplies	900
Repairs	300
	$46,200

If a static budget approach is used, the performance report appears as follows:

Mills Industries, Inc.
The Direct-Labor and Variable Overhead Budget
Assembly Department
for the Month of June

	Budget	Actual*	Variance (U or F)**
Production in units	6,000	5,800	200U
Direct labor	$39,000	$38,500	$500F
Variable overhead costs:			
Indirect labor	6,000	5,950	50F
Supplies	900	870	30F
Repairs	300	295	5F
	$46,200	$45,615	$585F

*Given.
**A variance represents the deviation of actual cost from the standard or budgeted cost. U and F stand for "unfavorable" and "favorable," respectively.

These cost variances are useless because they compare "apples and oranges." The problem is that the budget costs are based on an activity level of 6,000 units, whereas the actual costs were incurred at an activity level below this (5,800 units). From a control standpoint, it makes no sense to try to compare costs at one activity level with costs at a different activity level. Such comparisons would make a production manager look good only as long as the actual production is less than the budgeted production. Using the cost-volume formula and generating the budget based on the 5,800 actual units gives the following performance report:

Mills Industries, Inc.
Performance Report
Assembly Department for the Month of June

Budgeted production   6,000 units
Actual production   5,800 units

	Cost-volume formula	Budget 6,000 units	Actual 5,800 units	Variance (U or F)
Direct labor	$6.50 per unit	$37,700	$38,500	$800U
Variable overhead:				
Indirect labor	1.00	5,800	5,950	150U
Supplies	.15	870	870	0
Repairs	.05	290	295	5U
	$7.70	$44,660	$45,615	$955U

Notice that all cost variances are unfavorable (U), as compared to the favorable cost variances on the performance report based on the static-budget approach.

FIXED-OVERHEAD VARIANCES

By definition, fixed overhead does not change over a relevant range of activity; the amount of fixed overhead per unit varies inversely with the level of production. In order to calculate variances for fixed overhead, it is necessary to determine a standard fixed-overhead rate, which requires the selection of a predetermined (denominator) level of activity. This activity should be measured on the basis of standard inputs allowed. The formula is:

$$\text{Standard fixed-overhead rate} = \frac{\text{Budgeted fixed overhead}}{\text{Budgeted level of activity}}$$

Total fixed overhead variance is simply under- or overapplied overhead. It is the difference between actual fixed overhead incurred and fixed overhead applied to production (generally, on the basis of standard direct-labor hours allowed for actual production). The total fixed-overhead variance combines fixed-overhead spending (flexible-budget) variance and fixed-overhead volume (capacity) variance.

Fixed-Overhead Spending (Flexible-Budget) Variance

This is the difference between actual fixed overhead incurred and budgeted fixed overhead. This variance is not affected by the level of production. Fixed overhead, by definition, does not change with the level of activity. The spending (flexible-budget) variance is caused solely by events such as unexpected changes in prices and unforeseen repairs.

Fixed-Overhead Volume (Capacity) Variance

This variance results when the actual level of activity differs from the denominator activity used in determining the standard fixed overhead rate. Note that the denominator used in the formula is the expected annual activity level. The fixed-overhead volume variance is a measure of the cost of failure to operate at the denominator (budgeted) activity level, and may be caused by such factors as failure to meet sales targets, idleness due to poor scheduling, and machine breakdowns. The volume variance is calculated as follows:

Fixed overhead	= (Budgeted fixed overhead) – (fixed overhead applied)
	or
	= (Denominator activity – standard hours allowed) × standard fixed overhead rate

When denominator activity exceeds standard hours allowed, the volume variance is unfavorable (U), because it is an index of less-than-denominator utilization of capacity.

It is important to note that there are no efficiency variances for fixed overhead. Fixed overhead does not change regardless of whether productive resources are used efficiently or not. (For example, property taxes, insurance, and factory rents are not affected by whether production is efficient or not.)

Figure 14-5 illustrates the relationship between the various elements of fixed overhead, and the possible variances.

Incurred: Actual Hours × Actual Rate (1)	Flexible Budget Based on Actual Hours (2)	Flexible Budget Based on Standard Hours Allowed (3)	Applied (4)
3-way Analysis	Spending variance (1) – (2)	Efficiency variance (not applicable)	Volume variance (3) – (4)
2-way Analysis	Flexible budget variance (1) – (3)		Volume variance (3) – (4)

(1) – (4)
Under- or Overapplied

FIG. 14-5. *Fixed overhead variances.*

EXAMPLE 5

The Geige Manufacturing Company has the following standard cost of factory overhead at a normal monthly production (denominator) volume of 1,300 direct-labor hours:

Variable overhead (1 hour @ $2)
Fixed overhead (1 hour @ $5)

Fixed overhead budgeted is $6,500 per month. During the month of March, the following events occurred:

(a) Actual overhead costs incurred (for 1,350 hours) were:

Variable $2,053
Fixed $6,725

(b) Standard hours allowed, 1,250 hours (1 hour × 1,250 units of output)

Note that:

(a) Flexible budget formula:
Variable overhead rate $2 per direct-labor hour
Fixed overhead budgeted $6,500

(b) Standard overhead applied rates:
Variable $2 per direct-labor hour
Fixed $5 per direct-labor hour

Figure 14-6 shows all the variances for variable overhead as well as fixed overhead.

	Incurred: Actual Hours × Actual Rate (1,350 hrs.) (1)	Flexible Budget Based on Actual Hours (1,350 hrs.) (2)	Flexible Budget Based on Standard Hours Allowed (1,250 hrs.) (3)	Applied (1,250 hrs.) (4)
V	$2,853	$2,700 (1,350 × $2)	$2,500 (1,250 × $2)	$2,500
F	6,725	6,500	6,500	6,250
	$9,578	$9,200	$9,000	$8,750

(3-way)	Spending variance (1) − (2)	Efficiency variance (NA*)	Volume variance (3) − (4)
V	$153 U	$200 U	NA*
F	225 U	NA*	$250 U
	$378 U	$200 U	$250 U

(2-way)	Flexible Budget Variance (1) − (3)	Volume Variance (3) − (4)
V	$353 U	NA*
F	225 U	$250 U
	$578 U	$250 U

	Under- or Overapplied (1) − (4)
V	$353 U
F	475 U
	$828 U

---

* Not applicable.

FIG. 14-6. *Variance analysis for variable and fixed overhead.*

The fixed overhead volume variance can also be calculated as:

Fixed overhead = (Denominator activity – standard hours allowed)
volume variance   × standard fixed overhead rate
           = (1,300 hours – 1,250 hours) × \$5
           = 50 hours × \$5 = \$250 U

METHODS OF VARIANCE ANALYSIS FOR FACTORY OVERHEAD

Variance analysis for factory overhead consists of a two-, three-, or four-way method of computation, depending on the significance of the variance amounts compared to the cost of analysis. These methods are indicated in Figure 14-5 and Figure 14-6.

The two-way analysis computes two variances: budget variance (sometimes called the flexible-budget or controllable variance) and volume variances, which means:

    (a) Budget variance = Variable-spending variance + Fixed-spending (budget) variance + Variable-efficiency variance
    (b) Volume variance = Fixed-volume variance

The three-way analysis computes three variances: spending, efficiency, and volume variances. Therefore,

    (a) Spending variance = Variable-spending variance + Fixed-spending (budget) variance
    (b) Efficiency variance = Variable-efficiency variance
    (c) Volume variance = Fixed-volume variance

The four-way analysis includes the following:

    (a) Variable-spending variance
    (b) Fixed-spending (budget) variance
    (c) Variable-efficiency variance
    (d) Fixed-volume variance

PRODUCTION MIX AND YIELD VARIANCES

The production mix variance is a cost variance that arises if the actual production mix deviates from the standard or budgeted mix. In a multiproduct, multi-input situation, the mix variances explain the portion of the quantity (usage, or efficiency) variance caused by using inputs (direct materials and direct labor) in ratios different from standard proportions, thus helping determine how efficiently mixing operations are performed.

The material mix variance indicates the impact on material costs of the deviation from the budgeted mix. The labor mix variance measures the impact of changes in the labor mix on labor costs.

■■ Material Mix Variance: (Actual Units used at standard mix − Actual Units used at actual mix) × Standard Unit Price

■■ Labor Mix Variance: (Actual Hours used at standard mix − Actual Hours used at actual mix) × Standard Hourly Rate

Probable causes of unfavorable production mix variances are as follows:

1. Capacity restraints force substitution.
2. Poor production scheduling.
3. Lack of certain types of labor.
4. Certain materials are in short supply.

EXAMPLE 6

J Company produces a compound composed of Materials Alpha and Beta, which is marketed in 20-pound bags. Material Alpha can be substituted for Material Beta. Standard cost and mix data have been determined as follows:

	Unit Price	Standard Unit	Standard Mix Proportions
Material Alpha	$3	5 lbs.	25%
Material Beta	4	15	75
		20 lbs.	100%

Processing each 20 lbs. of materials requires 10 hrs. of labor. The company employs two types of labor, "skilled" and "unskilled," working on two processes, assembly and finishing. The following standard labor cost has been set for a 20-pound bag.

	Standard Hours	Standard Wage Rate	Total	Standard Mix Proportions
Unskilled	4 hrs.	$2	$8	40%
Skilled	6	3	18	60
	10 hrs.	$2.60	26	100%

At standard cost, labor averages $2.60 per unit. During the month of December, 100 20-lb. bags were completed with the following labor costs:

	Actual Hrs.	Actual Rate	Actual Wages
Unskilled	380 hrs.	$2.50	$950
Skilled	600	3.25	1,950
	980 hrs.	$2.96	$2,900

We now want to determine the following variances from standard costs.

    (a) Material purchase price
    (b) Material mix
    (c) Material quantity
    (d) Labor rate
    (e) Labor mix
    (f) Labor efficiency

Material records show:

	Beginning Inventory	Purchase	Ending Inventory
Material Alpha	100 lbs.	800 @ $3.10	200 lbs.
Material Beta	225	1,350 @ $3.90	175

We will also prepare appropriate journal entries.

We will show how to compute these variances in a tabular form as follows:

(a) *Material Purchase Price Variance*

	Material Price per Unit			Actual Quantity Purchased	Variance ($)
	Standard	Actual	Difference		
Material Alpha	$3	$3.10	$.10 U	800 lbs.	$80 U
Material Beta	4	3.90	.10 F	1,350	135 F
					$55 F

(b) *Material Mix Variance*

	Unit That Should Have Been Used at Standard Mix*	Actual Unit at Actual Mix**	Difference	Standard Unit Price	Variance ($)
Material Alpha	525 lbs.	700 lbs.	175 U	$3	$525 U
Material Beta	1,575	1,400	175 F	4	700 F
	2,100 lbs.	2,100 lbs.			$175 F

The material mix variance measures the impact on material costs of the deviation from the standard mix. Therefore, it is computed holding the total quantity used constant at its actual amount and

---

*This is the standard mix proportion of 25% and 75% applied to the actual material units used of 2,100 lbs.
**Actual units used = beginning inventory + purchases − ending inventory. Therefore,
    Material Alpha: 700 lbs. = 100 + 800 − 200
    Material Beta: 1,400 lbs. = 225 + 1,350 − 175

allowing the material mix to vary between actual and standard. As shown above, due to a favorable change in mix, we ended up with a favorable material mix variance of $175.

(c) *Material Quantity Variance*

	Should Have Been Used at Standard Mix	Standard Units at Actual Mix	Difference	Standard Unit Price	Variance ($)
Material Alpha	525 lbs.	500 lbs.	25 U	$3	$75 U
Material Beta	1,575	1,500	75 U	4	300 U
	2,100 lbs.	2,000 lbs.			$375 U

The total material variance is the sum of the three variances:

Purchase price variance	$55 F
Mix variance	175 F
Quantity variance	375 U
	$145 U

The increase of $145 in material costs was due solely to an unfavorable quantity variance of 100 lbs. of material Alpha and Beta. The unfavorable quantity variance, however, was compensated largely by favorable mix and price variances. J Company must look for ways to cut down waste and spoilage.

The labor cost increase of $300 ($2,900 − $2,600) is attributable to three causes:

1. An increase of $.50 per hour in the rate paid to skilled labor and $.25 per hour in the rate paid to unskilled labor.
2. An unfavorable mix of skilled and unskilled labor.
3. A favorable labor efficiency variance of 20 hours.

Three labor variances are computed below.

(d) *Labor Rate Variance*

	Labor Rate per Hr.			Actual Hrs. Used	Variance ($)
	Standard	Actual	Difference		
Unskilled	$2	$2.50	$.5 U	380 U	$190 U
Skilled	3	3.25	.25 U	600	150 U
					$340 U

(e) *Labor Mix Variance*

	Actual Hrs. at Standard Mix*	Actual Hrs. at Actual Mix	Difference	Standard Rate	Variance ($)
Unskilled	392 hrs.	380 hrs.	12 F	$2	$24 F
Skilled	588	600	12 U	3	36 U
	980 hrs.	980 hrs.			$12 U

*This is the standard proportions of 40% and 60% applied to the actual total labor hrs. used of 980.

(f) *Labor Mix Variance*

	Actual Hrs. at Standard Mix	Standard Hrs. at Actual Mix	Difference	Standard Price	Variance ($)
Unskilled	392 hrs.	400 hrs.	8 F	$2	$16 F
Skilled	588	600	12 F	3	36 F
	980 hrs.	1,000 hrs.			$52 F

The total labor variance is the sum of these three variances:

Rate variance	$340 U
Mix variance	12 U
Efficiency variance	52 F
	$300 U

which is proved to be:

(g) *Total Labor Variance*

	Actual Hrs. Used	Actual Rate	Total Actual Cost	Standard Hrs. Allowed	Standard Hrs. Rate	Total Cost	Variance ($)
Unskilled	380 hrs.	$2.50	$950	400	$2	$800	$150 U
Skilled	600	3.25	1,950	600	3	1,800	150 U
			$2,900			$2,600	$300 U

The unfavorable labor variance, as evidenced by the cost increase of $300, may be due to:

1. Overtime necessary because of poor production scheduling resulting in a higher average labor cost per hour; and/or
2. unnecessary use of more expensive skilled labor. J Company should put more effort into better production scheduling.

PRODUCTION YIELD VARIANCE

The production yield variance is the difference between the actual yield and the standard yield. Yield is a measure of productivity. In other words, it is a measure of output from a given amount of input. For example, in the production of potato chips, we might expect a certain yield such as 40% yield or 40 pounds of chips for 100 pounds of potatoes.

If the actual yield is less than the expected or standard yield for a given level of input, the yield variance is unfavorable. A yield variance is computed for labor as well as materials. A labor yield variance is considered the result of the quantity and/or the quality of labor used. The yield variance explains the remaining portion of the quantity variance and is caused by a yield of finished product that does not correspond with the quantity that actual inputs should have produced. When there is no mix variance, the yield variance equals the quantity variance.

▬ Material Yield Variance: (Actual Units used at standard mix – Actual Output Units used at standard mix) × Standard Unit Price

▬ Labor Yield Variance: (Actual Hours used at standard mix – Actual Output Hours used at standard mix) × Standard Hourly Rate

The probable causes of unfavorable production yield variances are:

1. Use of low-quality materials and/or labor.
2. Existence of faulty equipment.
3. Use of improper production methods.
4. Improper or costly mix of materials and/or labor.

EXAMPLE 7

The Giffen Manufacturing Company uses a standard cost system for its production of a chemical product. This chemical is produced by mixing three major raw materials, A, B, and C. The company has the following standards:

36 lbs. of Material A	@1.00	=	$36.00
48 lbs. of Material B	@2.00	=	$96.00
36 lbs. of Material C	@1.75	=	$63.00
120 lbs. of standard mix	@1.625	=	$195.00

The company should produce 100 lbs. of finished product at a standard cost of $1.625 per lb. ($195/120 lbs.). To convert 120 lbs. of materials into 100 lbs. of finished chemical requires 400 direct-labor hours at $3.50 per hour, or $14 per lb. During the month of December, the company completed 4,250 lbs. of output with the following labor: direct labor 15,250 hours @$3.50. Material records show:

	Materials Purchased During the Month	Materials Used During the Month
Material A	1,200 @ $1.00	1,160 lbs.
Material B	1,800 @ 1.95	1,820
Material C	1,500 @ 1.80	1,480

The material *price variance is isolated at the time of purchase.* We want to compute the material purchase price, quantity, mix and yield variances.

Also, we want to prepare appropriate journal entries. We will show the computations of variances in a tabular form as follows.

(a) *Material Variances*

Material Purchase Price Variance

	Material Price per Unit			Actual Quantity Purchased	Variance ($)
	Standard	Actual	Difference		
Material A	$1.00	$1.10	$.10 U	1,200 lbs.	$120 U
Material B	2.00	1.95	.05 F	1,800	90 F
Material C	1.75	1.80	.05 U	1,500	75 U
					$105 U

The material quantity variance computed below results from the change in the mix of materials as well as from changes in the total quantity of materials. The standard input allowed for actual production consists of 1,275 lbs. of Material A, 1,700 lbs. of Material B, and 1,275 lbs. of Material C, a total of 4,250 lbs. The actual input consisted of 1,160 lbs. of Material A, 1,820 lbs. of Material B, and 1,480 lbs. of Material C. The total of variance is subdivided into a material mix variance and a material yield variance, as shown below.

Material Quantity Variance

	Actual Unit Used at Actual Mix	"Should Have Been" Inputs Based upon Actual Output	Difference	Standard Unit Price	Variance ($)
Material A	1,160 lbs.	1,275 lbs.	115 F	$1.00	$115
Material B	1,820	1,700	120 U	2.00	240 F
Material C	1,480	1,275			358.75 U
	4,460 lbs.	4,250 lbs.			$483.75 U

The computation of the material mix variance and the material yield variance for the Giffen Manufacturing Company is given below.

Material Mix Variance

	"Should Have Been" Individual Input Based upon Total Actual Throughput*	Actual Units Used at Actual Output*	Difference	Standard Unit Price	Variance ($)
Material A	1,338 lbs.	1,160 lbs.	178 F	$1.00	$178 F
Material B	1,784	1,820	36 U	2.00	72 U
Material C	1,338	1,480	142 U	1.79	248.5 U
	4,460 lbs.	4,460 lbs.			$142.5 U

*This is the standard mix proportions of 30%, 40%, and 30% applied to the actual material units used of 4,460 lbs.

Material Yield Variance

	Expected Input Units at Standard Mix	"Should Have Been" Inputs Based upon Actual Output*	Difference	Standard Unit Price	Variance ($)
Material A	1,338 lbs.	1,275 lbs.	63 U	$1.00	$63 U
Material B	1,784	1,700	84 U	2.00	168 U
Material C	1,338	1,275	63 U	1.75	110.25 U
	4,460 lbs.	4,420 lbs.			$341.25 U**

*This is the standard mix proportions of 30%, 40%, and 30% applied to the actual throughput of 4,460 lbs. or *output* of 4,250 lbs.
**The material yield variance of $341.25 U can be computed alternatively as follows.

> Actual input quantity at standard prices
>
> Material A 1,338 lbs. @$1.00 = $1,338
> Material B 1,784 lbs. @ 2.00 = 3,568
> Material C 1,338 lbs. @ 1.75 = 2,341.5 $7,247.50
>
> Hence, $7,247.5 – $4,906.25 = $341.25 U

The material mix and material yield variances are unfavorable, indicating that a shift was made to a more expensive (at standard) input mix and that an excessive quantity of material was used. Poor production scheduling requiring an unnecessarily excessive use of input material and an undesirable mix of Material A, B, and C was responsible for this result. To remedy the situation, the company must ensure that:

1. The material mix is adhered to in terms of the least cost combination without affecting product quality.
2. The proper production methods are being implemented:

Inefficiencies, waste, and spoilage are within the standard allowance.

3. Quality materials, consistent with established standards are being used.

Journal Entries

To record material purchases

Material and Supplies	7,425*	
Material Purchase Price Variance	105 U	
Cash (or Accounts Payable)		7,530**

*Actual quantities purchased at standard prices:

Material A (1,200 lbs. @$1.00)	$1,200	
Material B (1,800 @ 2.00)	3,600	
Material C (1,500 @ 1.75)	2,625	$7,425

**Actual quantities purchased at actual prices:

Material A (1,200 lbs. @$1.10)	$1,320	
Material B (1,800 @ 1.95)	3,510	
Material C (1,500 @ 1.80)	2,700	$7,530

To charge materials into production

Work-in-Process	7,247.50*	
Material Mix Variance	142.50 U	
Materials and Supplies		7,390**

*Actual quantities used at standard mix at standard prices:

Material A (1,338 lbs. @$1.00)	$1,338.00	
Material B (1,784 @ 2.00)	3,568.00	
Material C (1,480 @ 1.75)	2,341.50	$7,247.50

**Actual quantities used at standard prices:

Material A (1,160 lbs. @$1.00)	$1,160	
Material B (1,820 @ 2.00)	3,640	
Material C (1,480 @ 1.75)	2,590	$7,390

To transfer material costs to finished goods

Finished Goods	6,906.25*	
Material Yield Variance	341.25 U	
Work-in-Process		7,240.50*

*See the previous page for the numerical computations.

Employees seldom complete their operations according to standard times. Two factors should be brought out in computing labor variances if the analysis and computation will be used to fix responsibility:

1. The change in labor cost resulting from the efficiency of the workers, measured by a labor efficiency variance. (In finding the change, allowed hours are determined through the material input.)
2. The change in labor cost due to a difference in the yield, measured by a labor yield variance. (In computing the change, actual output is converted to allowed input hours.)

For the Giffen Manufacturing Company, more efficient workers resulted in a savings of 383.33 hours (15,250 hrs. − 14,866.67 hrs.). Priced at the standard rate per hour, this produced an unfavorable labor efficiency variance of $1,341.66 as shown below:

Labor Efficiency Variance

Actual hrs. at standard rate	$53,375
Actual hrs. at expected output	
(4,460 hrs. × 400/120 = 14,866.67 hrs. @$3.5	52,033.3
	$1,341.6

With a standard yield of 83 1/3% (=100/120), 4,250 lbs. of finished material should have required 17,000 hrs. of direct labor (4,250 lbs. × 400 DLH/100). Comparing the hours allowed for the actual input, 14,866.67 hrs. with the hours allowed for actual output, 17,000 hrs., we find a favorable labor yield variance of $7,466.66, as shown below.

Labor Yield Variance

Actual hrs. at expected output	$52,033.3
Actual output (4,250 lbs. × 400/100 =	
17,000 hrs. @$3.5 or 4,250 lbs. @$14.00)	59,500
	$7,466.6

The labor efficiency variance can be combined with the yield variance to give us the *traditional* labor efficiency variance, which turns out to be favorable as follows.

Labor efficiency variance	$1,341.66 U
Labor yield variance	7,466.66 F
	$6,125 F

This division is necessary when there is a difference between the actual yield and standard yield, if responsibility is to be fixed. The producing department cannot be rightfully credited with a favorable efficiency variance of $6,125. Note, however, that a favorable yield variance, which is a factor most likely outside the control of the producing department, more than offsets the *unfavorable* labor efficiency variance of $1,341.66, which the producing department rightfully should have been responsible for.

Journal Entries

To transfer labor costs to work-in-process

Work-in-Process	52,033.34	
Labor Efficiency Variance	1,341.66 U	
Payroll		53,375.00

To transfer labor costs to finished goods

Finished Goods	59,500	
Labor Yield Variance	7,466.66 F	
Work-in-Process		52,033.34

GROSS PROFIT ANALYSIS

Profit variance analysis, often called gross profit analysis, deals with how to analyze the profit variance that constitutes the departure between actual profit and the previous year's income or the budgeted figure. The primary goal of profit variance analysis is to improve performance and profitability.

Profit, whether it is gross profit in absorption costing or contribution margin in direct costing, is affected by at least three basic items: sales price, sales volume, and costs. In addition, in a multiproduct firm, if not all products are equally profitable, profit is affected by the mix of products sold.

The difference between budgeted and actual profits are due to one or more of the following:

1. Changes in unit sales price and cost, called sales price and cost price variances, respectively. The difference between the sales price variance and cost price variance is often called a contribution-margin-per-unit variance or a gross-profit-per-unit variance, depending upon what type of costing system is being referred to, that is, absorption costing or direct costing. Contribution margin is, however, a better measure of product profitability because it deducts from sales revenue only the variable costs that are controllable in terms of fixing responsibility. Gross profit does not reflect cost-volume-profit relationships, nor does it consider directly traceable marketing costs.

2. Changes in the volume of products sold summarized as the sales volume variance and the cost volume variance. The difference between the two is called the total volume variance.

3. Changes in the volume of the more profitable or less profitable items referred to as the sales mix variance.

Detailed analysis is critical to management when multiproducts exist. The volume variances may be used to measure a change in volume, while holding the mix constant, and the mix may be employed to evaluate the effect of a change in sales mix, while holding the quantity constant. This type of variance analysis is useful when the products are substituted for each other, or when products that are not necessarily substitutes for each other are marketed through the same channel.

Types of Standards in Profit Variance Analysis

To determine the various causes for a favorable variance (an increase) or an unfavorable variance (a decrease) in profit, we need some kind of yardsticks to compare against the actual results. The yardsticks may be based on the prices and costs of the previous year, or any year selected as the base periods. Some companies are summarizing profit variance analysis data in their annual report by showing departures from the previous year's reported income. However, one can establish a more effective control and budgetary method rather than the previous year's data. Standard or budgeted mix can be determined using such sophisticated techniques as linear and goal programming.

Single Product Firms

Profit variance analysis is simplest in a single product firm, as there is only one sales price, one set of costs (or cost price), and a unitary sales volume. An unfavorable profit variance can be broken down into four components: a sales price variance, a cost price variance, a sales volume variance, and a cost volume variance.

Sales Price Variance. The sales price variance measures the impact on the firm's contribution margin (or gross profit) of changes in the unit selling price. It is computed as:

Sales price variance = (actual price – budget price) × actual sales

If the actual price is lower than the budgeted price, for example, this variance is unfavorable; it tends to reduce profit.

Cost Price Variance. The cost price variance is simply the summary of price variances for materials, labor, and overhead.

(This is the sum of material price, labor rate, and factory overhead spending variances). It is computed as:

Cost price variance = (actual cost – budget cost) × actual sales

If the actual unit cost is lower than budgeted cost, for example, this variance is favorable; it tends to increase profit. We simplify the computation of price variances by taking the sales price variance less the cost price variance and call it the gross-profit-per-unit variance or contribution-margin-per-unit variance.

Sales Volume Variance. The sales volume variance indicates the impact on the firm's profit of changes in the unit sales volume. This is the amount by which sales would have varied from the budget if nothing but sales volume had changed. It is computed as:

Sales volume variance = (actual sales – budget sales) × budget price

If actual sales volume is greater than budgeted sales volume, this is favorable; it tends to increase profit.

Cost Volume Variance. The cost volume variance has the same interpretation. It is:

(Actual sales – budget sales) × budget cost per unit

The difference between the sales volume variance and the cost volume variance is called the *total volume variance.*

Multiproduct Firms

When a firm produces more than one product, there is a fourth component of the profit variance. This is the sales mix variance, the effect on profit of selling a different proportionate mix of products than the one that has been budgeted. This variance arises when different products have different contribution margins. In a multiproduct firm, actual sales volume can differ from that budgeted in two ways. The total number of units sold could differ from the target aggregate sales. In addition, the mix of the products actually sold may not be proportionate to the target mix. Each of these two different types of changes in volume is reflected in a separate variance.

The total volume variance is divided into two: the sales mix variance and the sales quantity variance. These two variances should be used to evaluate the marketing department. The sales mix variance shows how well the department has done in terms of selling the more profitable products, while the sales quantity variance measures how well the firm has done in terms of its overall sales volume. They are computed as:

▆▆▆ Sales Mix Variance. (Actual Sales at budget mix – Actual Sales at actual mix) × Budget CM (or gross profit/unit)

▆▆▆ Sales Quantity Variance. (Actual Sales at budget mix – Budget Sales at budget mix) × Budget CM (or gross profit/unit)

▆▆▆ Sales Volume Variance. (Actual Sales at actual mix – Budget Sales at budget mix) × Budget CM (or gross profit/unit)

EXAMPLE 8

The Lake Tahoe Ski Store sells two ski models—Model X and Model Y. For the years 20X1 and 20X2, the store realized a gross profit of $246,640 and $211,650, respectively. The owner of the store was astounded since the total sales volume in dollars and in units was higher for 20X2 than for 20X1, yet the gross profit achieved actually declined. Given below are the store's unaudited operating results for 20X1 and 20X2. No fixed costs were included in the cost of goods sold per unit.

| | | Model X | | | | Model Y | | |
| | Selling Price | Cost of Goods Sold per Unit | Sales in Units | Sales Revenue | Selling Price | Cost of Goods Sold per Unit | Sales in Units | Sales Revenue |
Year								
1	$150	$110	2,800	$420,000	$172	$121	2,640	$454,080
2	160	125	2,650	424,000	176	135	2,900	510,400

Explain why the gross profit declined by $34,990. Include a detailed variance analysis of price changes and changes in volume both for sales and cost. Subdivide the total volume variance into change in price and change in quantity.

Sales price and sales volume variances measure the impact on the firm's CM (or GM) of changes in the unit selling price and sales volume. In computing these variances, all costs are held constant in order to stress changes in price and volume. Cost price and cost volume variances are computed in the same manner, holding price, and volume constant. All these variances for the Lake Tahoe Ski Store are computed below.

Sales Price Variance

Actual sales for 20X2:
  Model X 2,650 × $160 = $424,000
  Model Y 2,900 × 176 = 510,400 $934,400
Actual 20X2 sales at 20X1 prices:
  Model X 2,650 × $150 = $397,500
  Model Y 2,900 × 172 = 498,800   896,300
                                   $38,100 F

Sales Volume Variance

Actual 20X2 sales at 20X1 prices:	$896,300
Actual 20X1 sales (at 20X1 prices):	
Model X 2,800 × $150 = $420,000	
Model Y 2,640 × 172 = 454,080	874,080
	$ 22,220 F

Cost Price Variance

Actual cost of goods sold for 20X2:	
Model X 2,650 × $125 = $331,250	
Model Y 2,900 × 135 = 391,500	$722,750
Actual 20X2 sales at 20X1 costs:	
Model X 2,650 × $110 = $291,500	
Model Y 2,900 × 121 = 350,900	642,400
	$ 80,350 U

Cost Volume Variance

Actual 20X2 sales at 20X1 costs:	
Actual 20X1 sales (at 20X1 costs):	
Model X 2,800 × $110 = $308,000	
Model Y 2,640 × 121 = 319,440	627,440
	$14,960 U

Total volume variance = sales volume variance − cost volume variance
= $22,220 F − $14,960 U = $7,260 F

The total volume variance is computed as the sum of a sales mix variance and a sales quantity variance as follows:

Sales Mix Variance

	20X2 Actual Sale at 20X1 Mix*	20X2 Actual Sale at 20X2 Mix	Difference	20X1 Gross Profit per Unit	Variance ($)
Model X	2,857	2,650	207 U	$40	$8,280 U
Model Y	2,693	2,900	207 F	51	10,557 F
	5,500	5,550			$2,277 F

*This is the 20X1 mix (used as standard or budget) proportions of 51.47% (or 2,800/5,440 = 51.47%) and 48.53% (or 2,640/5,440 = 48.53%) applied to the actual 20X2 sales figure of 5,550 units.

Sales Quantity Variance

	20X2 Actual Sale at 20X1 Mix*	20X2 Actual Sale at 20X1 Mix	Difference	20X1 Gross Profit per Unit	Variance ($)
Model X	2,857	2,800	57 F	$40	$2,280 F
Model Y	2,693	2,640	52 F	51	2,703 F
	5,550	5,440			$4,983 F

A favorable total volume variance is due to a favorable shift in the sales mix (that is, from Model X to Model Y) and also to a favorable increase in sales volume (by 110 units), which is shown as follows.

Sale mix variance	$2,277 F
Sales quantity variance	4,983 F
	$7260

However, there remains the decrease in gross profit. The decrease in gross profit of $34,990 can be explained as follows.

	Gains	Losses
Gain due to increased sales price	$38,100 F	
Loss due to increased cost		80,350
Gain due to increase in units sold	4,983 F	
Gain due to shift in sales mix	2,277 F	
	$45,360 F	$80,350

Hence, net decrease in gross profit = $80,350 − $45,360 = $34,990 U

Despite the increase in sales price and volume and the favorable shift in sales mix, the Lake Tahoe Ski Store ended up losing $34,990 compared to 20X1. The major reason for this comparative loss was the tremendous increase in cost of goods sold, as costs for both Model X and Model Y went up quite significantly over 20X1. The store has to take a close look at the cost picture; variable and fixed costs should be analyzed in an effort to cut down on controllable costs. In doing that, it is essential that responsibility be clearly assigned to given individuals. In a retail business like the Lake Tahoe Ski Store, operating expenses such as advertising and payroll of store employees must also be scrutinized.

EXAMPLE 9

Shim and Siegel, Inc., sells two products, C and D. Product C has a budgeted unit CM (Contribution Margin) of $3.00 and Product D has a budgeted unit CM of $6.00. The budget for a recent month called for sales of 3,000 units of C and 9,000 of D, for a total of 12,000 units. Actual sales totaled 12,200 units, 4,700 of C and 7,500 of D. Compute the sales volume variance and break this variance down into the (a) sales quantity variance, and (b) sales mix variance.

Shim and Siegel's sales volume variance is computed below. As we can see, while total unit sales increased by 200 units, the shift in sales mix resulted in a $3,900 unfavorable sales volume variance.

Sales Volume Variance

	Actual Sales at Actual Mix	Standard Sales at Budgeted Mix	Difference	Budgeted CM per Unit	Variance ($)
Product C	4,700	3,000	1,700 F	$3	$5,100 F
Product D	7,500	9,000	1,500 U	6	9,000 U
	12,200	12,000			$3,900 U

In multiproduct firms, the sales volumes variance is further divided into a sales quantity variance and a sales mix variance. The computations of these variances are shown below.

Sales Quantity Variance

Product C	3,050	3,000	50 F	$3	$150 F
Product D	9,150	9,000	150 F	6	900 F
	12,200	12,000			$1,050 F

Sales Mix Variance

	Actual Sales at Budgeted Mix	Standard Sales at Actual Mix	Difference	Standard CM per Unit	Variance ($)
Product C	3,050	4,700	1,650 F	$3	$4,950 F
Product D	9,150	7,500	1,650 U	6	9,900 U
	12,200	12,200			$4,950 U

The sales quantity variance reflects the impact on the CM or GM (gross margin) of deviations from the standard sales volume, whereas the sales mix variance measures the impact on the CM of deviations from the budgeted mix. In the case of Shim and Siegel, Inc., the sales quantity variance came out to be favorable, i.e., $1,050 F, and the sales mix variance came out to be unfavorable, i.e., $4,950 U. These variances indicate that while there was a favorable increase in sales volume by 200 units, it was obtained by an unfavorable shift in the sales mix, that is, a shift from Product D, with a high margin, to Product C, with a low margin.

The sales volume variance of $3,900 U is the algebraic sum of the following two variances.

Sales quantity variance	$1,050 F
Sales mix variance	4,950 U
	$3,900 U

In conclusion, the product emphasis on high margin sales is often a key to success for multiproduct firms. Increasing sales volume is one side of the story; selling the more profitable products is another.

Managerial Planning and Decision Making
In view of the fact that Shim and Siegel, Inc., experienced an unfavorable sales volume variance of $3,900 due to an unfavorable (less profitable) mix in sales volume, the company is advised to put more emphasis on increasing the sale of Product D.

In doing that the company might wish to:
1. Increase the advertising budget for succeeding periods to boost Product D sales.
2. Set up a bonus plan in such a way that the commission is based on quantities sold rather than higher rates for higher margin items such as Product D, or revise the bonus plan to consider the sale of product D.
3. Offer more lenient credit terms for Product D to encourage its sale.
4. Reduce the price of Product D enough to maintain the present profitable mix while increasing the sale of the product. This strategy must take into account the price elasticity of demand for Product D.

Sales Mix Analysis
Many product lines include a lower-margin price leader model, and often a high-margin deluxe model. For example, the automobile industry includes in its product line low-margin energy-efficient small cars and higher-margin deluxe models. In an attempt to increase overall profitability, management would

wish to emphasize the higher-margin expensive items, but salespeople might find it easier to sell lower-margin cheaper models. Thus, a salesperson might meet his or her unit sales quota with each item at its budgeted price, but because of mix shifts, he or she could be far short of contributing his or her share of budgeted profit.

Management should realize that

1. Greater proportions of more profitable products mean higher profits.
2. Higher proportions of lower-margin sales reduce overall profit despite the increase in overall sales volume. That is to say that an unfavorable mix may easily offset a favorable increase in volume, and vice versa.

Performance Reports

Profit variance analysis aids in fixing responsibility by separating the causes of the change in profit into price, volume, and mix factors. With responsibility resting in different places, the segregation of the total profit variance is essential. The performance reports based on the analysis of profit variances must be prepared for each responsibility center, indicating the following:

- Is it controllable?
- Is it favorable or unfavorable?
- If it is unfavorable, is it significant enough for further investigation?
- Who is responsible for what portion of the total profit variance?
- What are the causes for an unfavorable variance?
- What is the remedial action to take?

The performance report must address these types of questions. The report is useful in two ways: (1) in focusing attention on situations in need of management action and (2) in increasing the precision of planning and control of sales and costs. The report should be produced as part of the overall standard costing and responsibility accounting system.

CHAPTER PERSPECTIVE

Variance analysis is essential in an organization for the appraisal of all aspects of the business. This chapter was concerned with the control of cost centers through standard costs. It discussed the basic mechanics of how the two major variances—the price variance and the quantity variance—are calculated for direct materials, direct labor, variable overhead, and fixed overhead. The managerial significance of these variances were also discussed. The use of flexible budgeting was emphasized in an attempt to correctly measure the efficiency of the cost center. We noted that the fixed overhead volume variance has a limited usefulness at the level of a cost center, since only top management has the power to expand or contract fixed facilities. This chapter has also been concerned with the analysis and evaluation of profit center performances. *Gross profit analysis* (or profit variance analysis) was discussed in detail.

Cost Analysis for Nonroutine Decisions

INTRODUCTION AND MAIN POINTS

This chapter builds on material presented in Chapter 11. In that chapter, we discussed how contribution margin is computed. In this chapter, we use the contribution-margin approach to solve various types of business problems, such as whether to accept a lower selling price for a product or service and what price to bid on a contract.

Contribution-margin analysis is an important tool to use in decision making. It can be employed to appraise the performance of department managers, their departments, and particular programs. When performing the manufacturing and selling functions, you are constantly faced with the problem of choosing between alternative courses of action. Typical questions to be answered include: What to make? How to make it? Where to sell the product? What price should be charged? In the short run, you will experience many nonroutine, nonrecurring types of decisions.

In this chapter, you will learn:
━━ How to compute contribution margin and the contribution-margin ratio.
━━ How to prepare a contribution-margin income statement.
━━ What costs are relevant for a particular decision.
━━ Whether further processing of a product should take place.
━━ What the best way of utilizing capacity is.
━━ If an order should be accepted at below the normal selling price.
━━ How to determine the bid price on a contract for a product or service.
━━ Whether to drop an old product line or add a new one.
━━ How much to cut costs or raise selling price to achieve the same profit as last year when sales volume decreases.

CONTRIBUTION-MARGIN INCOME STATEMENT

In the contribution-margin approach, expenses are categorized as either fixed or variable. The variable costs are deducted from sales to obtain the *contribution margin*. Fixed costs are then subtracted from contribution margin to obtain net income. The contribution-margin ratio equals contribution margin divided by sales. The contribution-margin income statement looks at cost behavior. It shows the relationship between variable and fixed costs, irrespective of the function a given cost item is associated with. This information helps you (1) decide whether to drop or push a product line, (2) evaluate alternatives arising from production, special advertising, and so on, and (3) appraise performance. For instance, contribution-margin analysis tells you how to optimize capacity utilization, how to formulate a bid price on a contract, and whether to accept an order even if it is below the normal selling price.

The format of the contribution margin income statement is as follows:

Sales
Less variable cost of sales
Manufacturing contribution margin
Less variable selling and administrative expenses
Contribution margin
Less fixed cost
Net income

The advantages of the contribution-margin income statement are:

▬ Aids in decision making, such as whether to drop or push a product line

▬ Aids in deciding whether to ask a selling price that is below the normal price

Tip: When idle capacity exists, an order should be accepted at below the normal selling price as long as a contribution margin is earned, since fixed cost will not change.

The disadvantages of the contribution-margin income statement are:

▬ Not accepted for financial reporting or tax purposes

▬ Ignores fixed overhead as a product cost

▬ Difficult to segregate fixed cost and variable cost

Let us now determine contribution margin per unit and the contribution-margin ratio. Although these computations were presented in Chapter 11, it is useful to review them again before proceeding.

EXAMPLE 1

If the selling price is $10 per unit and the variable cost is $8 per unit, a contribution margin of $2 per unit is earned. The contribution margin ratio is 20% ($2/$10).

The format of the contribution-margin income statement is sales less variable costs equals contribution margin less fixed costs equals net income. An example of a contribution-margin income statement follows.

EXAMPLE 2

You sell 40,000 units of a product at $20 per unit. The variable cost per unit is $5, and the fixed cost is $250,000: the contribution-margin income statement is as follows:

Sales (40,000 × $20)	$800,000
Less: Variable cost (40,000 × $5)	200,000
Contribution margin (40,000 × $15)	$600,000
Less: Fixed cost	250,000
Net income	$350,000

The contribution-margin income statement may be presented in more detail to provide useful information by distinguishing between variable and fixed (1) manufacturing costs and (2) selling and administrative costs. Also, beginning and ending inventories may be presented.

EXAMPLE 3

Assume the following information:

Selling price	$15
Variable manufacturing cost per unit	$7
Variable selling cost per unit	$2
Fixed manufacturing overhead	$150,000
Fixed selling and administrative expenses	$60,000
Sales volume	600,000

Beginning inventory	50,000 units
Ending inventory	70,000 units

Production is:

Sales	600,000
Add ending inventory	70,000
Need	670,000
Less beginning inventory	50,000
Production	620,000

The contribution-margin income statement follows:

Sales (600,000 × $15)		$9,000,000
Less variable cost of sales		
Beginning inventory (50,000 × $7)	$350,000	
Variable cost of goods manufactured		
(620,000 × $7)	4,340,000	
Variable cost of goods available	$4,690,000	
Less ending inventory (70,000 × $7)	490,000	
Total variable cost of sales		4,200,000
Manufacturing contribution margin		$4,800,000
Less variable selling and administrative		
expenses (600,000 × $2)		1,200,000
Contribution margin		$3,600,000
Less fixed costs		
Fixed overhead	$150,000	
Fixed selling and administrative	60,000	
Total fixed costs		210,000
Net income		$3,390,000

RELEVANT COSTS

Not all costs are of equal importance in decision making, and you must identify the costs that are relevant to a decision. Such costs are called *relevant costs*. The relevant costs are the expected future costs (and also revenues), which differ according to decision alternatives. Therefore, the *sunk costs* (past and historical costs) are not considered relevant in the decision at hand. What is relevant are the incremental or differential costs. The decision involves the following steps:

1. Gather all costs associated with each alternative.
2. Drop the sunk costs.
3. Drop those costs which do not differ between alternatives.
4. Select the best alternative based on the remaining cost data.

Should Further Processing of a Product Occur?

You are sometimes faced with a decision whether to process an item further. This will be done when incremental profitability occurs. One application is a decision of whether to sell a product at the split-off point or process it further and sell it at the final point.

EXAMPLE 4

Honey may be sold at split-off or processed further. Relevant data follow:

Production	Sales value at Split-off	Additional cost and sales value for further processing	
		Sales	Cost
5,000	$95,000	$120,000	$18,000

Incremental revenue ($120,000 – $95,000)	$25,000
Incremental cost	18,000
Incremental gain	$7,000

You should process this product further, because it results in incremental earnings.

UTILIZATION OF CAPACITY

Contribution-margin analysis can be used to ascertain the best way of utilizing capacity. In general, the emphasis on products with higher contribution margin minimizes the company's total net income, even though sales may decrease. This is not true, however, where there are constraining factors and scarce resources. The constraining factor is the factor that restricts or limits the production or sale of a given product. The constraining factor may be machine-hours, labor-hours, or cubic feet of warehouse space. In the presence of these constraining factors, maximizing total profits depends on getting the highest contribution margin *per unit* of the constraining factor (rather than the highest contribution margin per unit of product output).

EXAMPLE 5

You can make a raw metal that can either be sold at this stage or worked on further and sold as an alloy. Relevant data follow:

	Raw Metal	Alloy
Selling price	$200	$315
Variable cost	90	120

Total fixed cost is $400,000, and 100,000 hours of capacity are interchangeable between the products. There is unlimited demand for both products. Three hours are required to produce the raw material, and five hours are needed to make the alloy. The constraining factor is the production hours.

Contribution margin per hour follows:

	Raw Metal	Alloy
Selling price	$200	$315
Less variable cost	90	120
Contribution margin	$110	$195
Hours per ton	3	5

Contribution margin
per hour $\dfrac{\$110}{3} = \$36.67$ $\dfrac{\$195}{5} = \$39$

You should sell only the alloy, because it results in the highest contribution margin per hour. Fixed costs are not considered, because they are constant and are incurred irrespective of which product is manufactured.

Should an Order Be Accepted Below the Normal Selling Price?

Let's say you often receive a short-term, special order for products at lower prices than usual. In normal times, you may refuse such an order since it will not yield a satisfactory profit. If times are bad, however, such an order should be accepted if the incremental revenue obtained from it exceeds the incremental costs. Fixed costs are constant at idle capacity. You are better off to receive some revenue above its variable costs than to receive nothing at all. Such a price, one lower than the regular price, is called a *contribution price*. This approach is more appropriate under the following conditions:

▪ When operating in a distress situation
▪ When there is idle capacity
▪ When faced with sharp competition or in a competitive bidding situation

EXAMPLE 6

You currently sell 8,000 units at $30 per unit. Variable cost per unit is $15. Fixed costs are $60,000 (fixed cost per unit is thus $60,000/8,000 = $7.50). Idle capacity exists. A potential customer is willing to purchase 500 units at $21 per unit.

You should accept this order, because it increases your profitability.

Sales (500 × $21)	$10,500
Less variable costs (500 × $15)	7,500
Contribution margin	3,000
Less fixed costs	0
Net income	$3,000

Note: If idle capacity exists, the acceptance of an additional order does not increase fixed cost. If fixed cost were to increase, say by $1,200 to buy a special tool for this job, it still is financially attractive to accept this order, because a positive profit of $1,800 ($3,000 − $1,200) would arise.

Let us now look at an example involving the possible sale of a manufactured item at a significant discount off the normal selling price.

EXAMPLE 7

You manufacture a product. You can produce 200,000 units per year at a total variable cost of $800,000 and a total fixed cost of $500,000. You estimate that you can sell 150,000 units at a normal selling price of $9 each. Further, a special order has been placed by a customer for 50,000 units at a 25% discount.

Your profit will rise by $137,500 due to this special order:

Special order price 0.75 × $9	$6.75
Variable cost per unit $800,000/200,000	4.00
Incremental profit per unit	$2.75
Incremental earnings $2.75 × 50,000 units = $137,500	

In the next example, we consider the profit effect of a special order when variable manufacturing costs and variable selling costs must be computed first.

EXAMPLE 8

Financial data for your department follows:

Selling price	$15
Direct material	$2
Direct labor	$1.90
Variable overhead	$0.50
Fixed overhead ($100,000/20,000 units)	$5

Selling and administrative expenses are fixed except for sales commissions, which are 14% of the selling price. Idle capacity exists.

You receive an additional order for 1,000 units from a potential customer at a selling price of $9.

Even though the offered selling price of $9 is much less than the current selling price of $15, the order should be accepted.

Sales (1,000 x $9)	$9,000
Less variable manufacturing costs (1,000 × $4.40)*	4,400
Manufacturing contribution margin	$4,600
Less variable selling and administrative	
expenses (14% × $9,000)	1,260
Contribution margin	$3,340
Less fixed cost	0
Net income	$3,340

*Variable manufacturing cost = $2 + $1.90 + $0.50 = $4.40.

In yet another example of a special order situation, variable overhead is directly tied to direct-labor cost.

EXAMPLE 9

You want a markup of 40% over cost on a product. Relevant data regarding the product appears below:

Direct material	$5,000
Direct labor	12,000
Overhead	4,000
Total cost	$21,000
Markup on cost (40%)	8,400
Selling price	$29,400

Total direct labor for the year is $1,800,000. Total overhead for the year is 30% of direct labor. The overhead consists of 25% fixed and 75% variable. A customer offers to buy the item for $23,000. There is idle capacity. You should accept the incremental order, since additional profitability arises.

Selling price		$23,000
Less variable costs		
Direct material	$5,000	
Direct labor	12,000	
Variable overhead ($12,000 × 22.5%)*	2,700	19,700
Contribution margin		$3,300
Less fixed cost		0
Net income		$3,300

*Total overhead 0.30 × $1,800,000 = $540,000; variable overhead = 22.5% of direct labor, computed as follows:

$$\frac{\text{Variable overhead}}{\text{Direct labor}} = \frac{0.75 \times \$540,000}{\$1,800,000} = \frac{\$405,000}{\$1,800,000} = 22.5\%$$

BID-PRICE DETERMINATION

Pricing policies using contribution-margin analysis may be helpful in contract negotiations for a product or service. Often such business is sought during the slack season, when it may be financially beneficial to bid on extra business at a competitive price that covers all variable costs and makes some contributions to fixed costs plus profits. A knowledge of your variable and fixed costs is necessary to make an accurate bid-price determination.

EXAMPLE 10

You receive an order for 10,000 units. You wish to know the minimum bid price that will result in a $20,000 increase in profits. The current income statement follows:

Sales (50,000 units × $25)		$1,250,000
Less cost of sales		
Direct material	$120,000	
Direct labor	200,000	
Variable overhead ($200,000 × 0.30)	60,000	
Fixed overhead	100,000	
		480,000
Gross margin		$770,000
Less selling and administrative expenses		
Variable (includes freight costs of		
$0.40 per unit)	$60,000	
Fixed	30,000	90,000
Net income		$680,000

In the event the contract is awarded, cost patterns for the incremental order are the same except that:

■ Freight costs will be borne by the customer
■ Special tools of $8,000 will be required for this order and will not be used again
■ Direct-labor time for each unit under the order will be 20% longer

Preliminary computations:

	Per Unit Cost
Direct material ($120,000/50,000)	$2.40
Direct labor ($200,000/50,000)	4.00
Variable selling and administrative expense	
($60,000/50,000)	1.20

A forecasted income statement follows:

Forecasted Income Statement

	Current	Forecasted	Explanation
Units	50,000	60,000	
Sales	$1,250,000	$1,372,400	Computed Last[a]
Cost of sales			
Direct material	$120,000	$144,000	($2.40 × 60,000)
Direct labor	200,000	248,000	($200,000 + [10,000 × $4.80[b]])
Variable overhead	60,000	74,400	($248,000 × .30)
Fixed overhead	100,000	108,000	
Total	$480,000	$574,400	
Selling and administrative expenses			
Variable	$60,000	$68,000	($60,000 + [10,000 × $.80[c]])
Fixed	30,000	30,000	
Total	$90,000	$98,000	
Net income	$680,000	$700,000[d]	

[a]Net income + selling and administrative expenses + cost of sales = sales $700,000 + $98,000 + $574,400 = $1,372,400
[b]$4 × 1.2 = $4.80
[c]$1.20 – $.40 = $.80
[d]$680,000 + $20,000 = $700,000

The contract price for the 10,000 units should be $122,400 ($1,372,400 – $1,250,000), or $12.24 per unit ($122,400/10,000).

The contract price per unit of $12.24 is below the $25 current selling price per unit. Keep in mind that total fixed cost is the same except for the $8,000 expenditure on the special tool.

ADDING OR DROPPING A PRODUCT LINE

The decision whether to drop an old product line or add a new one must take into account both qualitative and quantitative factors. However, any final decision should be based primarily on the impact the decision will have on contribution margin or net income. The effect of dropping a product on the net income of the company is illustrated in the next example.

EXAMPLE 11

The General Foods Company has three major product lines: pie, meat, and cereal. The company is considering the decision to drop the meat line, because the income statement shows it is being sold at a loss. Note the income statement for these product lines below:

	Pie	Meat	Cereal	Total
Sales	$10,000	$15,000	$25,000	$50,000
Less: Variable costs	6,000	8,000	12,000	26,000
Contribution margin	$4,000	$7,000	$13,000	$24,000
Less: Fixed costs				
Direct	$2,000	$6,500	$4,000	$12,500
Allocated	1,000	1,500	2,500	5,000
Total	$3,000	$8,000	$6,500	$17,500
Net income	$1,000	($1,000)	$6,500	$6,500

Direct fixed costs are those costs that are identified directly with each of the product lines, whereas allocated fixed costs are the amount of common fixed costs allocated to the product lines using some base such as space occupied. The amount of common fixed costs typically continues regardless of the decision and thus cannot be saved by dropping the product line to which it is distributed.

If meat is dropped, we have the following:

Sales revenue lost		$15,000
Gains:		
Variable cost avoided	$8,000	
Direct fixed costs avoided	6,500	14,500
Increase (decrease) in net income		$ (500)

By dropping meat the company will lose an additional $500. Therefore, the meat product line should be kept. One of the great dangers in allocating common fixed costs is that such allocations can make a product line look less profitable than it really is. Because of such an allocation, the meat product line showed a loss of $1,000, but in effect contributes $500 ($7,000 − $6,500) to the recovery of the company's common fixed costs.

THE MAKE-OR-BUY DECISION

The decision whether to produce a component part internally or to buy it from an outside supplier may have to be made. This decision involves both quantitative and qualitative factors. The qualitative factors include ensuring product quality and the necessity for long-run business relationships with the supplier. The quantitative factors deal with cost. The quantitative effects of the make-or-buy decision are best seen through the relevant cost approach.

EXAMPLE 12

Assume the following cost estimates for the manufacture of a subassembly component based on an annual production of 8,000 units:

	Per Unit	Total
Direct materials	$5	$40,000
Direct labor	4	32,000
Variable factory overhead applied	4	32,000
Fixed factory overhead applied		
(150% of direct labor cost)	6	48,000
Total cost	$19	$152,000

The supplier has offered to provide the subassembly at a price of $16 each. Two-thirds of fixed factory overhead, which represents executive salaries, rent, depreciation, and taxes, continue regardless of the decision. Should you buy or make the product?

The key to the decision lies in the investigation of those relevant costs that change between the make-or-buy alternatives. Assuming that the productive capacity will be idle if not used to produce the subassembly, the analysis takes the following form:

Schedule of Make-or-Buy

	Per Unit		Total of 8,000 Units	
	Make	Buy	Make	Buy
Purchase price		$16		$128,000
Direct materials	$5		$40,000	
Direct labor	4		32,000	
Variable overhead	4		32,000	
Fixed overhead that can be				
avoided by not making	2		16,000	
Total relevant costs	$15	$16	$120,000	$128,000
Difference in favor of				
making		$1		$8,000

The make-or-buy decision must be investigated, along with the broader perspective of considering how best to utilize available facilities. The alternatives are:

- Leaving facilities idle
- Buying the parts and renting out idle facilities
- Buying the parts and using idle facilities for other products

DESIRE TO MAINTAIN SAME PROFIT WITH LOWER SALES BASE

Contribution-margin analysis assists in determining how to derive the same profit as last year even though there is a drop in sales volume.

EXAMPLE 13

In 20X1, sales volume was 200,000 units, selling price was $25, variable cost per unit was $15, and fixed cost was $500,000. Therefore, the contribution margin per unit equals:

Selling price	$25
Less: Variable cost	15
Contribution margin	$10

In 20X2, sales volume is expected to total 150,000 units. As a result, fixed costs have been slashed by $80,000. On 4/1/20X2, 40,000 units have already been sold. You wish to compute the contribution margin that has to be earned on the remaining units for 20X2.

Net income computation for 20X1:

$$Sales = Fixed\ Cost + Variable\ Cost + Profit$$

$$\$25 \times 200,000 = \$500,000 + (\$15 \times 200,000) + P$$
$$\$1,500,00 = P$$

Contribution margin to be earned in 19X2:

Total fixed cost ($500,000 – $80,000)	$420,000
Net income	1,500,000
Contribution margin needed for year	$1,920,000
Contribution margin already earned:	
(Selling price variable cost) × units	
($25 – $15) = $10 × 40,000 units	400,000
Contribution margin remaining	$1,520,000

$$Contribution\ margin\ per\ unit\ needed = \frac{Contribution\ margin\ remaining}{Units\ remaining}$$

$$= \frac{\$1,520,000}{110,000} = \$13.82$$

Since you need a new contribution margin per unit of $13.82 on the remaining units while the original contribution margin per unit was $10, you must increase your contribution margin per unit by $3.82. This may be done by raising the selling price by $3.82, assuming you expect no loss in sales by doing so, by reducing your variable costs by $3.82 per unit, or some combination of the two. However, reducing variable costs by about 25.5% ($3.82/$15) may not be possible in many cases.

CHAPTER PERSPECTIVE

Contribution-margin analysis aids you in making sound departmental decisions. Is an order worth accepting even though it is below the normal selling price? Which products should be emphasized? What should the price of your product or service be? What should the bid price be on a contract? Is a proposed agreement advantageous? What is your incremental profitability? What is the best way of using departmental capacity and resources?

In some cases, your bonus may be based on the contribution margin you earn for your department. Thus, an understanding of the computation of contribution margin is necessary.

How to Make Capital-Budgeting Decisions

INTRODUCTION AND MAIN POINTS

Capital budgeting is the process of making long-term planning decisions for alternative investment opportunities. There are many investment decisions that the company may have to make in order to grow. Examples of capital-budgeting applications are product-line selection, decisions about whether to keep or sell a business segment, leasing vs. buying, and which asset to invest in.

After studying the material in this chapter:

■ You will know the types and special features of capital-budgeting decisions.

■ You will be able to calculate, interpret, and evaluate five capital-budgeting techniques.

■ You will be able to select the best mix of projects with a limited capital spending budget.

WHAT ARE THE TYPES OF INVESTMENT PROJECTS?

There are typically two types of long-term investment decisions made by your company:

1. *Selection decisions* about obtaining new facilities or expanding existing facilities. Examples include:
   (a) Investments in property, plant, and equipment, as well as other types of assets.
   (b) Resource commitments in the form of new-product development, market research, introduction of a computer, refunding of long-term debt, etc.
   (c) Mergers and acquisitions in the form of buying another company to add a new product line. Also see Chapter 17.
2. *Replacement decisions* about replacing existing facilities with new facilities. Examples include replacing an old machine with a high-tech machine.

WHAT ARE THE FEATURES OF INVESTMENT PROJECTS?

Long-term investments have three important features:

1. They typically involve a large number of initial cash outlays, which tend to have a long-term impact on the firm's future profitability. Therefore, this initial cash outlay needs to be justified on a cost-benefit basis.
2. There are expected recurring cash inflows (for example, increased revenues, savings in cash operating expenses, etc.) over the life of the investment project. This frequently requires considering the *time value of money*. The time value of money means that money is worth a different sum at different periods. (For more about this concept and its applications, refer to *Financial Management*, another book in Barron's Business Library series.)
3. Income taxes could make a difference in the accept-or-reject decision. Income tax factors must be taken into account in every capital budgeting decision.

HOW DO YOU MEASURE INVESTMENT WORTH?

There are several methods of evaluating investment projects:

1. Payback period
2. Accounting rate of return (ARR)
3. Net present value (NPV)
4. Internal rate of return (IRR)
5. Profitability index (or cost/benefit ratio)

The NPV method and the IRR method are called discounted cash flow (DCF) methods. Each of these methods is discussed below.

Payback Period

The payback period measures the length of time required to recover the amount of initial investment. It is computed by dividing the initial investment by the cash inflows through increased revenues or cost savings.

EXAMPLE 1

Assume:

Cost of investment	$18,000
Annual after-tax cash savings	$3,000

Then, the payback period is:

$$\text{Payback period} = \frac{\text{Initial investment}}{\text{Cost savings}} = \frac{\$18,000}{\$3,000} = 6 \text{ years}$$

Decision rule: Choose the project with the shorter payback period. The rationale behind this choice is: The shorter the payback period, the less risky the project and the greater the liquidity.

EXAMPLE 2

Consider the two projects whose after-tax cash inflows are not even. Assume each project costs $1,000.

	Cash inflow	
Year	A($)	B($)
1	100	500
2	200	400
3	300	300
4	400	100
5	500	
6	600	

When cash inflows are not even, the payback period has to be found by trial and error. The payback period of project A is ($1,000 = $100 + $200 + $300 + $400) 4 years. The payback period of project B is ($1,000 = $500 + $400 + $100):

$$2 \text{ years} + \frac{\$100}{\$300} = 2^{1}/_{3} \text{ years}$$

Project B is the project of choice in this case, since it has the shorter payback period.

The advantages of using the payback-period method of evaluating an investment project are that (1) it is simple to compute and easy to understand, and (2) it handles investment risk effectively.

The shortcomings of this method are that (1) it does not recognize the time value of money, and (2) it ignores the impact of cash inflows received after the payback period; cash flows after the payback period determine profitability of an investment.

Accounting Rate of Return

Accounting rate of return (ARR) measures profitability from the conventional accounting standpoint by relating the required investment—or sometimes the average investment—to the future annual net income.

Decision rule: Under the ARR method, choose the project with the higher rate of return.

EXAMPLE 3

Consider the following investment:

Initial investment	$6,500
Estimated life	20 years
Cash inflows per year	$1,000
Depreciation per year (using straight line)	$325

The accounting rate of return for this project is:

$$\text{ARR} = \frac{\text{net income}}{\text{investment}} = \frac{\$1,000 - \$325}{\$6,500} = 10.4\%$$

If average investment (usually assumed to be one-half of the original investment) is used, then:

$$\text{ARR} = \frac{\$1,000 - \$325}{\$3,250} = 20.8\%$$

The advantages of this method are that it is easily understandable, that it is simple to compute, and that it recognizes the profitability factor. The shortcomings of this method are that it fails to recognize the time value of money, and it uses accounting data instead of cash flow data.

Net Present Value

Net present value (NPV) is the excess of the present value (PV) of cash inflows generated by the project over the amount of the initial investment (I):

$$NPV = PV - I$$

The present value of future cash flows is computed using the so-called cost of capital (or minimum required rate of return) as the discount rate. When cash inflows are uniform, the present value would be

$$PV = A \times T_4 (i, n),$$

where A is the amount of the annuity. The value of T_4 is found in Table 4 of the Appendix.

Decision rule: If NPV is positive, accept the project. Otherwise reject it.

EXAMPLE 4

Consider the following investment:

Initial investment	$12,950
Estimated life	10 years
Annual cash inflows	$3,000
Cost of capital (minimum required rate of return)	12%

Present value of the cash inflows is:

$$
\begin{aligned}
PV &= A \times T_4 (i, n) \\
&= \$3,000 \times T_4(12\%, 10 \text{ years}) \\
&= \$3,000 (5,650) \qquad\qquad \$16,950
\end{aligned}
$$

Initial investment (I)   12,950

Net present value (NPV = PV − I) $4,000

Since the NPV of the investment is positive, the investment should be accepted.

The advantages of the NPV method are that it obviously recognizes the time value of money and that it is easy to compute whether the cash flows form an annuity or vary from period to period.

Internal Rate of Return

Internal rate of return (IRR) is defined as the rate of interest that equates I with the PV of future cash inflows. In other words, at IRR,

$$I = PV$$

or

$$NPV = 0$$

Decision rule: Accept the project if the IRR exceeds the cost of capital. Otherwise, reject it.

EXAMPLE 5

Assume the same data given in Example 4, and set the following equality (I = PV):

$$\$12,950 = \$3,000 \times T_4 (i, 10 \text{ years})$$

$$T_4 (i, 10 \text{ years}) = \frac{\$12,950}{\$3,000} = 4.317,$$

which stands somewhere between 18% and 20% in the 10-year line of Table 4 in the Appendix. The interpolation follows:

PV of an annuity of $1 factor
$T_4 (i, 10 \text{ years})$

18%	4.494	4.494
IRR	4.317	
20%		4.192
Difference	0.177	0.302

Therefore,

$$IRR = 18\% + \frac{0.177}{0.302} \ (20\% - 18\%)$$

$$= 18\% + 0.586\,(2\%) = 18\% + 1.17\% = 19.17\%$$

Since the IRR of the investment is greater than the cost of capital (12%), accept the project.

The advantage of using the IRR method is that it does consider the time value of money, and therefore is more exact and realistic than the ARR method. The shortcomings of this method are that (1) it is time-consuming to compute, especially when the cash inflows are not even, although most financial calculators and PCs have a key to calculate IRR, and (2) it fails to recognize the varying sizes of investment in competing projects.

Can a Computer Help?

Spreadsheet programs can be used in making IRR calculations. For example, *Excel* has a function IRR (*values, guess*). Excel considers negative numbers as cash outflows such as the initial investment and positive numbers as cash inflows. Many financial calculators have similar features. As in Example 5, suppose you want to calculate the IRR of a $12,950 investment (the value-12,950 entered in year 0) that is followed by 10 monthly cash inflows of $3,000. Using a guess of 12% (the value of 0.12), which is in effect the cost of capital, your formula would be @IRR(values, 0.12) and Excel would return 19.15%, as shown below.

Year 0	1	2	3	4	5	6	7	8	9	10
$ (12,950)	3,000	3,000	3,000	3,000	3,000	3,000	3,000	3,000	3,000	3,000

IRR = 19.15%
NPV = $4,000.67

Note: The *Excel* formula for NPV is NPV (discount rate, cash inflow values) + I, where I is given as a negative number.

Profitability Index

The profitability index is the ratio of the total PV of future cash inflows to the initial investment—that is, PV/I. This index is used as a means of ranking projects in descending order of attractiveness.

Decision rule: If the profitability index is greater than 1, accept the project.

Using the data in Example 4, the profitability index is:

$$\frac{PV}{I} = \frac{\$16,950}{\$12,950} = 1.31$$

Since this project generates $1.31 for each dollar invested (i.e., its profitability index is greater than 1), accept the project.

The profitability index has the advantage of putting all projects on the same relative basis regardless of size.

HOW TO SELECT THE BEST MIX OF PROJECTS WITH A LIMITED BUDGET

Many firms specify a limit on the overall budget for capital spending. Capital rationing is concerned with the problem of selecting the mix of acceptable projects that provides the highest overall NPV. The profitability index is used widely in ranking projects competing for limited funds.

EXAMPLE 6

The Westmont Company has a fixed budget of $250,000. It needs to select a mix of acceptable projects from the following:

Projects	I($)	PV($)	NPV($)	Profitability index	Ranking
A	70,000	112,000	42,000	1.6	1
B	100,000	145,000	45,000	1.45	2
C	110,000	126,500	16,500	1.15	5
D	60,000	79,000	19,000	1.32	3
E	40,000	38,000	–2,000	0.95	6
F	80,000	95,000	15,000	1.19	4

The ranking resulting from the profitability index shows that the company should select projects A, B, and D.

	I	PV
A	$70,000	$112,000
B	100,000	145,000
D	60,000	79,000
	$230,000	$336,000

Therefore:
$$NPV = \$336,000 - \$230,000 = \$106,000$$

HOW TO HANDLE MUTUALLY EXCLUSIVE INVESTMENTS

A project is said to be mutually exclusive if the acceptance of one project automatically excludes the acceptance of one or more other projects. In the case where one must choose between mutually exclusive investments, the NPV and IRR methods may result in contradictory indications. The conditions under which contradictory rankings can occur are:

1. Projects that have different life expectancies.
2. Projects that have different sizes of investment.
3. Projects whose cash flows differ over time. For example, the cash flows of one project increase over time, while those of another decrease.

The contradictions result from different assumptions with respect to the reinvestment rate on cash flows from the projects.

1. The NPV method discounts all cash flows at the cost of capital, thus implicitly assuming that these cash flows can be reinvested at this rate.
2. The IRR method implies a reinvestment rate at IRR. Thus, the implied reinvestment rate will differ from project to project.

The NPV method generally gives correct ranking, since the cost of capital is a more realistic reinvestment rate.

EXAMPLE 7
Assume the following:

Cash Flows

	0	1	2	3	4	5
A	(100)	120				
B	(100)					201.14

Computing IRR and NPV at 10% gives the following different rankings:

	IRR	NPV at 10%
A	20%	9.01
B	15%	24.90

The NPVs plotted against the appropriate discount rates form a graph called an NPV profile (Figure 16-1).

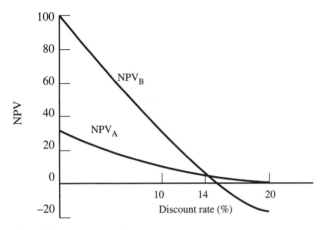

FIG. 16-1. *NPV profile.*

At a discount rate larger than 14%, A has a higher NPV than B. Therefore, A should be selected. At a discount rate less than 14%, B has the higher NPV than A, and thus should be selected. The correct decision is to select the project with the higher NPV, since the NPV method assumes a more realistic reinvestment rate—that is, the cost of capital.

CHAPTER PERSPECTIVE

We have examined the process of evaluating investment projects. We have also discussed five commonly used criteria for evaluating capital-budgeting projects, including the net present value (NPV) and internal rate of return (IRR) methods. The problems that arise with mutually exclusive investments and capital rationing were addressed.

How Does Income Tax Affect Investment Decisions?

INTRODUCTION AND MAIN POINTS

Income taxes make a difference in many capital budgeting decisions. Income taxes typically affect both the amount and the timing of cash flows. Since net income, not cash flows, is subject to tax, after-tax cash inflows are not usually the same as after-tax net income.

After studying the material in this chapter:
▬ You will have an understanding of how income-tax factors affect investment decisions.
▬ You will be able to calculate after-tax cash flows.
▬ You will understand various depreciation methods.
▬ You will be familiar with the effect of the Accelerated Cost Recovery System (ACRS) on capital-budgeting decisions.

HOW DOES INCOME TAX AFFECT INVESTMENT DECISIONS?

Income taxes make a difference in many capital budgeting decisions. In other words, the project that is attractive on a before-tax basis may have to be rejected on an after-tax basis and vice versa. Income taxes typically affect both the amount and the timing of cash flows. Since net income, not cash inflows, is subject to tax, after-tax cash flows are not usually the same as after-tax net income.

HOW TO CALCULATE AFTER-TAX CASH FLOWS

The terms in the calculations are defined as follows:

S = sales
E = cash operating expenses
d = depreciation
t = tax rate

Then, before-tax cash inflows (or cash savings) = $S - E$ and net income = $S - E - d$.

By definition,

$$\text{After-tax cash inflows} = \text{before-tax cash inflows} - \text{taxes}$$
$$= (S - E) - (S - E - d)(t)$$

Rearranging gives the shortcut formula:

$$\text{After-tax cash inflows} = (S - E)(1 - t) + (d)(t)$$

As can be seen, the deductibility of depreciation from sales in arriving at taxable net income reduces income-tax payments and thus serves as a *tax shield*.

$$\text{Tax shield} = \text{tax savings on depreciation} = (d)(t)$$

EXAMPLE 1
Assume:

$$S = \$12,000$$
$$E = \$10,000$$
$$d = \$500 \text{ per year using the straight-line method}$$
$$t = 30\%$$

Then:

$$\text{After-tax cash inflow} = (\$12,000 - \$10,000)(1 - .3) + (\$500)(.3)$$
$$= (\$2,000)(.7) + (\$500)(.3)$$
$$= \$1,400 + \$150 = \$1,550$$

Note that:

$$\text{Tax shield} = \text{tax savings on depreciation} = (d)(t)$$
$$= (\$500)(.3) = \$150$$

Since the tax shield is $(d)(t)$, the higher the depreciation deduction, the higher the tax savings on depreciation. Therefore, an accelerated depreciation method (such as double-declining balance) produces higher tax savings than the straight-line method. Accelerated methods produce higher present values for the tax savings, which may make a given investment more attractive.

EXAMPLE 2
The Shalimar Company estimates that it can save $2,500 a year in cash operating costs for the next ten years if it buys a special-purpose machine at a cost of $10,000. No residual value is expected. Assume that the income tax rate is 30% and the after-tax cost of capital (minimum required rate of return) is 10%. After-tax cash savings can be calculated as follows:

Note that depreciation by straight-line is $10,000/10 = $1,000 per year. Thus:

$$\text{After-tax cash savings} = (S - E)(1 - t) + (d)(t)$$
$$= \$2,500(1 - .3) + \$1,000(.3)$$
$$= \$1,750 + \$300 = \$2,050$$

To see if this machine should be purchased, the net present value can be calculated:

$$PV = \$2,050 \ T^4(10\%, \ 10 \ \text{years}) = \$2,050(6.145) = \$12,597.25$$

Thus:

$$NPV = PV - I = \$12,597.25 - \$10,000 = \$2,597.25$$

Since NPV is positive, the machine should be bought.

TYPES OF DEPRECIATION METHODS

We saw that depreciation provided the tax shield in the form of (d)(t). Among the commonly used depreciation methods are straight-line and accelerated methods. The two major accelerated methods are sum-of-the-years'-digits (SYD) and double-declining balance (DDB).

Straight-Line Method

This is the easiest and most popular method of calculating depreciation. It results in equal periodic depreciation charges. The method is most appropriate when an asset's usage is uniform from period to period, as is the case with furniture. The annual depreciation expense is calculated by using the following formula:

$$\text{Depreciation expense} = \frac{\text{Cost} - \text{salvage value}}{\text{Number of years of useful life}}$$

EXAMPLE 3

An auto is purchased for $20,000 and has an expected salvage value of $2,000. The auto's estimated life is 8 years. Its annual depreciation is calculated as follows:

$$\text{Depreciation expense} = \frac{\text{Cost} - \text{salvage value}}{\text{Number of years of useful life}}$$

$$= \frac{\$20,000 - \$2,000}{8 \ \text{years}} = \$2,250/\text{year}$$

An alternative means of computation is to multiply the *depreciable* cost ($18,000) by the annual depreciation rate, which is 12.5% in this example. The annual rate is calculated by dividing the number of years of useful life into one (1/8 = 12.5%). The result is the same: $18,000 × 12.5% = $2,250.

Sum-of-the-Years'-Digits (SYD) Method

In this method, the number of years of life expectancy is enumerated in reverse order in the numerator, and the denominator is the sum of the digits. For example, if the life expectancy of a machine is 8 years, write the numbers in reverse order: 8, 7, 6, 5, 4, 3, 2, 1. The sum of these digits is 36, or $(8 + 7 + 6 + 5 + 4 + 3 + 2 + 1)$. The fraction for the first year is 8/36, while the fraction for the last year is 1/36. The sum of the eight fractions equals 36/36, or 1. At the end of 8 years, the machine is completely written down to its salvage value.

The following formula may be used to quickly find the sum-of-the-years' digits (S):

$$S = \frac{(N)(N + 1)}{2}$$

where N represents the number of years of expected life.

EXAMPLE 4

In Example 3, the *depreciable* cost is $18,000 ($20,000 − $2,000). Using the SYD method, the computation for each year's depreciation expense is:

$$S = \frac{(N)(N + 1)}{2} = \frac{8(9)}{2} = \frac{72}{2} = 36$$

Year	Fraction	×	Depreciation Amount ($)	=	Depreciation Expense
1	8/36		$18,000		$4,000
2	7/36		18,000		3,500
3	6/36		18,000		3,000
4	5/36		18,000		2,500
5	4/36		18,000		2,000
6	3/36		18,000		1,500
7	2/36		18,000		1,000
8	1/36		18,000		500
Total					$18,000

Double-Declining Balance (DDB) Method

Under this method, depreciation expense is highest in the earlier years and lower in the later years. First, a depreciation rate is determined by doubling the straight-line rate. For example, if an asset has a life of 10 years, the straight-line rate is 1/10 or 10%, and the double-declining rate is 20%. Second, depreciation expense is computed by multiplying the rate by the book value of the asset at the beginning of each year. Since book value declines over time, the depreciation expense decreases each successive period.

This method ignores salvage value in the computation. However, the book value of the fixed asset at the end of its useful life cannot be below its salvage value.

EXAMPLE 5

Assume the data in Example 3. Since the straight-line rate is 12.5% (1/8), the double-declining balance rate is 25% (2 × 12.5%). The depreciation expense is computed as follows:

Year	Book value at beginning of year	×	Rate (%)	=	Depreciation expense	Year-end book value
1	$20,000		25%		$5,000	$15,000
2	15,000		25		3,750	11,250
3	11,250		25		2,813	8,437
4	8,437		25		2,109	6,328
5	6,328		25		1,582	4,746
6	4,746		25		1,187	3,559
7	3,559		25		890	2,669
8	2,669		25		667	2,002

Note: If the original estimated salvage value had been $2,100 instead of $2,000, the depreciation expense for the eighth year would have been $569 ($2,669 – $2,100) rather than $667, since the asset cannot be depreciated below its salvage value.

Units of Production Method

Under this method, depreciation varies with output.

$$\text{Depreciation per unit} = \frac{\text{Cost} - \text{salvage value}}{\text{Estimated total units that can be produced in the asset's lifetime}}$$

Depreciation = units of output for year × depreciation per unit

EXAMPLE 6

The cost of a machine is $11,000 with a salvage value of $1,000. The estimated total units are 5,000. The units produced in the first year are 400.

$$\text{Depreciation per unit} = \frac{\$11,000 - \$1,000}{5,000} = \$2 \text{ per unit}$$

Depreciation in year 1 = 400 units × $2 = $800

WHICH METHOD TO USE

1. Of course, over the life of the fixed asset, the total depreciation charge will be the same no matter what depreciation method is used; only the timing of the tax savings will differ.
2. The depreciation method used for financial reporting purposes should be realistic for that type of fixed asset. For example, depreciation on an automobile may be based on mileage.
3. The accelerated methods such as SYD and DDB are advantageous for tax purposes, since higher depreciation charges in the earlier years result in less income and thus less taxes. The tax savings may then be invested for a return.

CAPITAL BUDGETING DECISIONS AND THE MODIFIED ACCELERATED COST RECOVERY SYSTEM (MACRS)

Although traditional depreciation methods still can be used for computing depreciation for book purposes, 1981 saw a new way of computing depreciation deductions for tax purposes. The current rule is called the *Modified Accelerated Cost Recovery System* (MACRS) rule, as enacted by Congress in 1981 and then modified somewhat in 1986 under the Tax Reform Act of 1986. This rule is characterized as follows:

1. It abandons the concept of useful life and accelerates depreciation deductions by placing all depreciable assets into one of eight age property classes. It calculates deductions, based on an allowable percentage of the asset's original cost (see Tables 17-1 and 17-2).

    With a shorter asset tax life than useful life, the company would be able to deduct depreciation more quickly and save more in income taxes in the earlier years, thereby making an investment more attractive. The rationale behind the system is that by doing this the government encourages the company to invest in facilities and increase its productive capacity and efficiency. Remember that the higher d is, the larger the tax shield (d)(t).

2. Since the allowable percentages in Table 17-1 add up to 100%, there is no need to consider the salvage value of an asset in computing depreciation.

3. The company may elect the straight-line method. The straight-line convention must follow what is called the *half-year convention*. This means that the company can deduct only half of the regular straight-line depreciation amount in the first year. The reason for electing to use the MACRS optional straight-line method is that some firms may prefer to stretch out depreciation deductions using the straight-line method rather than to accelerate them. Those firms are the ones that just start out or have little or no income and wish to show more income on their income statements.

EXAMPLE 7

Assume that a machine falls under a three-year property class and costs $3,000 initially. The straight-line option under MACRS differs from the traditional straight-line method in that under this method the company would deduct only $500 depreciation in the first year and the fourth year ($3,000/3 years = $1,000; $1,000/2 = $500). The table below compares the straight-line with half-year convention with the MACRS.

Year	Straight-line (half-year) Depreciation	Cost	MACRS%	MACRS Deduction
1	$ 500	$3,000	× 33.3%	$ 999
2	1,000	3,000	× 44.5	1,335
3	1,000	3,000	× 14.8	444
4	500	3,000	× 7.4	222
	$3,000			$3,000

EXAMPLE 8

A machine costs $10,000. Annual cash inflows are expected to be $5,000. The machine will be depreciated using the MACRS rule and will fall under the three-year property class. The cost of capital after taxes is 10%. The estimated life of the machine is four years. The salvage value of the machine at the end of the fourth year is expected to be $1,200. The tax rate is 30%.

The formula for computation of after-tax cash inflows, $(S - E)(1 - t) + (d)(t)$ needs to be computed separately. The NPV analysis can be performed as follows:

					Present value factor @ 10%	Present value
Initial investment: $10,000					1.000	$(10,000.00)
$(S - E)(1 - t)$:						
$5,000(1 - .3) = $3,500 for 4 years					3.170[a]	$11,095.00
(d)(t):						

Year	Cost	MACRS%	d	(d)(t)		
1	$10,000 ×	33.3%	$3,330	$ 999	.909[b]	908.09
2	$10,000 ×	44.5	4,450	1,335	.826[b]	1,102.71
3	$10,000 ×	14.8	1,480	444	.751[b]	333.44
4	$10,000 ×	7.4	740	222	.683[b]	151.63

Salvage value:

$1,200 in year 4: $1,200 (1 - .3) = 840[c]		.683[b]	573.72
Net present value (NPV)			$4,164.59

[a] From Table 4 in the Appendix.

[b] From Table 3 in the Appendix.

[c] Any salvage value received under the MACRS rules is a *taxable gain* (the access of the selling price over book value, $1,200 in this example), since the book value will be zero at the end of the life of the machine.

Since NPV = PV – I = $4,164.59 is positive, the machine should be bought.

Table 17-1
Modified Accelerated Cost Recovery System
Classification of Assets

Property class

Year	3-year	5-year	7-year	10-year	15-year	20-year
1	33.3%	20.0%	14.3%	10.0%	5.0%	3.8%
2	44.5	32.0	24.5	18.0	9.5	7.2
3	14.8*	19.2	17.5	14.4	8.6	6.7
4	7.4	11.5*	12.5	11.5	7.7	6.2
5		11.5	8.9*	9.2	6.9	5.7
6		5.8	8.9	7.4	6.2	5.3
7			8.9	6.6*	5.9*	4.9
8			4.5	6.6	5.9	4.5*
9				6.5	5.9	4.5
10				6.5	5.9	4.5
11				3.3	5.9	4.5

12				5.9	4.5
13				5.9	4.5
14				5.9	4.5
15				5.9	4.5
16				3.0	4.4
17					4.4
18					4.4
19					4.4
20					4.4
21					2.2
Total	100.0%	100.0%	100.0%	100.0%	100.0%	100.0%

*Denotes the year of changeover to straight-line depreciation.

CHAPTER PERSPECTIVE

Since income taxes could make a difference in the accept-or-reject decision, tax factors must be taken into account in every decision.

Although the traditional depreciation methods still can be used for computing depreciation for book purposes, 1981 saw a new way of computing depreciation deductions for tax purposes. The new rule is called the modified accelerated cost recovery system (MACRS). It was enacted by Congress in 1981 and then modified somewhat under the Tax Reform Act of 1986. We presented an overview of the traditional depreciation methods and illustrated the use of MACRS.

Table 17-2
MACRS Tables by Property Class

MACRS property class and depreciation method	Useful life (ADR Midpoint Life*)	Examples of assets
3-year property 200% declining-balance	4 years or less	Most small tools are included; the law specifically *excludes* autos and light trucks from this property class.
5-year property 200% declining-balance	More than 4 years to less than 10 years	Autos and light trucks, computers, typewriters, copiers, duplicating equipment, heavy general-purpose trucks, and research and experimentation equipment are included.
7-year property 200% declining-balance	10 years or more to less than 16 years	Office furniture and fixtures and most items of machinery and equipment used in production are included.

10-year property 200% declining-balance	16 years or more to less than 20 years	Various machinery and equipment, such as that used in petroleum distilling and refining and in the milling of grain, are included.
15-year property 150% declining-balance	20 years or more to less than 25 years	Sewage treatment plants, telephone and electrical distribution facilities, and land improvements are included.
20-year property 150% declining-balance	25 years or more	Service stations and other real property with an ADR midpoint life of less than 27.5 years are included.
27.5-year property Straight-line	Not applicable	All residential rental property is included.
31.5-year property Straight-line	Not applicable	All nonresidential real property is included.

*The term *ADR midpoint life* means the "useful life" of an asset in a business sense; the appropriate ADR midpoint lives for assets are designated in the tax *Regulations*.

Cost Analysis for Transfer Pricing

INTRODUCTION AND MAIN POINTS

Goods and services are often exchanged between various divisions of a decentralized organization. Relatively autonomous responsibility centers buy from, and sell to, each other. For example, at General Motors, it is common for one division to buy direct materials from other divisions of the company. The *transfer price* is the selling price credited to the selling division and the cost charged to the buying division for an internal transfer of an assembled product or service. It is the same price for each as if an "arm's length" transaction had taken place between independent businesses. A transfer price has to be formulated so that a realistic and meaningful profit figure can be determined for each division. It should be established only after proper planning.

The choice of transfer prices not only affects divisional performance, but is also important in decisions involving make or buy, whether to sell or process further, and choosing between alternative production possibilities.

In this chapter, you will learn:
■ The attributes of a good transfer price.
■ How to establish a transfer price.
■ The various types of transfer prices that may be used and when each might be appropriate or inappropriate.
■ How to determine the profit of a division after using transfer prices.
■ When a buying division should be forced to buy inside the company rather than being allowed to go outside.

ATTRIBUTES OF A GOOD TRANSFER PRICE

A transfer price should satisfy the following characteristics:
■ Promote the goals of the company and harmonize divisional goals with organizational ones.
■ Be flexible and equitable to the different divisional managers. The transfer price should give the selling division enough credit

for its transfer of goods and services to the buying division. Will the transfer price hurt the performance of the selling division?

▬ Preserve autonomy, so the selling and buying division managers operate their divisions as decentralized entities.

▬ Minimize duplication and paperwork.

▬ Respond quickly to changing business conditions in domestic and international markets.

▬ Act as an incentive to keep costs under control.

▬ Minimize the conflict between buying and selling divisions.

▬ Put profits where you want them. For example, put higher profits in low-tax areas and lower profits in high-tax areas. It should minimize tariffs in international dealings. Also, put profits where they can best be used, such as constructing a new building.

▬ Conform to legal requirements.

▬ Result in cooperation across divisional and country lines.

SELECTION OF A TRANSFER PRICE

What monetary values should be assigned to exchanges? There are a number of ways in which a transfer price may be determined, including negotiated market value, budgeted cost plus profit markup, actual cost plus profit markup, cost, incremental cost, and dual pricing. Unfortunately, there is no single transfer price that will please everybody—that is, top management, the selling division, and the buying division—involved in the transfer. In practice, most companies use negotiated market value, but many companies select actual cost plus markup. We will now discuss how each type of transfer price is determined, when it would be appropriate, the advantages, and the disadvantages.

Negotiated Market Value

The best transfer price is the *negotiated market value* of the assembled product or service, since it is a fair price and treats each profit center as a separate economic entity. It equals the outside service fee or selling price for the item (a quoted price for a product or service is only comparable if the credit terms, grade, quality, delivery, and auxiliary conditions are precisely the same) less internal cost savings that result from dealing internally within the organization (e.g., advertising, sales commission, delivery charges, bookkeeping costs for customer's ledgers, credit and collection costs, and bad debts). Even if the selling center does not have a quantity discount policy, a discount may be considered into the transfer price. In many cases, if the buying center were an outside customer, the selling center would provide a volume discount, so a similar discount should be offered as an element of the transfer price. The market value of services performed is based on the going rate for a specific job (e.g., equipment tune-up) and/or the standard hourly rate (e.g., the hourly rate for a plumber). Market price may be determined from price catalogues, obtaining outside bids, and examining published data on completed market transactions. (*Caution*: An outside supplier may intentionally quote a low price to obtain the business with the thought of increasing the price at a later date.) If two divisions cannot agree on the transfer price, it will be settled by arbitration at a higher level. A temporarily low transfer price (due to oversupply of the item, for example) or high transfer price (due to a strike situation causing a supply shortage, for example) should not be employed. *Solution*: Use the average long-term market price.

A negotiated transfer price works best when outside markets for the intermediate product exist, all parties have access to market information, and one is permitted to deal externally if a negotiated settlement is impossible. If one of these conditions is violated, the negotiated price may break down and cause inefficiencies.

Budgeted Cost Plus Profit Markup

If the outside market price is not ascertainable (e.g., new product, absence of replacement market, or inappropriate, or too costly to be used for transfer pricing), you should use *budgeted cost plus profit markup,* because this transfer price approximates market value and will spot divisional inefficiencies. Budgeted cost includes the factory cost and any administrative cost applicable to production, such as cost accounting, production planning, industrial engineering, and research and development. Direct material, direct labor, and variable factory overhead are based on standard rates for the budget period. Fixed factory overhead and administrative expenses are unitized at normal volume. Use of normal volume is preferable, because it levels out the intracompany prices over the years. Profit markup should take into account the particular characteristics of the division rather than the overall corporate profit margin. Profit is often calculated based on a percentage return on capital which is budgeted to be used at the budgeted or normal volume used for unitizing fixed costs. This percentage is established by company policy. It may be the average expected return for the manufacturing unit, purchasing unit, or company. When budgeted cost plus profit is used as the transfer price, a provision usually exists to adjust for changes in raw-material prices and wage rates.

There is an incentive to the selling division to control its costs, because it will not be credited for an amount in excess of budgeted cost plus a markup. Thus, if the selling division's inefficiencies resulted in actual costs being excessive, it would have to absorb the decline in profit to the extent that actual cost exceeded budgeted cost. Profit markup should be as realistic as possible given the nature of the division and its product.

Actual Cost Plus Profit Markup

Another commonly used method of transfer pricing is *actual cost plus profit markup.* This approach has the drawback of passing on cost inefficiencies. In fact, the selling division is encouraged to be cost-inefficient, since the higher its actual cost, the higher will be its selling price (since it shows a greater profit).

Cost-Based

Some companies employ *actual cost* as the transfer price because of ease of use, but the problem with this approach is that no profit is shown by the selling division, and cost inefficiencies are passed on. Further, the cost-based method treats the divisions as cost centers rather than profit or investment centers. Therefore, measures such as return on investment and residual income cannot be used for evaluation purposes.

The *variable-cost-based* transfer price has an advantage over the full-cost method because in the short run it tends to ensure the best utilization of the overall company's resources. The reason is that, in the short run, fixed costs do not change. Any use of facilities, without incurrence of additional fixed costs, will increase the company's overall profits. In the case where division managers are responsible for costs in their divisions, the cost-price approach to transfer pricing is often used.

A transfer price based on cost may be appropriate when there are minimal services provided by one department to another. A company may have more than one department providing a product or service that is identical or very similar. It may be cost beneficial to centralize that product or service into one department. If more than one department provides an identical or very similar service, a cost-basis transfer price may be used since the receiving department will select the services of the department providing the highest quality. Thus, the providing department has an incentive to do a good job.

A company may use a *below-cost transfer price* to favor a division newly spun off by the parent. This may provide the new firm with a better competitive position, allowing it to get started in an industry other than that of the parent and compete effectively with established industry leaders.

Incremental Cost
Incremental cost is another transfer pricing possibility. *Incremental costs* are the variable costs of making and shipping goods and any costs directly and exclusively traceable to the product. This cost is quite good for use by the company as a whole, but does little for measuring divisional performance. The incremental-cost approach assumes the selling division has sufficient capacity to satisfy internal company demands as well as demands of outside customers.

Dual Pricing
Another way of setting the transfer price is *dual pricing.* It occurs when the buying division is charged with variable cost ($1) and the selling division is credited with full cost (variable cost and fixed cost) and markup ($1.50 plus 60%). Under dual pricing there is a motivational effect, since each division's performance is enhanced by the transfer. However, profit for the company as a whole will be less than the sum of the divisions' profits. The difference between the two transfer prices is debited to the corporate account.

DIVISIONAL PROFIT
The profit of a division equals its revenue less direct and indirect costs. Profit determination takes into account the transfer price that is either credited to the selling division or charged to the buying division. Examples of profit determination follow.

EXAMPLE 1
The Assembling division manufactures an assembled product that can be sold to outsiders or transferred to the Finishing division. Relevant information for the period follows:

Assembling Division	Units
Production	1,500
Transferred to finishing division	1,200
Sold outside	300
Selling price $25	
Unit cost $5	

The units transferred to the Finishing division were processed further at a cost of $7. They were sold outside at $45. Transfers are at market value.

Division profit is:

	Assembling Division	Finishing Division	Company
Sales	$7,500	$54,000	$61,500
Transfer price	30,000		
	$37,500	$54,000	$61,500
Product cost	$7,500	$8,400	$15,900
Transfer price		30,000	
	$7,500	$38,400	$15,900
Profit	$30,000	$15,600	$45,600

EXAMPLE 2

Emerson Electric manufactures radios. It has two production divisions (assembly and finishing) and one service division (maintenance). The assembly division both sells assembled radios to other companies and transfers them for further processing to the finishing division. The transfer price used is market value. Relevant data follow.

Assembly Division

Outside sales: 1,000 assembled radios at $30 (included in the price is selling commission fees of $1 per unit and freight costs of $2 per unit). Transferred to finishing division: 10,000 assembled radios.

Direct costs	$80,000
Indirect costs	$45,000

Finishing Division

Outside sales: 10,000 finished radios at $55

Direct costs	$90,000
Indirect costs	$30,000

Maintenance Division

Direct costs (direct labor, parts)	$80,000
Indirect costs	$25,000

9,000 hours rendered for servicing to assembly division
12,000 hours rendered for servicing to finishing division
Standard hourly rate: $8

A schedule of the gross profit of the separate divisions and the gross profit of Emerson Electric Corporation is shown in Table 18-1.

Table 18-1
Gross Profit, Emerson Electric Corporation

	Assembly	Finishing	Maintenance	Transfers	Emerson
Revenue					
Sales	$30,000	$550,000			$580,000
Transfers	270,000			$270,000	
			$72,000	72,000	
			96,000	96,000	
Total	$300,000	$550,000	$168,000	$438,000	$580,000
Costs					
Direct	$80,000	$90,000	$80,000		$250,000
Indirect	45,000	30,000	25,000		100,000
Transfers:					
Maintenance	72,000	96,000		168,000	
Assembly		270,000		270,000	
Total costs	$197,000	$486,000	$105,000	$438,000	$350,000
Gross profit	$103,000	$64,000	$63,000	—	$230,000

Assembly revenue: Sales, $30 × 1000; transfer price, $27 × 10,000.

WHETHER TO BUY INTERNALLY OR OUTSIDE

The *maximum transfer price* that should be charged is the *outside price*, since the selling division should not gain from inefficiencies. Whether the buying division will be forced to buy inside or be permitted to buy outside depends on what is best for corporate profitability.

EXAMPLE 3

An assembly division wants to charge a finishing division $80 per unit for an internal transfer of 800 units. The variable cost per unit is $50. Total fixed cost in the assembly division is $200,000. Current production is 10,000 units. Idle capacity exists. The finishing division can purchase the item outside for $73 per unit.

The maximum transfer price should be $73, which is the cost to buy it from outside. The finishing division should not have to pay a price greater than the outside market price.

Should the buying division buy the item outside or be required to buy inside? Let us look at the impact on overall profit. Typically, the buying division is required to purchase inside at a maximum transfer price ($73), since the selling division still has to meet its fixed cost when idle capacity exists. The impact on corporate profitability of having the buying division go outside is determined as follows:

Cost savings to assembly division (units × variable cost per unit): 800 × $50	$40,000
Cost to finishing division (units × outside selling price): 800 × $73	58,400
Savings from staying inside	$18,400

The buying division will be asked to purchase inside the company, because if it went outside, corporate profitability would decline by $18,400.

CHAPTER PERSPECTIVE

A transfer price is the one charged between divisions for an internal transfer of an assembled product or service. In this way, divisional profitability may be determined. In practical terms, the best transfer price to use is negotiated market value. However, when that is not available—say, for example, there is a new product—budgeted cost plus profit markup should be used. Other transfer pricing bases are also used by companies, such as actual cost plus markup and actual cost. In any event, the buying division should never be charged a transfer price that exceeds the outside market price. Whether the buying division is allowed to buy outside or stay inside depends on what is best for corporate profitability.

Quantitative Applications for Cost Analysis

INTRODUCTION AND MAIN POINTS

The use of quantitative tools is commonplace in cost analysis. Also, in recent years much attention has been given to using a variety of quantitative models in financial decision making. With the rapid development of personal computers (PCs), cost analysts find it increasingly easy to use quantitative techniques. A knowledge of mathematical and statistical methods will greatly aid the managerial accountant in performing his/her functions. The so-called Decision Support System (DSS) is in effect the embodiment of this trend.

The term *quantitative models,* also known as *operations research (OR)* and *management science*, describes sophisticated mathematical and statistical techniques in the solution of planning and decision making problems. There are numerous tools available under these subject headings. We will explore five of the most important of these techniques; all five have been widely applied in managerial accounting and cost analysis. They are:

1. Statistical analysis and evaluation
2. Linear programming and opportunity costs
3. Learning curve
4. Inventory planning
5. Program Evaluation and Review Technique (PERT)

After studying the material in this chapter:

■ You will be able to utilize various quantitative techniques for various decision situations.

■ You will be able to identify which technique is appropriate for a given decision situation.

■ You will gain an understanding of how each of the quantitative methods works and what they are used for.

STATISTICAL ANALYSIS AND EVALUATION

In many situations, cost analysts and managerial accountants have a large volume of data that need to be analyzed. These data could be earnings, cash flows, accounts receivable balances, weights of an incoming shipment, etc. The most commonly used statistics to describe the characteristics of the data are the *mean* and the *standard deviation*. These statistics are also used to measure the return on and risk in investment and financial decision making in which the managerial accountant may be asked to participate by the business entity.

Standard Deviation

The standard deviation measures the tendency of data to be spread out. Cost analysts and managerial accountants can make important inferences from past data with this measure. The standard deviation, denoted with the Greek letter σ (sigma) is defined as follows:

$$\sigma = \frac{\sqrt{(x - \overline{x})^2}}{n - 1}$$

where x is the mean (arithmetic average) and n = number of observations.

More specifically, the standard deviation can be calculated, step by step, as follows:

1. Subtract the mean from each element of the data.
2. Square each of the differences obtained in step 1.
3. Add together all the squared differences.
4. Divide the sum of all the squared differences by the number of values minus one.
5. Take the square root of the quotient obtained in step 4.

The standard deviation can be used to measure the variation of such items as the expected contribution margin (CM) and expected variable manufacturing costs. It can also be used to assess the risk associated with investment decisions.

EXAMPLE 1

One and one-half years of quarterly returns are listed below for United Motors stock.

Time period	x	$(x - \overline{x})$	$(x - \overline{x})^2$
1	10%	0	0
2	15	5	25
3	20	10	100
4	5	−5	25
5	−10	−20	400
6	20	10	100
	60		650

From the table, note that

$$\overline{x} = 60/6 = 10\%$$

$$\sigma = \sqrt{(x - \overline{x})/n - 1} = \sqrt{650/(6 - 1)} = \sqrt{130} = 11.40\%$$

The United Motors stock has returned on the average 10% over the last six quarters, and the variability about its average return was 11.40%. The high standard deviation (11.40%) relative to the average return of 10% indicates that the stock is very risky.

LINEAR PROGRAMMING AND OPPORTUNITY COSTS

Linear programming (LP) is a mathematical technique designed to determine an optimal decision (or an optimal plan) chosen from a large number of possible decisions. The *optimal decision* is the one that meets the specified objective of the company, subject to various restrictions or constraints. It concerns itself with the problem of allocating scarce resources among competing activities in an optimal manner. The optimal decision yields the highest profit, contribution margin (CM), or revenue, or the lowest cost. A linear programming model consists of two important ingredients:

1. *Objective function.* The company must define the specific objective to be achieved.
2. *Constraints.* Constraints are in the form of restrictions on availability of resources or meeting minimum requirements.

As the name "linear programming" indicates, both the objective function and constraints must be in linear form.

EXAMPLE 2

A firm wishes to find an optimal product mix. The optimal mix would be the one that maximizes its total CM within the allowed budget and production capacity. Or the firm may want to determine a least-cost combination of input materials while meeting production requirements, employing production capacities, and using available employees.

Applications of LP

Applications of LP are numerous. They include:

1. Developing an optimal budget
2. Determining an optimal investment portfolio
3. Scheduling jobs to machines
4. Determining a least-cost shipping pattern
5. Scheduling flights
6. Gasoline blending

Formulation of LP

To formulate an LP problem, certain steps are followed. They are:

1. Define what are called *decision variables* that you are trying to solve for.
2. Express the objective function and constraints in terms of these decision variables. All the expressions must be in *linear* form.

In the following example, we will use this technique to find the optimal product mix.

EXAMPLE 3

The JKS Furniture Manufacturing Company produces two products: desks and tables. Both products require time in two processing departments, assembly and finishing. Data on the two products are as follows:

	Products		Available
Processing	Desk	Table	hours
Assembly	2	4	100 hours
Finishing	3	2	90
Contribution margin per unit	$25	$40	

The company wants to find the most profitable mix of these two products.

Step 1: Define the decision variables as follows:

$$A = \text{Number of units of product A to be produced}$$
$$B = \text{Number of units of product B to be produced}$$

Step 2: The objective function to maximize total contribution margin (CM) is expressed as:

$$\text{Total CM} = 25A + 40B$$

Then formulate the constraints as inequalities:

$$2A + 4B \leq 100 \text{ (assembly constraint)}$$
$$3A + 2B \leq 90 \text{ (finishing constraint)}$$

In addition, implicit in any LP formulation are the constraints that restrict A and B to be non-negative—i.e.:

$$A, B \geq 0$$

Our LP model is:

$$\text{Maximize:} \quad \text{Total CM} = 25A + 40B$$
$$\text{Subject to:} \quad 2A + 4B \leq 100$$
$$3A + 2B \leq 90$$
$$A, B \geq 0$$

Computation Methods of LP

There are solution methods available to solve LP problems. They include:

1. The simplex method
2. The graphical method

The simplex method is the technique most commonly used to solve LP problems. It is an algorithm, which is an iteration method of computation that moves from one solution to another until it reaches the best solution. *Note:* Virtually all computer software for LP uses this method of computation.

The graphical solution is easier to use but limited to the LP problems involving two (or at most three) decision variables. The graphical method follows these steps:

Step 1: Change inequalities to equalities.

Step 2: Graph the equalities.

Step 3: Identify the correct side for the original inequalities.

Step 4: Identify the feasible region, the area of feasible solutions (values of decision variables that satisfy all the constraints simultaneously).

Step 5: Determine the contribution margin at all corners in the feasible region.

EXAMPLE 4

Using the data and the LP model from Example 3, follow steps 1 through 4. We obtain the feasible region shown by the shaded area in Figure 19-1.

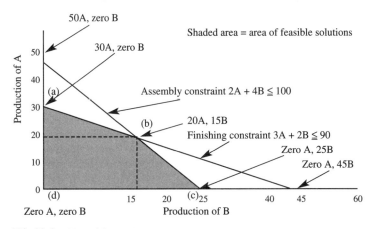

FIG. 19-1. *Feasible region.*

Then we evaluate all of the corner points in the feasible region in terms of their CM, as follows:

| | Corner Points | | Contribution Margin |
	A	B	$25A + $40B
(a)	30	0	$25(30) + $40(0) = $750
(b)	20	15	25(20) + 40(15) = 1,100
(c)	0	25	25(0) + 40(25) = 1,000
(d)	0	0	25(0) + 40(0) = 0

The corner, 20A, 15B produces the most profitable solution.

Opportunity Costs (Shadow Prices)

A cost analyst who has solved an LP problem might wish to know whether it pays to add capacity in hours in a particular department. The analyst might be interested in the monetary value to the firm of adding, say, an hour per week of assembly time. This monetary value is usually the additional profit that could be earned. This amount is the *opportunity cost* (also known as the *shadow price*), the profit that would be lost by not adding an additional hour of capacity. To justify a decision in favor of a short-term capacity decision, the manager must be sure that the shadow price exceeds the actual price of that expansion.

For example, suppose that the shadow price of an hour of assembly capacity is $6.50 while the actual market price is $8.00. That means it does not pay to obtain an additional hour of assembly capacity.

Shadow prices are computed, step by step, as follows:
1. Add one hour (preferably more than one hour, to make it easier to show graphically) to the constraint of a given LP problem under consideration.
2. Resolve the problem and find the maximum CM.
3. Compute the difference between the CM of the original LP problem and the CM determined in step 2, which is the shadow price.

EXAMPLE 5

Using the data from the preceding two examples, we compute the shadow price of the assembly capacity. To make it easier to show graphically, add 8 hours of capacity of the assembly department, rather than one hour. The new assembly constraint and the resulting feasible region is shown in Figure 19-2.

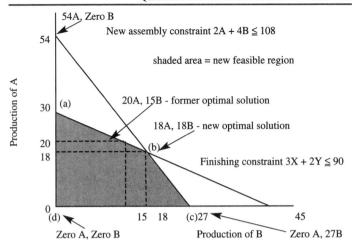

FIG. 19-2. *New feasible region.*

Then we evaluate all of the corner points in the *new* feasible region in terms of their CM, as follows:

	Corner Points		Contribution Margin
	A	B	$25A + $40B
(a)	30	0	$25(30) + $40(0) = $750
(b)	18	18	25(18) + 40(18) = 1,170
(c)	0	27	25(0) + 40(27) = 1,080
(d)	0	0	25(0) + 40(0) = 0

The new optimal solution of 18A, 18B has total CM of $1,170 per week. Therefore, the shadow price of the assembly capacity is $70 ($1,170 – $1,100 = $70), or $8.75 per hour ($70/8 hours = $8.75). The firm would be willing to pay up to $70 to obtain an additional 8 hours of the assembly capacity per week, or $8.75 per hour per week. In other words, the firm's opportunity cost of not adding an additional hour is $8.75.

Use of Computer LP Software
We can use a computer LP software package, such as LINDO (Linear Interactive and Discrete Optimization), to quickly solve an LP problem. Figure 19-3 shows a computer output by an LP program for our LP model set up in Example 3. Figure 19-4 presents Excel LP output.

Note: The printout shows the following optimal solution:

$$X_1 = A = 20 \text{ units}$$
$$X_2 = B = 15 \text{ units}$$
$$CM = \$1,100$$

Shadow prices are:

Assembly capacity = \$8.75
Finishing capacity = \$2.50

INFORMATION ENTERED

NUMBER OF CONSTRAINTS	2	
NUMBER OF VARIABLES	2	*Note:*
NUMBER OF ≦ CONSTRAINTS	2	$X_1 = A$
NUMBER OF = CONSTRAINTS	0	$X_2 = B$
NUMBER OF ≧ CONSTRAINTS	0	

MAXIMIZATION PROBLEM

$$25 \text{ X } 1 \qquad +40 \text{ X } 2$$

SUBJECT TO

$$2 \text{ X } 1 \quad + 4 \text{ X } 2 \quad \leqq 100$$
$$3 \text{ X } 1 \quad + 2 \text{ X } 2 \quad \leqq 90$$

RESULTS

VARIABLE	VARIABLE VALUE	ORIGINAL COEFF.	COEFF. SENS.	
X1	20	25	0	Solution: $X_1 = A = 20$
X2	15	40	0	$X_2 = B = 15$

CONSTRAINT NUMBER	ORIGINAL RHS	SLACK OR SURPLUS	SHADOW PRICE	Shadow price of the assembly capacity
1	100	0	8.75	
2	90	0	2.5	←

OBJECTIVE FUNCTION VALUE: <u>1100</u> = CM

SENSITIVITY ANALYSIS

OBJECTIVE FUNCTION COEFFICIENTS

VARIABLE	LOWER LIMIT	ORIGINAL COEFFICIENT	UPPER LIMIT
X1	20	25	60
X2	16.67	40	50

RIGHT HAND SIDE

CONSTRAINT NUMBER	LOWER LIMIT	ORIGINAL VALUE	UPPER LIMIT
1	60	100	180
2	50	90	150

FIG. 19-3. *Computer printout for LP.*

Microsoft Excel 8.0a Answer Report
Worksheet: [T06-JKS-LP1.XLS]JKS
Report Created: 3/31/99 8:27:04 PM

Target Cell (Max)

Cell	Name	Original Value	Final Value
$E$5	Unit Contribution Margin: TotalCM:	$0	$1,100

Adjustable Cells

Cell	Name	Original Value	Final Value
$B$4	Number to make: Desk	0	20
$C$4	Number to make: Table	0	15

Constraints

Cell	Name	Cell Value	Formula	Status	Slack
$D$8	Assembly Used	100	$D$8<=$E$8	Binding	0
$D$9	Finishing Used	90	$D$9<=$E$9	Binding	0
$B$4	Number to make: Desk	20	$B$4>=0	Not Binding	20
$C$4	Number to make: Table	15	$C$4>=0	Not Binding	15

FIG. 19-4. *Excel LP output.*

Microsoft Excel 8.0a Sensitivity Report
Worksheet: [T06-JKS-LP1.XLS]JKS
Report Created: 3/31/99 8:27:28 PM

Adjustable Cells

Cell	Name	Final Value	Reduced Gradient
$B$4	Number to make: Desk	20	0
$C$4	Number to make: Table	15	0

Constraints

Cell	Name	Final Value	Lagrange Multiplier
$D$8	Assembly Used	100	8.75
$D$9	Finishing Used	90	2.5

Microsoft Excel 8.0a Limits Report
Worksheet: [T06-JKS-LP1.XLS]JKS
Report Created: 3/31/99 8:27:54 PM

Cell	Target Name	Value
$E$5	Unit Contribution Margin: TotalCM:	$1,100

Cell	Adjustable Name	Value	Lower Limit	Target Result	Upper Limit	Target Result
$B$4	Number to make: Desk	20	0	600	20	1100
$C$4	Number to make: Table	15	0	500	15	1100

LEARNING CURVE

The learning curve is based on the proposition that labor-hours decrease in a definite pattern as labor operations are repeated. More specifically, it is based on the statistical findings that as the cumulative production doubles, the cumulative average time required per unit will be reduced by some constant percentage, ranging typically from 10% to 20%. By convention, learning curves are referred to in terms of the complements of their improvement rates. For example, an 80% learning curve denotes a 20% decrease in unit time with each doubling of repetitions. For example, a project is known to have an 80% learning curve. It has just taken a laborer 10 hours to produce the first unit. Then each time the cumulative output doubles, the time per unit for that amount should be equal to the previous time multiplied by the learning percentage. Thus:

Unit	Unit time	(hours)
1		10
2	.8(10)	= 8
4	.8(8)	= 6.4
8	.8(6.4)	= 5.12
16	.8(5.12)	= 4.096

An 80% learning curve is shown in Figure 19-5.

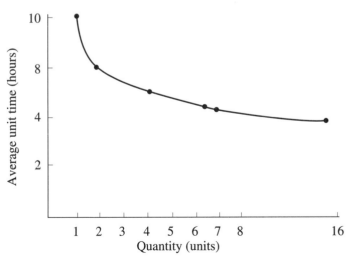

FIG. 19-5. *An 80% learning curve.*

This example, however, raises an interesting question: How do we compute time for values for three, five, six, seven, and other units that do not fall into this pattern? Fortunately, the time for these units can be quickly determined using Table 19-1 (Learning Curve Coefficients). The time for the nth unit is determined by multiplying the table value by the time required for the first unit.

EXAMPLE 6

NBRF Contractors, Inc., is negotiating a contract involving production of 20 jets. The initial jet required 200 labor-days of direct labor. Assuming an 80% learning curve, we will determine the expected number of labor-days for (1) the 20th jet, and (2) all 20 jets as follows:

Using Table 19-1 with $n = 20$ and an 80% learning rate, we find: Unit = .381 and Total = 10,485. Therefore,
  (1) Expected time for the 20th jet = 200(.381) = 76.2 labor-days.
  (2) Expected total time for all 20 jets = 200(10.485) = 2,097 labor-days.

The learning curve theory has found useful applications in many areas, including:
  1. Scheduling labor requirements
  2. Setting incentive wage rates
  3. Pricing new products
  4. Negotiated purchasing
  5. Budgeting, purchasing, and inventory planning

The following example illustrates the use of the learning-curve theory for the pricing of a contract.

EXAMPLE 7

Big Mac Electronics Products, Inc., finds that new-product production is affected by an 80% learning effect. The company has just produced 50 units of output at 100 hours per unit. Costs were as follows:

Materials 50 units @ $20	$1,000
Labor and labor-related costs:	
Direct labor—100 hours @ $8	800
Variable overhead—100 hours @ $2	200
	$2,000

The company has just received a contract calling for another 50 units of production. It wants to add a 50% markup to the cost of materials and labor and labor-related costs. To determine the price for this job, the first step is to build up the learning-curve table.

Quantity	Total time (hours)	Average time (per unit)
50	100	2 hours
100	160	1.6 (.8 × 2 hours)

For the new 50-unit job, it takes 60 hours total. The contract price is:

Materials 50 units @ $20	$1,000
Labor and labor-related costs:	
Direct labor—60 hours @ $8	480
Variable overhead—60 hours @ $2	120
	$1,600
50% markup	800
Contract price	$2,400

INVENTORY PLANNING

One of the most common problems facing managerial accountants is that of inventory planning. This is understandable, since inventory represents, on the average, more than 30% of total current assets in U.S. industry. Excessive money tied up in inventory is a drag on profitability. The purpose of inventory planning is to develop policies that will achieve an optimal investment in inventory. This objective is achieved by determining the level of inventory necessary to minimize inventory-related costs.

Inventory-related costs fall into three categories:
1. Ordering costs, which include all costs associated with preparing a purchase order.
2. Carrying (holding) costs, which include storage costs for inventory items plus the cost of money tied up in inventory.
3. Shortage (stockout) costs, which include those costs incurred when an item is out of stock. These include the lost contribution margin on sales plus lost customer goodwill.

There are many inventory-planning models available that try to answer the following two questions:
1. How much to order?
2. When to order?

Table 19-1
Learning Curve Coefficients

Unit number	70%		75%		80%		85%		90%	
	Unit time	Total time	Unit time	Total time	Unit time	Total time	Unit time	Total time	Unit time	Total time
1	1.000	1.000	1.000	1.000	1.000	1.000	1.000	1.000	1.000	1.000
2	.700	1.700	.750	1.750	.800	1.800	.850	1.850	.900	1.900
3	.568	2.268	.634	2.384	.702	2.502	.773	2.623	.846	2.746
4	.490	2.758	.562	2.946	.640	3.142	.723	3.345	.810	3.556
5	.437	3.195	.513	3.459	.596	3.738	.686	4.031	.783	4.339
6	.398	3.593	.475	3.934	.562	4.299	.657	4.688	.762	5.101
7	.367	3.960	.446	4.380	.534	4.834	.634	5.322	.744	5.845
8	.343	4.303	.422	4.802	.512	5.346	.614	5.936	.729	6.574
9	.323	4.626	.402	5.204	.493	5.839	.597	6.533	.716	7.290
10	.306	4.932	.385	5.589	.477	6.315	.583	7.116	.705	7.994
11	.291	5.223	.370	5.958	.462	6.777	.570	7.686	.695	8.689
12	.278	5.501	.357	6.315	.449	7.227	.558	8.244	.685	9.374
13	.267	5.769	.345	6.660	.438	7.665	.548	8.792	.677	10.052
14	.257	6.026	.334	6.994	.428	8.092	.539	9.331	.670	10.721
15	.248	6.274	.325	7.319	.418	8.511	.530	9.861	.663	11.384
16	.240	6.514	.316	7.635	.410	8.920	.522	10.383	.656	12.040
17	.233	6.747	.309	7.944	.402	9.322	.515	10.898	.650	12.690
18	.226	6.973	.301	8.245	.394	9.716	.508	11.405	.644	13.334

19	.220	7.192	.295	8.540	.338	10.104	.501	11.907	.639	13.974
20	.214	7.407	.288	8.828	.381	10.485	.495	12.402	.634	14.608
21	.209	7.615	.283	9.111	.375	10.860	.490	12.892	.630	15.237
22	.204	7.819	.277	9.388	.370	11.230	.484	13.376	.625	15.862
23	.199	8.018	.272	9.660	.364	11.594	.479	13.856	.621	16.483
24	.195	8.213	.267	9.928	.359	11.954	.475	14.331	.617	17.100
25	.191	8.404	.263	10.191	.355	12.309	.470	14.801	.613	17.713
26	.187	8.591	.259	10.449	.350	12.659	.466	15.267	.609	18.323
27	.183	8.774	.255	10.704	.346	13.005	.462	15.728	.606	18.929
28	.180	8.954	.251	10.955	.342	13.347	.458	16.186	.603	19.531
29	.177	9.131	.247	11.202	.338	13.685	.454	16.640	.599	20.131
30	.174	9.305	.244	11.446	.335	14.020	.450	17.091	.596	20.727
31	.171	9.476	.240	11.686	.331	14.351	.447	17.538	.593	21.320
32	.168	9.644	.237	11.924	.328	14.679	.444	17.981	.590	21.911
33	.165	9.809	.234	12.158	.324	15.003	.441	18.422	.588	22.498
34	.163	9.972	.231	12.389	.321	15.324	.437	18.859	.585	23.084
35	.160	10.133	.229	12.618	.318	15.643	.434	19.294	.583	23.666
36	.158	10.291	.226	12.844	.315	15.958	.432	19.725	.580	24.246
37	.156	10.447	.223	13.067	.313	16.271	.429	20.154	.578	24.824
38	.154	10.601	.221	13.288	.310	16.581	.426	20.580	.575	25.339
39	.152	10.753	.219	13.507	.307	16.888	.424	21.004	.573	25.972
40	.150	10.902	.216	13.723	.305	17.193	.421	21.425	.571	26.543

They include the so-called economic order quantity (EOQ) model, the reorder point, and the determination of safety stock.

Economic Order Quantity

The economic order quantity (EOQ) determines the order quantity that results in the lowest sum of carrying and ordering costs. The EOQ is computed as:

$$EOQ = \sqrt{\frac{2\,OD}{C}}$$

where C = carrying cost per unit, O = ordering cost per order, and D = annual demand (requirements) in units.

If the carrying cost is expressed as a percentage of average inventory value (say, 12% per year to hold inventory), then the denominator value in the EOQ formula would be 12% times the price of an item.

EXAMPLE 8
Assume the Los Alamitos Store buys sets of steel at $40 per set from an outside vendor. It will sell 6,400 sets evenly throughout the year. The store desires a 16% return on its inventory investment, since the 16% represents the interest charge on the borrowed money. In addition, rent, taxes, etc., for each set in inventory is $1.60 per year. The ordering cost is $100 per order.

Then the carrying cost per dozen is 16% ($40) + $1.60 = $8.00 per year.

Therefore:

$$EOQ = \sqrt{\frac{2(6,400)(\$100)}{\$8.00}} = \sqrt{160,000} = 400 \text{ sets}$$

Total number of
orders per year $\quad=\;$ D/EOQ $\;=\;$ 6,400/400 $\;=\;$ 16 orders
Total inventory costs $\;=\;$ Carrying cost $\;+\;$ Ordering cost
$\qquad\qquad\qquad\;=\;$ C $\times$ (EOQ/2) $\;+\;$ O (D/EOQ)
$\qquad\qquad\qquad\;=\;$ ($8.00)(400/2) $\;+\;$ ($100)(6,400/400)
$\qquad\qquad\qquad\;=\;$ $1,600 $\;+\;$ $1,600 $\;=\;$ $3,200

Based on these calculations, the Los Alamitos Store's inventory policy should be the following:
1. The store should order 400 sets of steel each time it places an order and order 16 times during a year.
2. This policy will be most economical and cost the store $3,200 per year.

Reorder Point

Reorder point (ROP), which answers when to place a new order, requires a knowledge about the lead time, which is the time interval between placing an order and receiving delivery. ROP can be calculated as follows:

ROP = (average usage per unit of lead time × lead time) + safety stock

First, multiply average daily (or weekly) usage by the lead time in days (or weeks), yielding the lead time demand. Then add safety stock to this to provide for the variation in lead-time demand to determine the reorder point. If average usage and lead time are both certain, no safety stock is necessary and should be dropped from the formula.

EXAMPLE 9

Assume lead time in the preceding example is constant at one week, and that there are 50 working weeks in a year. The reorder point is 128 sets = (6,400 sets/50 weeks) × 1 week. Therefore, when the inventory level drops to 128 sets, the new order should be placed. Suppose, however, that the store is faced with variable usage for its steel and requires a safety stock of 150 additional sets to carry. Then the reorder point will be 128 sets plus 150 sets, or 278 sets.

Figure 19-6 shows this inventory system when the order quantity is 400 sets and the reorder point is 128 sets.

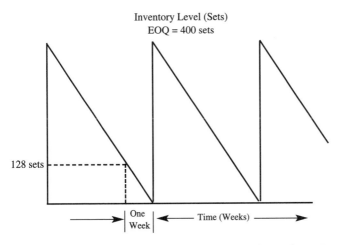

FIG. 19-6. *Basic inventory system with EOQ and reorder point.*

Assumptions and Applications

The EOQ model makes some assumptions. They are:

1. Demand is fixed and constant throughout the year.
2. Lead time is known with certainty.
3. No quantity discounts are allowed.
4. No shortages are permitted.

The assumptions may be unrealistic. However, the model still proves useful in inventory planning for many firms. In fact, many situations exist where a certain assumption holds or nearly holds. For example, subcontractors who must supply parts on a regular basis to a primary contractor face a constant demand. Even where demand varies, the assumption of uniform usage is not unrealistic. Demand for automobiles, for example, varies from week to week over a season, but the weekly fluctuations tend to cancel out each other so that seasonal demand can be assumed constant.

EOQ with Quantity Discounts

The economic-order-quantity (EOQ) model does not take into account quantity discounts, which is not realistic in many real-world cases. Usually, the more you order, the lower the unit price you pay. Quantity discounts are price reductions for large orders offered to buyers to induce them to buy in large quantities. If quantity discounts are offered, the buyer must weigh the potential benefits of reduced purchase price and fewer orders that will result from buying in large quantities against the increase in carrying costs caused by higher average inventories. Hence, the buyer's goal in this case is to select the order quantity that will minimize total costs, where total cost is the sum of carrying cost, ordering cost, and product cost:

$$\text{Total cost} = \text{Carrying cost} + \text{Ordering cost} + \text{Product cost}$$
$$= C \times (Q/2) + O \times (D/Q) + PD$$

where P = unit price and Q = order quantity.

A step-by-step approach in computing economic order quantity with quantity discounts is summarized as follows:

1. Compute the economic order quantity (EOQ) when price discounts are ignored and the corresponding costs are based on the new cost formula given above.
   Note: $\text{EOQ} = \sqrt{2OD/C}$.

2. Compute the costs for those quantities greater than the EOQ at which price reductions occur.

3. Select the value of Q that will result in the lowest total cost.

EXAMPLE 10

In Example 8, assume that the Los Alamitos Store was offered the following price discount schedule:

Order quantity (Q)	Unit price (P)
1 to 499	$40.00
500 to 999	39.90
1,000 or more	39.80

First, the EOQ with no discounts is computed as follows:

$$\text{EOQ} = \sqrt{2(6,400)(100)/8.00} = \sqrt{160,000} = 400 \text{ sets.}$$

$$\text{Total cost} = \$8.00(400/2) + \$100(6,400/400) + \$40.00(6,400)$$

$$= \$1,600 + 1,600 + 256,000 = \$259,200$$

The annual costs associated with varying order quantities are shown in Table 19-2.

Table 19-2
Annual Costs with Varying Order Quantities

Order quantity (Q)	400	500	1,000
Purchase price (P)	$40	$39.90	$39.80
Carrying cost (C × Q/2) $8 × (order quantity/2)	$1,600	$2,000	$4,000
Ordering cost (O × D/Q) $100 × (6,400/order quantity)	1,600	1,280	640
Product cost (PD) Unit price × 6,400	256,000	255,360	254,720
Total cost	$259,200	$258,640	$259,360

Note that C = $8.00, O = $100, and D = 6,400 for all possible orders.

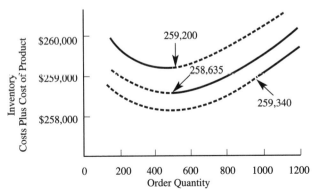

FIG. 19-7. *Inventory cost and quantity.*

We see that the value that minimized the sum of the carrying cost and the ordering cost but not the purchase cost was EOQ = 400 sets. As can been seen in Figure 19-7, the further we move from the point 400, the greater will be the sum of the carrying and ordering costs. Thus, 400 is obviously the only candidate for the minimum total-cost value within the first price range. Q = 500 is the only candidate within the $39.90 price range and Q = 1,000 is the only candidate within the $39.80 price bracket. These three quantities are evaluated in Table 19-2 and illustrated in Figure 19-7. We find that the EOQ with price discounts is 500 sets. Hence, ABC store is justified in going to the first price break, but the extra carrying cost of going to the second price break more than outweighs the savings in ordering and in the cost of the product itself.

Advantages and Disadvantages of Quantity Discounts

Buying in large quantities has some advantages and disadvantages. The advantages are lower unit costs, lower ordering costs, fewer stockouts, and lower transportation costs. On the other hand, there are disadvantages, such as higher inventory carrying costs, greater capital requirement, and higher probability of obsolescence and deterioration.

Determination of Safety Stock

When lead time and demand are not certain, the firm must carry extra units of inventory, called safety stock, as protection against possible stockouts. Stockouts can be quite expensive. Lost sales and disgruntled customers are examples of resulting external costs. Idle machine and disrupted production scheduling are examples of resulting internal costs. We will illustrate the probability approach to show how the optimal stock size can be determined in the presence of stockout costs.

EXAMPLE 11

In Examples 8 and 9, suppose that total usage for the Los Alamitos Store over a one-week period is expected to be:

Total usage	Probability
78	.2
128	.4
178	.2
228	.1
278	.1
	1.00

Suppose further that a stockout cost is estimated at $12.00 per set. Recall that the carrying cost is $8.00 per set.

Table 19-3 shows the computation of safety stock. The computation shows that the total costs are minimized at $1,200, when a safety stock of 150 sets is maintained. Therefore, the reorder point is: 128 sets + 150 sets = 278 sets.

Table 19-3
Computation of Safety Stock

Safety stock levels in units	Stockout and probability	Average stockout in units	Average stockout costs	No. of orders	Total annual stockout costs	Carrying costs	Total
0 {	50 with .2 / 100 with .1 / 150 with .1	35*	$420**	16	$6,720***	0	$7,140
50 {	50 with .1 / 100 with .1	15	180	16	2,880	400****	3,280
100	50 with .1	5	60	16	960	800	1,760
150	0	0	0	16	0	1,200	1,200

*50(.2) + 100(.1) + 150(.1) = 10 + 10 + 15 = 35 units.
**35 units × $12.00 = $420.
***$420 × 16 times = $6,720.
****50 units × $8.00 = $400.

PROGRAM EVALUATION AND REVIEW TECHNIQUE (PERT)

Program Evaluation and Review Technique (PERT) is a useful management tool for planning, scheduling, costing, coordinating, and controlling complex projects such as:

- Formulation of a master budget
- Construction of buildings
- Installation of computers
- Scheduling the closing of books
- Assembly of a machine
- Research-and-development activities
  Questions to be answered by PERT include:
- When will the project be finished?
- What is the probability that the project will be completed by any given time?

The PERT technique involves the diagrammatic representation of the sequence of activities comprising a project by means of a network. The network (1) visualizes all of the individual tasks (activities) to complete a given job or program; (2) points out interrelationships; and (3) consists of activities (represented by arrows) and events (represented by circles), as shown below.

1. Arrows. Arrows represent "tasks" or "activities," which are distinct segments of the project requiring time and resources.

2. Nodes (circles). Nodes symbolize "events," or milestone points in the project representing the completion of one or more activities and/or the initiation of one or more subsequent activities. An event is a point in time and does not consume any time in itself, as does an activity.

In a real-world situation, the estimates of completion times of activities are seldom certain. To cope with the uncertainty in activity time estimates, the PERT proceeds by estimating three possible duration times for each activity. In Figure 19-8, the numbers appearing on the arrows represent these three time estimates for activities needed to complete the various events. These time estimates are:

■ The most optimistic time (labeled a)
■ The most likely time (m)
■ The most pessimistic time (b)

For example, the optimistic time for completing activity H is 2 days, the most likely time is 4 days, and the pessimistic time is 12 days. The next step is to calculate an expected time, which is determined as follows:

$$t_e \text{ (expected time)} = (a + 4m + b)/6$$

For example, for activity H, the expected time is

$$[2 + 4(4) + 12]/6 = 30/6 = 5 \text{ days}$$

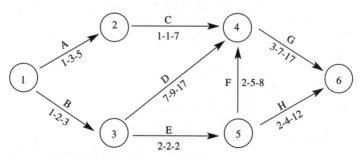

FIG. 19-8. *Network diagram.*

Note: This formula is based on the assumption that the uncertain activity times are best described by a *beta probability distribution*. This distribution assumption, which was judged to be reasonable by the developers of PERT, provides the time distribution for activity H as shown in Figure 19-9.

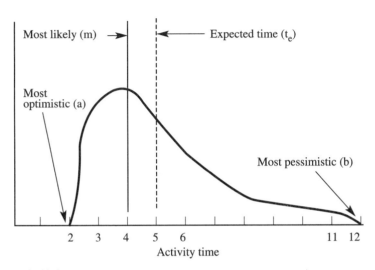

FIG. 19-9. *Activity time distribution for activity H.*

As a measure of variation (uncertainty) about the expected time, the standard deviation is calculated as follows:

$$\sigma = (b - a)/6$$

For example, the standard deviation of completion time for activity H is:

$$(12 - 2)/6 = 10/6 = 1.67 \text{ days}$$

Note: This formula is based on the notion that a standard deviation is approximately 1/6 of the difference between the extreme values of the distribution.

Expected activity times and their standard deviations are computed in this manner for all the activities of the network and arranged in the tabular format as follows.

Activity	Predecessors	a	m	b	t_e	σ
A	None	1	3	5	3.0	.67
B	None	1	2	3	2.0	.33
C	A	1	1	7	2.0	1.00
D	B	7	9	17	10.0	1.67
E	B	2	2	2	2.0	0.00
F	E	2	5	8	5.0	.67
G	C,D,F	3	7	17	8.0	2.33
H	E	2	4	12	5.0	1.67

To answer the first question, we need to determine the network's critical path. A path is a sequence of connected activities. In Figure 19-8, 1-2-4-6 would be an example of a path. The critical path for a project is the path that takes the longest amount of time. The sum of the estimated times for all activities on the critical path is the total time required to complete the project. These activities are "critical" because any delay in their completion will cause a delay in the project.

The time to do all the activities on the critical path represents the minimum amount of time needed for the completion of the project. Thus, to speed up the project, the activities along this path must be shortened. Activities not on the critical path are not critical, since they will be worked on simultaneously with critical-path activities and their completion could be delayed up to a point without delaying the project as a whole.

An easy way to find the critical path involves following two steps:
1. Identify all possible paths of a project and calculate their completion times.
2. Pick the one with the longest amount of completion time, which is the critical path.

(When the network is large and complex, we need a more systematic and efficient approach, which is beyond the scope of this book.)

In the example, we have:

Path	Completion time
A-C-G	13 days (3 + 2 + 8)
B-D-G	20 days (2 + 10 + 8)
B-E-F-G	17 days (2 + 2 + 5 + 8)
B-E-H	9 days (2 + 2 + 5)

The critical path is B-D-G, which means it takes 20 days to complete the project.

The next important information we want to obtain is "what is the chance that the project will be completed within a contract time—say, 21 days?" To answer the question, we introduce the standard deviation of total project time around the expected time, which is determined as follows:

$$\text{Standard deviation (project)} = \sqrt{\begin{array}{l}\text{the sum of the squares of the standard}\\ \text{deviations of all critical path activities}\end{array}}$$

Using this formula, the standard deviation of completion time (the path B-D-G) for the project is as follows:

$$\sqrt{(.33)^2 + (1.67)^2 + (2.33)^2} = \sqrt{.1089 + 2.7889 + 5.4289} = \sqrt{8.3267}$$
$$= 2.885 \text{ days}$$

Using the standard deviation and table of areas under the normal distribution curve (Table 5 of the Appendix), the probability of completing the project within any given time period can be determined. Assume the expected delivery time is 21 days. The first step is to compute z, which is the number of standard deviations from the mean represented by our given time of 21 days. The formula for z is:

$$z = (\text{delivery time} - \text{expected time})/\text{standard deviation}$$

$$z = (21 \text{ days} - 20 \text{ days})/2.885 \text{ days} = .35$$

The next step is to find the probability associated with the calculated value of z by referring to a table of areas under a normal curve.

From Appendix Table 5 we see the probability is .6368, which means there is close to a 64% chance that the project will be completed in less than 21 days.

To summarize what we have obtained:

1. The expected completion time of the project is 20 days.
2. There is a better-than-60% chance of finishing before 21 days. *(Note:* We can also obtain the chances of meeting any other deadline if we wish. All we need to do is change the delivery time and recalculate the z value.)
3. Activities B-D-G are on the critical path; they must be watched more closely than the others, for if they fall behind, the whole project falls behind.
4. If extra effort is needed to finish the project on time or

before the deadline, we have to borrow resources (such as money and labor) from any activity not on the critical path.

5. It is possible to reduce the completion time of one or more activities, which will require an extra expenditure of cost. The benefit from reducing the total completion time of a project by accelerated efforts on certain activities must be balanced against the extra cost of doing so. A related problem is to determine which activities must be accelerated to reduce the total project completion time. The critical path method (CPM), also known as PERT/COST, is widely used to deal with this subject.

It should be noted that PERT is a technique for project management and control. It is not an optimizing-decision model, since the decision to undertake a project is initially assumed. It won't evaluate an investment project according to its attractiveness or time specifications.

CHAPTER PERSPECTIVE

Quantitative applications and modeling in corporate cost management and analysis have been on the rise, coupled with the advent of microcomputers and software for various quantitative decision-making tools. Cost managers and analysts should take advantage of the advances in new technology to analyze and solve a variety of financial problems faced by the business.

Total Quality Management and Quality Costs

In order to be globally competitive in today's world-class manufacturing environment, firms place an increased emphasis on quality and productivity. Total quality management (TQM) is an effort in this direction. Simply put, it is a system for creating a competitive advantage by focusing the organization on what is important to the customer. Total quality management can be broken down into:

1. *Total*—the whole organization is involved and understands that customer satisfaction is everyone's job.
2. *Quality*—the extent to which products and services satisfy the requirements of internal and external customers.
3. *Management*—the leadership, infrastructure, and resources that support employees as they meet the needs of those customers.

After studying this chapter, you should be able to:

■ Define quality and explain how quality of design and quality of conformance differ.

■ Describe TQM and explain its relationship to quality costs.

■ Identify and discuss the four types of quality costs.

■ Explain the difference between the tranditional view of acceptable quality level and the zero-defect view.

■ Prepare four different types of quality performance reports.

QUALITY DEFINED

A quality product is a product that conforms to customer expectations. Generally, there are two types of product quality.

1. Quality of design refers to quality differences of products that serve the same function but have different design specifications, such as the type and quality of materials used in the product.

   Usually, higher design quality results in higher manufacturing costs and higher selling prices. For example, 14 karat gold jewelry has a higher design value than the same jewelry that is gold plated.

2. Quality of conformance is a measure of how a product meets its design specifications. Is the product manufactured as the design specifies? When quality experts refer to improving quality, they are referring to reducing the incidence of nonconformance. Quality refers to doing it right the first time.

TOTAL QUALITY MANAGEMENT (TQM)

TQM is supported by two key beliefs that quality is what the customer says it is, and that it must be thoroughly integrated into the very fabric of the organization, including its basic strategies, culture, and management systems. It is essentially an endless quest for perfect quality. It is a *zero-defects* approach. It views the optimal level of quality costs as the level where zero defects are produced. This approach to quality is opposed to the traditional belief, called *acceptable quality level (AQL)*, which allows a predetermined level of defective units to be produced and sold. AQL is the level at which the number of defects allowed minimizes total quality costs. The rationale behind the traditional view is that there is a tradeoff between prevention and appraisal costs and failure costs. As you increase prevention and appraisal costs, you expect to see failure costs decrease. Figure 20-1 graphically illustrates the relationship between these two cost components under two different views.

Studies indicate that the total cost of poor quality, or the cost of not doing the right things right the first time, is 20% of gross sales for manufacturing companies and 30% for service industries. If U.S. production of goods and services is estimated at $4.5 trillion, as it was in 1994, then the potential for savings from improved quality is a staggering almost $1 trillion that can be saved or redirected for better use. Quality experts maintain that the optimal quality level should be about 2.5% of sales. The accounting department should be a major force in the firm that keeps track of and reports quality costs.

Principles of TQM

Making a product right the first time is one of the principal objectives of TQM. Implementing a successful TQM program will in fact reduce costs rather than increase them. There is no question that better quality will result in better productivity. This is based on the principle that when less time is spent on rework or repair, more time is available for manufacturing, which will increase productivity.

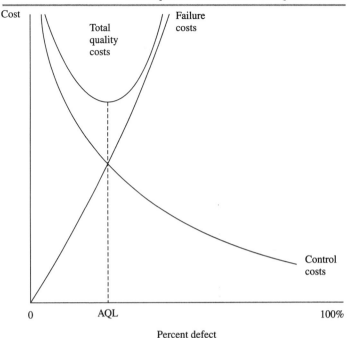

FIG. 20-1. *Traditional view.*

When an organization maintains accurate records of its cost of quality, TQM will demonstrate that effective quality assurance geared toward prevention versus correction will pay for itself. A good example of this is the situation in which it is possible to eliminate 100% inspection with a good statistical process control (SPC) program. Elimination of high reject rates results in fewer products being repaired, reworked, or scrapped with the obvious reductions in cost.

Tying the cost of quality to TQM is necessary in order to motivate management, which is cost motivated in both industry and government. In a TQM environment, management will start utilizing the cost data to measure the success of the program. The corporate financial planner can determine that overall product costs are being reduced by the TQM program. Given this success in the prevention of defects, the following failure costs will be reduced or eliminated:

1. Rework or repair.
2. Inspection of rework.

3. Testing of rework.
4. Warranty costs.
5. Returned material.
6. Discounts, adjustments, and allowances.

It is obvious that the cost of prevention in TQM is minor when taken against the above-listed failure costs.

A checklist of TQM features are as follows:

- A systematic way to improve products and services.
- A structured approach in identifying and solving problems.
- Long term.
- Conveyed by management's actions.
- Supported by statistical quality control.
- Practiced by everyone.

Elements of TQM

The major elements of TQM are straightforward and embrace a commonsense approach to management. However, each of the individual elements must be integrated into a structured whole to succeed. The elements are as follows:

A Focus on the Customer. Every functional unit has a customer, whether it be an external consumer or an internal unit. TQM advocates that managers and employees become so customer-focused that they continually find new ways to meet or exceed customers' expectations. We must accept that quality is defined by the customer. Meeting the customer's needs and expectations is the strategic goal of TQM.

A Long-term Commitment. Experience in the United States and abroad shows that substantial gains come only after management makes a long-term commitment, usually five years or more, in improving quality. Customer focus must be constantly renewed to keep that goal foremost.

Top Management Support and Direction. Top management must be the driving force behind TQM. Senior managers must exhibit personal support by using quality-improvement concepts in their management style, incorporating quality in their strategic-planning process, and providing financial and staff support.

Employee Involvement. Full employee participation is also an integral part of the process. Each employee must be a partner in achieving quality goals. Teamwork involves managers, supervisors, and employees in improving service delivery, solving systemic problems, and correcting errors in all parts of work processes.

Effective and Renewed Communications. The power of internal communication, both vertical and horizontal, is central to employee involvement. Regular and meaningful communication from all levels must occur. This will allow an agency to adjust its ways of operating and reinforce the commitment of TQM at the same time.

Reliance on Standards and Measures. Measurement is the springboard to involvement, allowing the organization to initiate corrective action, set priorities, and evaluate progress. Standards and measures should reflect customer requirements and changes that need to be introduced in the internal business of providing those requirements. The emphasis is on "doing the right thing right the first time."

Commitment to Training. Training is absolutely vital to the success of TQM. The process usually begins with awareness training for teams of top-level managers. This is followed by courses for teams of mid-level managers, and finally by courses for nonmanagers. Awareness training is followed by an identification of areas of concentration, or of functional areas where TQM will first be introduced. Implementing TQM requires additional skills training, which is also conducted in teams.

Importance of Rewards and Recognition. Most companies practicing TQM have given wide latitude to managers in issuing rewards and recognition. Here, a common theme is that individual financial rewards are not as appropriate as awards to groups or team members, since most successes are group achievements.

Costs of Quality
Market shares of many U.S. firms have eroded because foreign firms have been able to sell higher-quality products at lower prices. In order to be competitive, U.S. firms have placed an increased emphasis on quality and productivity in order to:
1. produce savings such as reducing rework costs, and
2. improve product quality.

Studies indicate that costs of quality for American companies are typically 20–30% of sales. Quality experts maintain that the optimal quality level should be about 2.5% of sales.

Costs of quality are costs that occur because poor quality may exist or actually does exist. More specifically, quality costs are the total of the costs incurred by (1) investing in the prevention of nonconformances to requirements; (2) appraising a product or service for conformance to requirements; and (3) failure to meet requirements.

Quality costs are classified into three broad categories (see Fig. 20–1): prevention, appraisal, and failure costs.

Prevention Costs. These are costs that are incurred to prevent defects. Amounts spent on quality training programs, researching customer needs, quality circles, and improved production equipment are considered in prevention costs. Expenditures made for prevention will minimize the costs that will be incurred for appraisal and failure.

Appraisal Costs. These are costs incurred for monitoring or inspection; these costs compensate for mistakes not eliminated through prevention.

Failure Costs. These may be internal, such as scrap and rework costs and reinspection, or external, such as product returns due to quality problems, warranty costs, lost sales due to poor product performance, and complaint department costs. Figure 2 summarizes these quality cost components.

Two Different Views Concerning Optimal Quality Costs

There are two views concerning optimal quality costs:
1. Traditional view that uses an acceptable quality level.
2. World-class view that uses total quality control.

Optimal Distribution of Quality Costs: Traditional View. The traditional approach uses an acceptable quality level (AQL) that permits a predetermined level of defective units to be produced and sold. AQL is the level where the number of defects allowed minimizes total quality costs. The reasoning of the traditional approach is that there is a tradeoff between failure costs and prevention and appraisal costs. As prevention and appraisal costs increase, internal and external failure costs are expected to decrease. As long as the decrease in failure costs is greater than the corresponding increase in prevention and failure costs, a company should continue increasing its efforts to prevent or detect defective units.

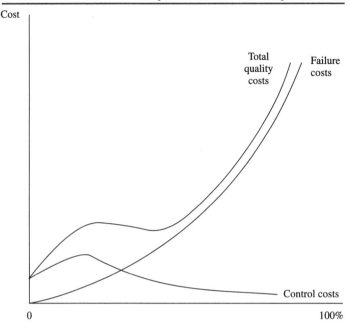

FIG. 20-2. *World-class view.*

Optimal Distribution of Quality Costs: World-Class View. The world-class view uses total quality control and views the optimal level of quality costs as the level where zero defects are produced. The zero-defects approach uses a quality performance standard that requires:

1. Products to be produced according to specifications.
2. Services to be provided according to requirements.

Zero defects reflects a total quality control philosophy used in JIT manufacturing.

Quality Cost and Performance Reports

The first step in a quality cost reporting system is to prepare a detailed listing of actual quality costs by category. Furthermore, each category of quality costs is expressed as a percentage of sales. This serves two purposes:

1. It permits managers to assess the financial impact of quality costs.
2. It reveals the relative emphasis placed on each category.

QUALITY COSTS—GENERAL DESCRIPTION

Prevention Costs. These are the costs of all activities specifically designed to prevent poor quality in products or services. Examples are the costs of new product review, quality planning, supplier capability surveys, process capability evaluations, quality improvement team meetings, quality improvement projects, and quality education and training.

Appraisal Costs. The costs associated with measuring, evaluating, or auditing products or services to assure conformance to quality standards and performance requirements. These include the costs of incoming and source inspection/test of purchased material, in-process and final inspection/test, product, process, or service audits, calibration of measuring and test equipment, and the costs of associated supplies and materials.

Failure Costs. The costs resulting from products or services not conforming to requirements or customer/user needs. Failure costs are divided into internal and external failure cost categories.

Internal Failure Costs. Failure costs occurring prior to delivery or shipment of the product, or the furnishing of a service, to the customer. Examples are the costs of scrap, rework, reinspection, retesting, material review, and downgrading.

External Failure Costs. Failure costs occurring after delivery or shipment of the product, and during or after furnishing of a service, to the customer. Examples are the costs of processing customer complaints, customer returns, warranty claims, and product recalls.

Total Quality Costs. The sum of the above costs. It represents the difference between the actual cost of a product or service, and what the reduced cost would be if there was no possibility of substandard service, failure of products, or defects in their manufacture.

How to Use Quality Cost Reports

Quality cost reports can be used to point out the strengths and weaknesses of a quality system. Improvement teams can use them to describe the monetary benefits and ramifications of proposed changes. Return-on-investment (ROI) models and other financial analyses can be constructed directly from quality cost data to justify proposals to management. In practice, quality costs can define activities of quality program and quality improvement efforts in a language that management can understand and act on—dollars.

The negative effect on profits, resulting from a product or service of less than acceptable quality or from ineffective quality management, is almost always dynamic. Once started, it continues to mushroom until ultimately the company finds itself in serious financial difficulty due to the two-pronged impact of an unheeded increase in quality costs coupled with a declining performance image. Management that clearly understands this understands the economics of quality.

In the quality cost report, quality costs are grouped into one of four categories:

1. Prevention costs.
2. Appraisal costs.
3. Internal failure costs.
4. External failure costs.

In addition, each category of quality costs is expressed as a percentage of sales. There are four types of performance reports to measure a company's quality improvement. They are:

Interim Quality Performance Report. It measures the progress achieved within the period relative to the planned level of progress for the period (see Figure 20-3).

One-Year Quality Trend Report. It compares the current year's quality cost ratio with the previous year's ratio. More specifically, it compares (1) the current year's variable quality cost ratio with the previous year's variable quality cost ratio, and the current year's actual fixed quality costs with the previous year's actual fixed quality costs (see Figure 20-4).

Multiple-Period Quality Report. It shows the overall trend of quality costs by category since the inception of the quality enhancement program (see Figure 20-5).

Allison Products
Quality Cost Report
for the Year Ended March 31, 20X2

	Quality Costs		Percentage of Sale[a]
Prevention costs:			
Quality training	$30,000		
Reliability engineering	79,000	$109,000	3.73%
Appraisal costs:			
Materials inspection	$19,000		
Product acceptance	10,000		
Process acceptance	35,000	$64,000	2.19%
Internal failure costs:			
Scrap	$40,000		
Rework	34,000	$74,000	2.53%
External failure costs:			
Customer complaints	$24,000		
Warranty	24,000		
Repair	15,000	$63,000	2.16%
Total quality costs		$310,000	10.62%[b]

[a] Actual sales of $2,920,000.
[b] $310,000/$2,920,000 = 10.62 percent. Difference is rounding error.

FIG. 20-3. *Quality cost report.*

Long-range Quality Performance Report. It compares the current year's actual quality costs with the firm's intended long-range quality goal (see Figure 20-6).

Activity-Based Management and Optimal Quality Costs

Activity-based management supports the zero-defect view of quality costs. Activity-based management classifies activities as: (1) value-added activities and (2) nonvalue-added activities.

■ Quality-related activities (internal and external failure activities, prevention activities, and appraisal activities) can be classified as value-added and nonvalue-added.

■ Internal and external failure activities and their associated costs are nonvalue-added and should be eliminated.

■ Prevention activities that are performed efficiently are value-added. (Costs caused by inefficiency in prevention activities are nonvalue-added costs.)

■ Appraisal activities may be value-added or nonvalue-added, depending upon the activity. For example, quality audits may serve a value-added objective.

Allison Products
Interim Standard Performance Report
for the Year Ended March 31, 20X2

	Actual Costs	Budgeted Costs[a]	Variance
Prevention costs:			
Quality training	$30,000	$30,000	$0
Reliability engineering	79,000	80,000	1,000 F
Total prevention	$109,000	$110,000	$1,000 F
Appraisal costs:			
Materials inspection	$19,000	$28,000	$9,000 F
Product acceptance	10,000	15,000	5,000 F
Process acceptance	35,000	35,000	0
Total appraisal	$64,000	$78,000	$14,000 F
Internal failure costs:			
Scrap	$40,000	$44,000	$4,000 F
Rework	34,000	36,500	2,500 F
Total internal failure	$74,000	$80,500	$6,500 F
External failure costs:			
Fixed:			
Customer complaints	$24,000	$25,000	$1,000
Variable:			
Warranty	24,000	20,000	(4,000) U
Repair	15,000	17,500	2,500 F
Total external failure	$63,000	$62,500	($500) U
Total quality costs	$310,000	$331,000	$21,000 F
Percentage of actual sales[b]	10.62%	11.34%	0.72% F

[a] Based on actual sales.
[b] Actual sales of $2,920,000.

FIG. 20-4. *Interim standard performance report.*

Once the quality-related activities are identified for each category, resource drivers can be used to improve cost assignments to individual activities. Root or process drivers can also be identified and used to help managers understand what is causing the cost of the activities.

Using Quality Cost Information

The principal objective of reporting quality costs is to improve and facilitate managerial planning, control, and decision making.

Potential uses of quality cost information include:
1. Quality program implementation decisions.
2. Evaluation of the effectiveness of quality programs.

Allison Products
Quality Cost, One-Year Trend
for the Year Ended March 31, 20X2

	Actual Costs 20X2[a]	Budgeted Costs 20X1	Variance
Prevention costs:			
Quality training	$30,000	$36,000	$6,000 F
Reliability engineering	79,000	120,000	41,000 F
Total prevention	$109,000	$156,000	$47,000 F
Appraisal costs:			
Materials inspection	$19,000	$33,600	$14,600 F
Product acceptance	10,000	16,800	6,800 F
Process acceptance	35,000	39,200	4,200 F
Total appraisal	$64,000	$89,600	$25,600 F
Internal failure costs:			
Scrap	$40,000	$48,000	$8,000 F
Rework	34,000	40,000	6,000 F
Total internal failure	$74,000	$88,000	$14,000 F
External failure costs:			
Fixed:			
Customer complaints	$24,000	$33,000	$9,000 F
Variable:			
Warranty	24,000	23,000	(1,000) U
Repair	15,000	16,400	1,400 F
Total external failure	$63,000	$72,400	$9,400 F
Total quality costs	$310,000	$406,000	$96,000 F
Percentage of actual sales	10.62%	13.90%	3.29% F

[a] Based on actual sales = $2,920,000.

FIG. 20-5. *Quality cost, one-year trend.*

3. Strategic pricing decisions; for example, improved reporting of quality costs might be used by managers to target specific quality costs for reductions. A reduction in quality costs might enable a firm to reduce its selling price, improve its competitive position, and increase market share.
4. Inclusion of quality costs in cost-volume-profit analysis; for example, overlooking quality cost savings results in a higher break-even and possible rejection of a profitable project.

The control process involves comparing actual performance with quality standards. This comparison provides feedback that can be used to take corrective action, if necessary.

Allison Products
Long-range Performance Report
for the Year Ended March 31, 20X2

	Actual Costs	Target Costs[a]	Variance
Prevention costs:			
Quality training	$30,000	$14,000	($16,000) U
Reliability engineering	79,000	39,000	(40,000) U
Total prevention	$109,000	$53,000	($56,000) U
Appraisal costs:			
Materials inspection	$19,000	$7,900	($11,100) U
Product acceptance	10,000	0	(10,000) U
Process acceptance	35,000	12,000	(23,000) U
Total appraisal	$64,000	$19,900	($44,100) U
Internal failure costs:			
Scrap	$40,000	$0	($40,000) U
Rework	34,000	0	(34,000) U
Total internal failure	$74,000	$0	($74,000) U
External failure costs:			
Fixed:			
Customer complaints	$24,000	$0	($24,000) U
Variable:			
Warranty	24,000	0	(24,000) U
Repair	15,000	0	(15,000) U
Total external failure	$63,000	$0	($63,000) U
Total quality costs	$310,000	$72,900	($237,100) U
Percentage of actual sales	10.62%	2.50%	−8.12% U

[a] Based on actual sales of $2,920,000. These costs are value-added costs.

FIG. 20-6. *Long-range performance report.*

CHAPTER PERSPECTIVE

In today's tough competition, TQM is "the minimum requirement for staying in the game." Comparing total quality to the current hot managerial idea—reeningeering, both aim to increase productivity by rethinking processes. Reengineering may be more likely to come up with bold solutions because it starts with the question "Should we still be doing this at all?" rather than TQM's "How can we do this cheaper, faster, and better?"

In the long run, quality can be achieved only by involving the total organization in continuous improvement. TQM requires changes in how we lead, what we communicate, what is rewarded, and how decisions are made, as well as how accurately quality costs are accounted for and reported.

Appendix

The Appendix contains present value and future value tables so as to take into account the time value of money when analyzing costs. Other tables useful in cost analysis are also provided, including normal distribution and statistical sampling tables.

Table 1
The Future Value of $1.00
(Computed Amount of $1.00)

$$(1 + i)^n = T_1 (i, n)$$

Periods	4%	6%	8%	10%	12%	14%	20%
1	1.040	1.060	1.080	1.100	1.120	1.140	1.200
2	1.082	1.124	1.166	1.210	1.254	1.300	1.440
3	1.125	1.191	1.260	1.331	1.405	1.482	1.728
4	1.170	1.263	1.361	1.464	1.574	1.689	2.074
5	1.217	1.338	1.469	1.611	1.762	1.925	2.488
6	1.265	1.419	1.587	1.772	1.974	2.195	2.986
7	1.316	1.504	1.714	1.949	2.211	2.502	3.583
8	1.369	1.594	1.851	2.144	2.476	2.853	4.300
9	1.423	1.690	1.999	2.359	2.773	3.252	5.160
10	1.480	1.791	2.159	2.594	3.106	3.707	6.192
11	1.540	1.898	2.332	2.853	3.479	4.226	7.430
12	1.601	2.012	2.518	3.139	3.896	4.818	8.916

Periods	4%	6%	8%	10%	12%	14%	20%
13	1.665	2.133	2.720	3.452	4.364	5.492	10.699
14	1.732	2.261	2.937	3.798	4.887	6.261	12.839
15	1.801	2.397	3.172	4.177	5.474	7.138	15.407
16	1.873	2.540	3.426	4.595	6.130	8.137	18.488
17	1.948	2.693	3.700	5.055	6.866	9.277	22.186
18	2.026	2.854	3.996	5.560	7.690	10.575	26.623
19	2.107	3.026	4.316	6.116	8.613	12.056	31.948
20	2.191	3.207	4.661	5.728	9.646	13.743	38.338
30	3.243	5.744	10.063	17.450	29.960	50.950	237.380
40	4.801	10.286	21.725	45.260	93.051	188.880	1469.800

Table 2
The Future Value of an Annuity of $1.00*
(Compounded Amount of an Annuity of $1.00)

$$\frac{(1+i)^n - 1}{i} = T_2(i, n)$$

Periods	4%	6%	8%	10%	12%	14%	20%
1	1.000	1.000	1.000	1.000	1.000	1.000	1.000
2	2.040	2.060	2.080	2.100	2.120	2.140	2.200
3	3.122	3.184	3.246	3.310	3.374	3.440	3.640
4	4.247	4.375	4.506	4.641	4.779	4.921	5.368
5	5.416	5.637	5.867	6.105	6.353	6.610	7.442
6	6.633	6.975	7.336	7.716	8.115	8.536	9.930
7	7.898	8.394	8.923	9.487	10.089	10.730	12.916
8	9.214	9.898	10.637	11.436	12.300	13.233	16.499
9	10.583	11.491	12.488	13.580	14.776	16.085	20.799
10	12.006	13.181	14.487	15.938	17.549	19.337	25.959
11	13.486	14.972	16.646	18.531	20.655	23.045	32.150
12	15.026	16.870	18.977	21.385	24.133	37.271	39.580

Periods	4%	6%	8%	10%	12%	14%	20%
13	16.627	18.882	21.495	24.523	28.029	32.089	48.497
14	18.292	21.015	24.215	27.976	32.393	37.581	59.196
15	20.024	23.276	27.152	31.773	37.280	43.842	72.035
16	21.825	25.673	30.324	35.950	42.753	50.980	87.442
17	23.698	28.213	33.750	40.546	48.884	59.118	105.930
18	25.645	30.906	37.450	45.600	55.750	68.394	128.120
19	27.671	33.760	41.446	51.160	63.440	78.969	154.740
20	29.778	36.778	45.762	57.276	75.052	91.025	186.690
30	56.085	79.058	113.283	164.496	241.330	356.790	1181.900
40	95.026	154.762	259.057	442.597	767.090	1342.000	7343.900

*Payments (or receipts) at the *end* of each period.

Table 3
Present Value of $1.00

$$\frac{1}{(1+i)^n} = T_3\,(i, n)$$

Periods	4%	6%	8%	10%	12%	14%	16%	18%	20%	22%	24%	26%	28%	30%	40%
1	.962	.943	.926	.909	.893	.877	.862	.847	.833	.820	.806	.794	.781	.769	.714
2	.925	.890	.857	.826	.797	.769	.743	.718	.694	.672	.650	.630	.610	.592	.510
3	.889	.840	.794	.751	.712	.675	.641	.609	.579	.551	.524	.500	.477	.455	.364
4	.855	.792	.735	.683	.636	.592	.552	.516	.482	.451	.423	.397	.373	.350	.260
5	.822	.747	.681	.621	.567	.519	.476	.437	.402	.370	.341	.315	.291	.269	.186
6	.790	.705	.630	.564	.507	.456	.410	.370	.335	.303	.275	.250	.227	.207	.133
7	.760	.665	.583	.513	.452	.400	.354	.314	.279	.249	.222	.198	.178	.159	.095
8	.731	.627	.540	.467	.404	.351	.305	.266	.233	.204	.179	.157	.139	.123	.068
9	.703	.592	.500	.424	.361	.308	.263	.225	.194	.167	.144	.125	.108	.094	.048
10	.676	.558	.463	.386	.322	.270	.227	.191	.162	.137	.116	.099	.085	.073	.035
11	.650	.527	.429	.350	.287	.237	.195	.162	.135	.112	.094	.079	.066	.056	.025
12	.625	.497	.397	.319	.257	.208	.168	.137	.112	.092	.076	.062	.052	.043	.018
13	.601	.469	.368	.290	.229	.182	.145	.116	.093	.075	.061	.050	.040	.033	.013
14	.577	.442	.340	.263	.205	.160	.125	.099	.078	.062	.049	.039	.032	.025	.009
15	.555	.417	.315	.239	.183	.140	.108	.084	.065	.051	.040	.031	.025	.020	.006

Periods	4%	6%	8%	10%	12%	14%	16%	18%	20%	22%	24%	26%	28%	30%	40%
16	.534	.394	.292	.218	.163	.123	.093	.071	.054	.042	.032	.025	.019	.015	.005
17	.513	.371	.270	.198	.146	.108	.080	.060	.045	.034	.026	.020	.015	.012	.003
18	.494	.350	.250	.180	.130	.095	.069	.051	.038	.028	.021	.016	.012	.009	.002
19	.475	.331	.232	.164	.116	.083	.060	.043	.031	.023	.017	.012	.009	.007	.002
20	.456	.312	.215	.149	.104	.073	.051	.037	.026	.019	.014	.010	.007	.005	.001
21	.439	.294	.199	.135	.093	.064	.044	.031	.022	.015	.011	.008	.006	.004	.001
22	.422	.278	.184	.123	.083	.056	.038	.026	.018	.013	.009	.006	.004	.003	.001
23	.406	.262	.170	.112	.074	.049	.033	.022	.015	.010	.007	.005	.003	.002	
24	.390	.247	.158	.102	.066	.043	.028	.019	.013	.008	.006	.004	.003	.002	
25	.375	.233	.146	.092	.059	.038	.024	.016	.010	.007	.005	.003	.002	.001	
26	.361	.220	.135	.084	.053	.033	.021	.014	.009	.006	.004	.002	.002	.001	
27	.347	.207	.125	.076	.047	.029	.018	.011	.007	.005	.003	.002	.001	.001	
28	.333	.196	.116	.069	.042	.026	.016	.010	.006	.004	.002	.002	.001	.001	
29	.321	.185	.107	.063	.037	.022	.014	.008	.005	.003	.002	.001	.001	.001	
30	.308	.174	.099	.057	.033	.020	.012	.007	.004	.003	.002	.001	.001	.001	
40	.208	.097	.046	.022	.011	.005	.003	.001	.001						

Table 4
Present Value of an Annuity of \$1.00*

$$\frac{1}{i}\left[1 - \frac{1}{(1+i)^n}\right] = T_4\,(i, n)$$

Periods	4%	6%	8%	10%	12%	14%	16%	18%	20%	22%	24%	25%	26%	28%	30%	40%
1	0.962	0.943	0.926	0.909	0.893	0.877	0.862	0.847	0.833	0.820	0.806	0.800	0.794	0.781	0.769	0.714
2	1.886	1.883	1.783	1.736	1.690	1.647	1.605	1.566	1.528	1.492	1.457	1.440	1.424	1.392	1.361	1.224
3	2.775	2.673	2.577	2.487	2.402	2.322	2.246	2.174	2.106	2.042	1.981	1.952	1.923	1.868	1.816	1.589
4	3.630	3.465	3.312	3.170	3.037	2.914	2.798	2.690	2.589	2.494	2.404	2.362	2.320	2.241	2.166	1.849
5	4.452	4.212	3.993	3.791	3.605	3.433	3.274	3.127	2.991	2.864	2.745	2.689	2.635	2.532	2.436	2.035
6	5.242	4.917	4.623	4.355	4.111	3.889	3.685	3.498	3.326	3.167	3.020	2.951	2.885	2.759	2.643	2.168
7	6.002	5.582	5.206	4.868	4.564	4.288	4.039	3.812	3.605	3.416	3.242	3.161	3.083	2.937	2.802	2.263
8	6.733	6.210	5.747	5.335	4.968	4.639	4.344	4.078	3.837	3.619	3.421	3.329	3.241	3.076	2.925	2.331
9	7.435	6.802	6.247	5.759	5.328	4.946	4.607	4.303	4.031	3.786	3.566	3.463	3.366	3.184	3.019	2.379
10	8.111	7.360	6.710	6.145	5.650	5.216	4.833	4.494	4.192	3.923	3.682	3.571	3.465	3.269	3.092	2.414
11	8.760	7.887	7.139	6.495	5.938	5.453	5.029	4.656	4.327	4.035	3.776	3.656	3.544	3.335	3.147	2.438
12	9.385	8.384	7.536	6.814	6.194	5.660	5.197	4.793	4.439	4.127	3.851	3.725	3.606	3.387	3.190	2.456
13	9.986	8.853	7.904	7.103	6.424	5.842	5.342	4.910	4.533	4.203	3.912	3.780	3.656	3.427	3.223	2.468
14	10.563	9.295	8.244	7.367	6.628	6.002	6.468	5.008	4.611	4.265	3.962	3.824	3.695	3.459	3.249	2.477
15	11.118	9.712	8.559	7.606	6.811	6.142	5.575	5.092	4.675	4.315	4.001	3.859	3.726	3.483	3.268	2.484

Periods	4%	6%	8%	10%	12%	14%	16%	18%	20%	22%	24%	25%	26%	28%	30%	40%
16	11.652	10.106	8.851	7.824	6.974	6.265	5.669	5.162	4.730	4.357	4.033	3.887	3.751	3.503	3.283	2.489
17	12.166	10.477	9.122	8.022	7.120	6.373	5.749	5.222	4.775	4.391	4.059	3.910	3.771	3.518	3.295	2.492
18	12.659	10.828	9.372	8.201	7.250	6.467	5.818	5.273	4.812	4.419	4.080	3.928	3.786	3.529	3.304	2.494
19	13.134	11.158	9.604	8.365	7.366	6.550	5.877	5.316	4.844	4.442	4.097	3.942	3.799	3.539	3.311	2.496
20	13.590	11.470	9.818	8.514	7.469	6.623	5.929	5.353	4.870	4.460	4.110	3.954	3.808	3.546	3.316	2.497
21	14.029	11.764	10.017	8.649	7.562	6.687	5.973	5.384	4.891	4.476	4.121	3.963	3.816	3.551	3.320	2.498
22	14.451	12.042	10.201	8.772	7.645	6.743	6.011	5.410	4.909	4.488	4.130	3.970	3.822	3.556	3.323	2.498
23	14.857	12.303	10.371	8.883	7.718	6.792	6.044	5.432	4.925	4.499	4.137	3.976	3.827	3.559	3.325	2.499
24	15.247	12.550	10.529	8.985	7.784	6.835	6.073	5.451	4.937	4.507	4.143	3.981	3.831	3.562	3.327	2.499
25	15.622	12.783	10.675	9.077	7.843	6.873	6.097	5.467	4.948	4.514	4.147	3.985	3.834	3.564	3.329	2.499
26	15.983	13.003	10.810	9.161	7.896	6.906	6.118	5.480	4.956	4.520	4.151	3.988	3.837	3.566	3.330	2.500
27	16.330	13.211	10.935	9.237	7.943	6.935	6.136	5.492	4.964	4.524	4.154	3.990	3.839	3.567	3.331	2.500
28	16.663	13.406	11.051	9.307	7.984	6.961	6.152	5.502	4.970	4.528	4.157	3.992	3.840	3.568	3.331	2.500
29	16.984	13.591	11.158	9.370	8.022	6.983	6.166	5.510	4.975	4.531	4.159	3.994	3.841	3.569	3.332	2.500
30	17.292	13.755	11.258	9.427	8.055	7.003	6.177	5.517	4.979	4.534	4.160	3.995	3.842	3.569	3.332	2.500
40	19.793	15.046	11.925	9.779	8.244	7.105	6.234	5.548	4.997	4.544	4.166	3.999	3.846	3.571	3.333	2.500

*Payments (or receipts) at the *end* of each period.

Table 5
Normal Distribution Table

Areas Under the Normal Curve

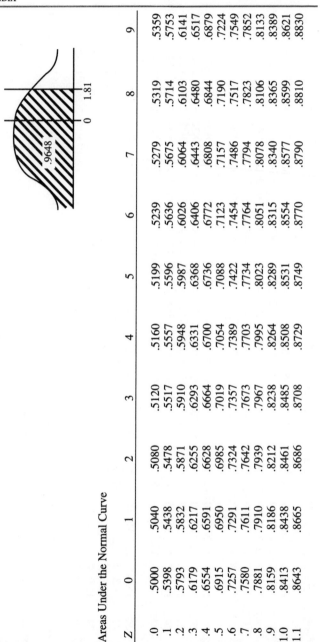

Z	0	1	2	3	4	5	6	7	8	9
.0	.5000	.5040	.5080	.5120	.5160	.5199	.5239	.5279	.5319	.5359
.1	.5398	.5438	.5478	.5517	.5557	.5596	.5636	.5675	.5714	.5753
.2	.5793	.5832	.5871	.5910	.5948	.5987	.6026	.6064	.6103	.6141
.3	.6179	.6217	.6255	.6293	.6331	.6368	.6406	.6443	.6480	.6517
.4	.6554	.6591	.6628	.6664	.6700	.6736	.6772	.6808	.6844	.6879
.5	.6915	.6950	.6985	.7019	.7054	.7088	.7123	.7157	.7190	.7224
.6	.7257	.7291	.7324	.7357	.7389	.7422	.7454	.7486	.7517	.7549
.7	.7580	.7611	.7642	.7673	.7703	.7734	.7764	.7794	.7823	.7852
.8	.7881	.7910	.7939	.7967	.7995	.8023	.8051	.8078	.8106	.8133
.9	.8159	.8186	.8212	.8238	.8264	.8289	.8315	.8340	.8365	.8389
1.0	.8413	.8438	.8461	.8485	.8508	.8531	.8554	.8577	.8599	.8621
1.1	.8643	.8665	.8686	.8708	.8729	.8749	.8770	.8790	.8810	.8830

Z	0	1	2	3	4	5	6	7	8	9
1.2	.8849	.8869	.8888	.8907	.8925	.8944	.8962	.8980	.8997	.9015
1.3	.9032	.9049	.9066	.9082	.9099	.9115	.9131	.9147	.9162	.9177
1.4	.9192	.9207	.9222	.9236	.9251	.9265	.9278	.9292	.9306	.9319
1.5	.9332	.9345	.9357	.9370	.9382	.9394	.9406	.9418	.9430	.9441
1.6	.9452	.9463	.9474	.9484	.9495	.9505	.9515	.9525	.9535	.9545
1.7	.9554	.9564	.9573	.9582	.9591	.9599	.9608	.9616	.9625	.9633
1.8	.9641	.9648	.9656	.9664	.9671	.9678	.9686	.9693	.9700	.9706
1.9	.9713	.9719	.9726	.9732	.9738	.9744	.9750	.9756	.9762	.9767
2.0	.9772	.9778	.9783	.9788	.9793	.9798	.9803	.9808	.9812	.9817
2.1	.9821	.9826	.9830	.9834	.9838	.9842	.9846	.9850	.9854	.9857
2.2	.9861	.9864	.9868	.9871	.9874	.9878	.9881	.9884	.9887	.9890
2.3	.9893	.9896	.9898	.9901	.9904	.9906	.9909	.9911	.9913	.9916
2.4	.9918	.9920	.9922	.9925	.9927	.9929	.9931	.9932	.9934	.9936
2.5	.9938	.9940	.9941	.9943	.9945	.9946	.9948	.9949	.9951	.9952
2.6	.9953	.9955	.9956	.9957	.9959	.9960	.9961	.9962	.9963	.9964
2.7	.9965	.9966	.9967	.9968	.9969	.9970	.9971	.9972	.9973	.9974
2.8	.9974	.9975	.9976	.9977	.9977	.9978	.9979	.9979	.9980	.9981
2.9	.9981	.9982	.9982	.9983	.9984	.9984	.9985	.9985	.9986	.9986
3.	.9987	.9990	.9993	.9995	.9997	.9998	.9998	.9999	.9999	1.0000

Glossary

A, B, and C depending on the value and importance of the item.

ABC analysis inventory control system that divides the inventory into three classes.

activity-based costing (ABC) a costing system which first traces costs to activities and then to products. It separates overhead costs into overhead cost pools, where each cost pool is associated with a different cost driver. A predetermined overhead rate is computed for each cost pool and each cost driver. In consequence, this method has enhanced product costing accuracy.

activity-based management (ABM) systemwide, integrated approach that focuses management's attention on activities with the goal of improving customer value, reducing costs, and the resulting profit.

analysis of variances (variance analysis) analysis and investigation of causes for variances between standard costs and actual costs. A variance is considered favorable if actual costs are less than standard costs; it is unfavorable if actual costs exceed standard costs. Unfavorable variances are the ones that need further investigation for their causes.

benchmarking searching for new and better procedures by comparing your own procedures to that of the very best.

beta distribution probability distribution often used to describe activity times.

break-even analysis a branch of cost-volume-profit (CVP) analysis that determines the break-even sales, which is the level of sales where total costs equal total revenue.

business process reengineering (BPR) approach aiming at making revolutionary changes as opposed to evolutionary changes by eliminating nonvalue-added steps in a business process and computerizing the remaining steps to achieve desired outcomes.

capacity rate at which work is capable of being produced.

capital budget a budget or plan of proposed acquisitions and replacements of long-term assets and their financing. A capital budget is developed using a variety of capital budgeting techniques such as the discount cash flow method.

capital rationing the problem of selecting the mix of acceptable projects that provides the highest overall net present value (NPV) where a company has a limit on the budget for capital spending.

cash budget a budget for cash planning and control presenting expected cash inflow and outflow for a designated time period. The cash budget helps management keep cash balances in reasonable relationship to its needs. It aids in avoiding idle cash and possible cash shortages.

cash flow (1) cash receipts minus cash disbursements from a given operation or asset for a given period. Cash flow and cash inflow are often used interchangeably. (2) the monetary value of the expected benefits and costs of a project. It may be in the form of cash savings in operating costs or the difference between additional dollars received and additional dollars paid out for a given period.

coefficient of determination a statistical measure of how good the estimated regression equation is. Simply put, it is a measure of "goodness of fit" in the regression.

common costs expense shared by different departments, products, jobs, also called joint costs or indirect costs.

continuous improvement (CI) also called *Kaizen* in Japanese, neverending effort for improvement in every part of the firm relative to all of its deliverables to its customers.

contribution margin (CM) the difference between sales and the variable costs of the product or service, also called marginal income. It is the amount of money available to cover fixed costs and generate profits.

conversion costs the sum of the costs of direct labor and factory overhead.

cost accumulation the collection of costs in an organized fashion by means of a cost accounting system. There are two primary approaches to cost accumulation: a job order system and process cost system.

cost behavior analysis analysis of mixed costs. Mixed costs must be separated into the variable and fixed elements in order to be included in a variety of business planning analyses such as cost-volume-profit (CVP) analysis.

cost center the unit within the organization in which the manager is responsible only for costs. A cost center has no control over sales or over the generating of revenue. An example is the production department of a manufacturing company.

cost driver a factor that causes a cost item to be incurred (e.g., direct-labor hours, number of setups, or number of inspections).

cost management a system that measures the cost of significant activities, recognizes non-value-added costs, and identifies activities that will improve overall performance.

cost of production report a summary of the unit and cost data of a production department in a process cost system.

cost pool a group of related costs that are assigned together to a set of cost objectives (such as jobs, products, or activities).

cost-volume formula a cost function in the form of y = a + bx. For example, the cost-volume formula for factory overhead is y = \$200 + \$10x where y = estimated factory overhead and x = direct-labor hours, which means that the factory overhead is estimated to be \$200 fixed, plus \$10 per hour of direct labor. Cost analysts use the formula for cost prediction and flexible budgeting purposes.

cost-volume-profit (CVP) analysis analysis that deals with how profits and costs change with a change in volume. It looks at the effects on profits of changes in such factors as variable costs, fixed costs, selling prices, volume, and mix of products sold.

decision tree a pictorial representation of sequential decisions, states of nature, probabilities attached to the state of nature, and conditional benefits and losses.

departmental rate a predetermined factory overhead rate for each production department.

direct method a method of allocating the costs of each service department directly to production departments on the basis of the relative portion of services rendered.

discretionary (fixed) costs those fixed costs that change because of managerial decisions, also called management (fixed) costs or programmed (fixed) costs. Examples of this type of fixed costs are advertising outlays, training costs, and research and development costs.

Du Pont formula the breakdown of return on investment (ROI) into profit margin and asset turnover.

economic order quantity (EOQ) the order size that should be ordered at one time to minimize the sum of carrying and ordering costs.

fixed overhead spending (budget) variance the difference between actual fixed overhead incurred and fixed overhead budgeted.

fixed overhead volume (denominator) variance the difference between budgeted fixed overhead and the fixed overhead costs applied to products. It is used as a measure of utilization of plant facilities.

flexible budget a budget based on cost-volume relationships and developed for the actual level of activity. An extremely useful tool for comparing the actual cost incurred to the cost allowable for the activity level achieved.

internal rate of return (IRR) the rate of interest that equates the initial investment with the present value of future cash inflows.

investment center a responsibility center within an organization that has control over revenue, cost, and investment funds. It is a profit center whose performance is evaluated on the basis of the return earned on invested capital.

job order costing the accumulation of costs by specific jobs, contracts, or orders. This costing method is appropriate when direct costs can be identified with specific units of production. Widely used by custom manufacturers such as printing, aircraft, construction, auto repair, and professional services.

just-in-time (JIT) a demand-pull system where demand for customer output (not plans for using input resources) triggers production. Production activities are "pulled," not "pushed," into action. JIT, in its purest sense, is buying and producing in very small quantities just in time for use.

just-in-time production approach to manufacturing in which items are produced only when needed in production.

KANBAN Japanese information system for coordinating production orders and withdrawals from in-process inventory to realize just-in-time production.

labor efficiency variance the difference between the amount of labor time that should have been used and the labor actually used, multiplied by the standard rate.

labor rate variance any deviation from standard in the average hourly rate paid to workers.

learning curve a curve that represents the efficiencies gained from experience. Based on the statistical findings that as the cumulative output doubles, the cumulative average labor input time required per unit will be reduced by some constant percentage, ranging between 10 and 40%.

least squares method a statistical technique for fitting a straight line through a set of points in such a way that the sum of the squared distances from the data points to the line is minimized.

linear programming (LP) a technique used to find an optimal solution to the resource allocation problem under constrained conditions.

master (comprehensive) budget a plan of activities expressed in monetary terms of the assets, equities, revenues, and costs which will be involved in carrying out the plans. A set of projected or planned financial statements.

materials price variance the difference between what is paid for a given quantity of materials and what should have been paid, multiplied by actual quantity of materials used.

materials quantity (usage) variance the difference between the actual quantity of materials used in production and the standard quantity of materials allowed for actual production, multiplied by the standard price per unit.

mixed costs costs that vary with changes in volume but, unlike variable costs, do not vary in direct proportion, also called semivariable costs.

multiple regression analysis a statistical procedure that attempts to assess the relationship between the dependent variable and two or more independent variables. For example, total factory overhead is related to both labor hours and machine hours.

net present value (NPV) the difference between the present value of cash inflows generated by the project and the amount of the initial investment.

opportunity cost the net benefit foregone by rejecting an alternative use of time or facilities.

out-of-pocket costs actual cash outlays made during the period for payroll, advertising, and other operating expenses.

payback period the length of time required to recover the initial amount of a capital investment.

predetermined overhead rates an overhead rate, based on budgeted factory overhead cost and budgeted activity, that is established before a period begins.

process costing a cost accumulation method used to assign costs to units of a homogeneous product as the units pass through one or more processes.

profit-volume chart a chart that determines how profits vary with changes in volume.

profitability index the ratio of the total present value of future cash inflows to the initial investment.

program evaluation and review technique (PERT) a useful management tool for planning, coordinating, and controlling large complex projects such as formulation of a master budget, construction of buildings, installation of computers, and scheduling the closing of books.

rate of return on investment (ROI) (1) for the company as a whole, net income after taxes divided by invested capital, (2) for the segment of an organization, net operating income divided by operating assets, (3) for capital budgeting purposes, also called simple accounting, or unadjusted rate of return, expected future net income divided by initial (or average) investment.

reciprocal method   a method of allocating service department costs to production departments, where reciprocal services are allowed between service departments; also known as the linear algebra method, the matrix method, the double-distribution method, the cross-allocation method, and simultaneous equation method.

regression analysis   a statistical procedure for mathematically estimating the average relationship between the dependent variable (sales, for example) and one or more independent variables (price and advertising, for example).

relevant cost   the expected future cost that will differ between the alternatives being considered.

residual income (RI)   the operating income which an investment center is able to earn above some minimum return on its assets.

responsibility accounting   the collection, summarization, and reporting of financial information about various decision centers (responsibility centers) throughout an organization. Also called activity accounting or profitability accounting.

responsibility center   a unit in the organization which has control over costs, revenues, or investment funds. For accounting purposes, responsibility centers are classified as cost centers, revenue centers, profit centers, and investment centers, depending on what each center is responsible for.

segmented reporting   the process of reporting activities of various segments of an organization such as divisions, product lines, or sales territories.

shadow price   profit that would be lost by not adding an additional hour of capacity.

simple regression   a regression analysis which involves one independent variable. For example, total factory overhead is related to one activity variable (either direct-labor hours or machine hours).

step method   the allocation of service department costs to other service departments as well as production departments in a sequential manner.

theory of constraints (TOC)   approach seeking to identify a company's constraints or bottlenecks and exploit them so that throughput is maximized and inventories and operating costs are minimized.

total quality management (TQM) concept of using quality methods and techniques to strategic advantage within firms.

total quality control (TQC) a quality program in which the goal is complete elimination of product defects.

variance (1) in statistics, the square of the standard deviation, (2) in cost analysis, the deviation between the actual cost and the standard cost.

volume-based cost driver a cost driver that is based on production volume, such as machine hours or direct-labor hours.

zero-base budgeting a method of budgeting in which cost and benefit estimates are built up from scratch, from the level of zero, and must be justified.

Index

Absorption costing, 175–179
Acceptable quality level (AQL), 120, 314
Accounting rate of return (ARR), 255–256
Action cost plus profit markup, 278
Activity-based costing, 2, 101–109, 114–116
Activity-based management (ABM), 109–114, 318–319
Activity driver, 111–112
After-tax cash flow, 263–265
Allocation bases, 76–77, 83–86. *See also* Costs allocation

Balance sheets, 23–24, 192–193
Benchmarking, 10
Bid-price determination, 247–248
Bottlenecks, 11
Break-even analysis, 153, 155–157, 168–169
Budgeted cost plus profit markup, 277–278
Budgeted income statement, 191
Budget(s) and budgeting:
    cash, 189–191
    comprehensive, 182–184
    computer-based models and software for, 193–200
    definition of, 181
    direct-labor, 187
    direct-material, 185–186
    ending inventory, 188
    factory overhead, 187–188
    flexible, 205, 213–215
    preparation of, 182–183
    production, 185
    sales, 184
    selling and administrative expense, 189
    static, 213–214
    types of, 182
    zero-base, 200–204
Business process reengineering, 10
By-products, 64–73

Capacity:
    description of, 35–36
    normal, 36
    planned, 36
    practical, 36
    theoretical, 36
    utilization of, 243–246
Capital budgeting, 253, 268
Cash break-even point, 157
Certified Cost Estimator/Analyst (CCEA), 13
Certified Internal Auditor (CIA), 12–13
Certified Management Accountant (CMA), 11–12
Coefficient of determination, 140–141
Continuous improvement, 9–10
Contribution income statement, 148–150
Contribution-margin income statement, 240–242
Contribution price, 244
Controllable costs, 20–21
Controller/Comptroller, 5–6
Correlation coefficient, 140–141
Cost accounting, 2, 8–9, 121
Cost Accounting Standards Board (CASB), 6–8
Cost analysis, 2–5, 87–94
Cost centers, 48, 205–207
Cost control, 3
Cost drivers, 100–101, 104–106
Costing:
    absorption, 175–179
    activity-based, 101–109, 114–116
    direct, 175–179
    just-in-time, 124
    overhead, 95–101
    process. *See* Process costing
    standard, 36
Cost management, 2–3, 121
Cost objective, 75
Cost planning, 2
Cost pool(s), 83–86, 102, 106–109
Cost prediction, 145–147
Costs:
    by-product, 64–66
    centralized, 77
    classification of, 15–16, 19

controllable, 20–21
direct, 18, 76
distribution, 87–94
fixed. *See* Fixed costs
incremental, 21–22, 279
indirect, 18, 76
joint. *See* Joint costs
manufacturing, 16–17
mixed, 19, 130–135
noncontrollable, 20–21
nonmanufacturing, 17
opportunity, 22–23, 288–289
out-of-pocket, 22
period, 18
product, 18, 31
quality, 17, 313–321
relevant, 22, 242–243
semidirect, 76
service, 79
standard, 21, 205–207
step-function, 163–165
sunk, 22, 63
total, 19–20, 42–43
unit, 19–20, 42–43, 55
variable, 19, 81–83, 129–130
Costs allocation:
approaches, 77–78
arbitrary, 78
aspects of, 75–76
bases for, 76–77
cautions associated with, 78
contribution approach, 87
distribution costs, 89–94
function of, 75
guidelines, 76–86
joint costs, 51–54, 56–73
segmental reporting and, 86–87
service department, 78–81
Cost-volume formula, 131, 150
Cost-volume-profit (CVP) analysis,
153–155, 158–160, 163–165,
167–172
Cost-volume-revenue (CVR) analysis,
167–172

Degree of completion estimating,
47–48
Depreciation methods, 265–268
Direct costing, 175–179
Direct costs, 18, 76
Distribution cost analysis, 87–94
Distribution costs, 87–94

Divisional profit, 279–281
Double-declining depreciation,
266–267
Dual pricing, 279
Dummy variables, 144–145

Economic order quantity (EOQ),
298–302
Equivalent units, 42–47

Factory overhead, 218
Factory overhead budget, 187–188
Financial accounting, 4
Financial leverage, 172–174
First-in, first-out (FIFO) method,
43–47
Fixed costs:
committed, 131
common, 87
definition of, 19, 130
description of, 81–83
direct, 87
discretionary, 130–131
Fixed-overhead variance, 215–218
Flexible budgets, 205, 213–215

Generally Accepted Accounting
Principles (GAAP), 4
Gross profit analysis, 228–236

Half-year convention, 269
High-low method, 133–135
Homogeneous cost pool, 102

Income statement:
under absorption costing, 177–178
budgeted, 191
contribution, 148–150
contribution-margin, 240–242
description of, 23–24
under direct costing, 176–177
Income tax, 263
Incremental costs, 21–22
Indirect costs, 18, 76
Institute of Management Accountants
(IMA), 11–12
Interactive Financial Planning System
(IFPS), 194–195
Internal rate of return (IRR), 257–258
Inventory planning, 295, 298–303
Investments, 253–254, 260–261

Job cost sheet, 25–26
Job-order costs:
    description of, 25, 37
    journal entries in, 32–35
    process costing and, 40
    standard costing and, 36
Joint costs, 51–54, 56–73
Joint products, 51–53, 62–66, 73
Just-in-time (JIT):
    benefits of, 121–122
    costing system, 124
    cost management and, 124–126
    definition of, 2, 10, 118
    description of, 117, 126–127
    examples of, 122–123
    product costing and, 124–126
    traditional manufacturing and,
        118–121

Labor variance, 210–211
Lean production, 10–11
Learning curve, 293–297
Least-squares method, 137–140
Leverage, 172–175
Linear programming (LP), 285–292
Line authority, 5

Make-or-buy decision, 249–251
Management accounting, 2–3, 8–9
Manufacturing cells, 119–120
Manufacturing cost per unit, 103
Manufacturing costs, 16–17
Margin of safety, 158
Material mix variance, 218–222
Materials variance, 207–209
Mixed costs, 19, 130–135
Modified Accelerated Cost Recovery
    System (MACRS), 268–273
Multiple regression, 143, 150

Negotiated market value, 276–277
Net present value (NPV), 256–257,
    261
Net realizable value:
    allocations based on, 56–73
    of by-product, 66
    definition of, 52
Noncontrollable costs, 20–21
Nonmanufacturing costs, 17
Nonvalue-added activity, 110–111
Normal capacity, 36

Operating leverage, 172–173
Operations research, 283
Opportunity costs, 22–23, 288–289
Out-of-pocket costs, 22
Overhead costing:
    accuracy of, 99–100
    categorization of, 106
    description of, 95
    multiple-product, 96–101
    non-volume-related, 100–101
    single-product, 95–96
Overhead rate, 29–32, 98–99

Parallel flow, 41
Payback period, 254–255
Performance report, 214–215, 236,
    315–317
Period costs, 18
Physical measure, 53, 56–73
Planned capacity, 36
Practical capacity, 36
Predetermined lump-sums, 82
Price variance, 206
Process costing:
    calculations, 42–43
    data, 48
    definition of, 39
    estimating degree of completion,
        47–48
    job-order cost system and, 40
    for management decision making,
        48–49
    overview of, 49
    product flow, 40–42
Process value analysis, 109
Product costs, 18, 31
Product flow, 40–42
Production department, 78–81
Production mix variance, 218–222
Production yield variance, 222–228
Product line, 248–249
Profitability index, 258–259
Profit budget, 2
Profit variance analysis. See Gross
    profit analysis
Profit-volume (P-V) chart, 156
Program Evaluation and Review
    Technique (PERT), 303–308

Quality, 309
Quality costs, 17, 313–321
Quantitative models, 283
Quantity variance, 206

Regression analysis:
  description of, 105, 137–139
  dummy variables, 144–145
  multiple, 143, 150
  spreadsheet program for, 142–143
  statistics, 140–142
Relative sales value method, 52
Relevant costs, 22, 242–243
Reorder point (ROP), 299

Sales mix analysis, 160–163
Segment, 86
Segmental reporting, 86–87
Selective flow, 41–42
Semidirect costs, 76
Sequential flow, 41
Service department, 78–81
Shadow price. *See* Opportunity costs
Split-off points, 60–66
Staff authority, 5
Standard costs, 21, 205–207
Standard deviation, 284–285
Standard error of the estimate, 141
Standard error of the regression
  coefficient, 142
Statistical process control, 10
Step-function costs, 163–165
Step method, of costs allocation,
  80–81
Straight-line depreciation, 265
Strategic cost analysis, 112–114
Sum-of-the-years'-digits depreciation,
  265
Sunk costs, 22, 63

Target income, 157–158
Tax shield, 264
Theoretical capacity, 36
Theory of constraints, 11

Total costs, 19–20, 42–43
Total leverage, 174–175
Total quality control (TQC), 120
Total quality management (TQM), 9,
  309–313, 321
Transfer price, 275–282
t-statistic, 142

Unit costs, 19–20, 42–43, 55
Unit manufacturing cost, 48
Units of production depreciation,
  267–268

Value-added activity, 110–111
Value chain, 112
Variable costs, 81–83, 129–130
Variable overhead variances, 211–213
Variance:
  cost price, 229–230
  cost volume, 230
  fixed-overhead, 215–218
  labor, 210–211
  material mix, 218–222
  materials, 207–209
  price, 206
  production mix, 218–222
  production yield, 222–228
  quantity, 206
  sales price, 229
  sales volume, 230
  variable overhead, 211–213
Variance analysis, 205, 218
Volume-based cost drivers, 100–101

Weight-average method, 43, 55

Yield variance, 222–228

Zero-base budgeting, 200–204